TEACHING TIPS FOR TERRIFIED TEACHERS*

A must have for children's Sunday school

*Also good for Terrific Teachers and those only Mildly Hysterical!

Scripture quotations are taken from the New Revised Standard Version of the Bible, copyright © 1989 by the Division of Christian Education of the National Council of the Churches of Christ in the USA, and used by permission.

TEACHING TIPS FOR TERRIFIED TEACHERS
Copyright ©1998 Abingdon Press
All rights reserved.

ISBN 0-687-08409-1
Manufactured in the United States of America

00 01 02 03 04 05 06 07 — 10 9 8 7 6 5 4 3 2

How To Use This Book

Teaching Tips for Terrified Teachers is a compilation of some of the best teaching helps from the quarterly publication, *Children's Teacher: News and How-tos for Christian Teaching*.

It was compiled by taking some of the questions teachers often ask and for which there are not always fast, handy solutions and by gathering the solutions into one easy-to-use resource.

Teaching Tips for Terrified Teachers is a book to help Christian educators, education chairpersons, Sunday school superintendents, pastors, and anyone who resources teachers. It brings knowledge and ideas from Christian educators and church teachers from around the country. You are no longer alone. This book will help you out.

Each article contains a specific way to help a teacher with a specific problem or idea. If you have a teacher with a question or a need, you will probably find an answer or an activity in this book.

For example, if a teacher comes to you because the teacher is having a problem with classroom discipline, you can give him or her a copy of the article, "The ABCs of Classroom Discipline". If your teacher wants some extra activities to spice up classroom time in the summer, you can give the teacher articles such as "Hosiery Games" or "A 'Messy Sunday' for All Ages."

What if your teacher or your education committee feels that a Halloween celebration is not appropriate for a church? Look up your article on "Hallowing Halloween: Putting the Hallow Back in All Hallow's Eve." It will enlighten your discussion and help people grow in their understanding of the holiday and how it can be celebrated with integrity in the church.

You can have all your answers handy at a moment's notice because you can store them in two different ways. You can leave them in this book for quick, easy reference or you can keep a photocopy in your files under the appropriate headings. We've already put the file tabs with the headings on the pages for you. All you need do is file them.

When the need arises, the original purchaser has permission to copy the articles for use in the immediate work setting or in personally led workshops. The appropriate copyright information is at the bottom of each article and must appear when duplicated.

Many of you will be leading workshops, and sometimes you need help with something specific. This book has lots of ideas on many topics that are often addressed in workshops.

Teaching Tips for Terrified Teachers is divided into seven areas to help you readily identify where to look for specific ideas.

ACTIVITY IDEAS gives some suggestions for specific activities that can enliven an educational setting. It includes a variety of things such as the use of boxes, how to make and use lanterns, and how to celebrate birthdays.

BIBLE TEACHING HELPS contains ways to enhance the learning of Bible stories and truths. It explains many ways to learn about the Bible, from how people lived in Bible times to ways for children to use their own Bibles.

CHILDREN IN MINISTRY helps you guide your children in how to do Christian ministry and missions. The whys and the how-tos are varied.

CHILDREN IN WORSHIP guides you in teaching your children about worship and related topics such as prayer.

TEACHING METHODS has suggestions of all kinds for helping train beginning teachers or even experienced teachers who just want fresh ways to teach. It helps with everything from equipping your classroom to how to teach songs to children.

RELATIONSHIPS helps your teachers with some of those tough problems that are caused by people being people. How do you relate to single parents? What do you do when there's been a death in a child's family? (Maybe more importantly – what you don't do.)

HOLIDAYS has some extra ideas for celebrating those special holidays of the church year. We can all use new ideas to spice up the celebrations of our faith.

If you have a favorite author of children's activities, just look in the index of authors. Many different authors are contributors. They all have years of experience with children.

Use and enjoy!

Contents

All Kinds of Box-Abilities!

by Ginna Minasian Dalton

A box in 1 Samuel 6:8,11,15 is connected to the ark of the covenant. Perfume boxes are referred to in Isaiah 3:20. Other references to boxes or containers occur throughout the Bible. Boxes protect treasures, store goods, and hide secrets. Boxes have been a part of our common human history.

But why would I use a box in church? Consider the environment. Every Christian must look at every opportunity to participate in the stewardship of God's creation. The lack of time and energy may tempt us to look for the path of least resistance and purchase something we could recycle, but teachers are called to be creative.

Cardboard boxes inspire creativity. They offer an opportunity to model good stewardship by recycling an existing product, and they are fun!

The Challenge of Space

With the ever-changing patterns of church membership, Sunday school attendance changes too. Some congregations find that their old buildings have too many rooms for the number of participants, and heating and cooling costs too much. Some churches combine classes and develop a broadly graded system. This makes it possible to use one large fellowship room for all groups. Some small congregations have only one or two rooms and struggle to create privacy and to provide storage at the same time. Growing churches need transitional space.

Boxes to the Rescue!

Slit a large refrigerator box down one side along the fold. Open up the box and you have a divider or one great wall. Encourage the children, youth, or adults to decorate or paint the printed side and use the plain side as an inside wall for the class.

Large TV and microwave oven boxes make wonderful tables for writing and painting. Don't worry about ruining these surfaces.

Boxes Create Fun

Don't buy wooden blocks! Cover all-size boxes with washable self-adhesive paper and you have safe and inexpensive toys instantly.

● Create playhouses from appliance boxes. These can be broken down for convenient storage. Recruit someone to paint a façade on these boxes to resemble a biblical home, a market, a tent, or a modern home from another country.

● Imagine a child's amazement when she whispers an idea into a story box painted like a person and then hears a voice coming from inside the box begin to tell a story.

● Push the story box idea further and decorate a box to look like a biblical character like Ruth or Paul; then have a person inside tell that person's story.

● Let the children take on the character of another person by playing inside the box.

Boxes Create Storage

Storage containers for large items like costumes, blocks, and posters are difficult to find or afford. Create a stackable pole using three or four sizable boxes. Use this pole to designate a particular area while using each box to store items that need to be put away. This is particularly helpful if your Sunday school space is used by another group, such as a weekday child care program. Decorate each box with the theme of a study unit. Displays like this allow other people to learn about your class.

Use boxes to store markers, rubber bands, paper bags, and other craft supplies. Label the outside of each box and stack the boxes to save space. Use smaller boxes for pins, cotton swabs, and smaller items. Labeling is important!

Sunday School Shoeboxes

In the nineteen fifties and sixties, Sunday school literature promoted the use of shoeboxes. Those ideas are still good ones. Here are some of them:

● Create a mini-theater. Have the children decorate the inside of a shoebox to resemble a scene from a Bible story.

● Cut out the back of a shoebox to create an opening for your hands in order to play a finger puppet skit. Add a curtain on a string glued at each end of the box.

● When you place the screen and paper on the bottom of a box, spatter-painting can be done inside, letting the sides catch the excess paint.

● After children spatter paint in a box, cut out facial openings and create masks to be used in Christmas celebrations, as the people of Ghana do. Masks are not to hide people, but to show a special inner quality.

Boxes Create Learning Opportunities

Give people privacy. Cut a box to leave three panels, in order to create an individual study carrel or quiet area.

Boxes also make great places for learning centers. Make openings for doors and windows. Cut holes large enough for hands to reach inside

and grab a game, instruction sheet, or storybook.

Here are some other ideas:

● When using a refrigerator box as a room divider, use one side as a bulletin board.

● Make a computer toy from a large box. Have the class members feed a biblical question in writing into the computer to stump it. The computer answers—on the paper with the question or orally. At the end, the pastor jumps out of the box. What a fun way to get to know your pastor!

● Collect sixty-six cereal or cracker boxes to help children learn the books of the Bible. Cover each box and label the spine with the name of a book of the Bible. Color-code the sections of books in each literary type to emphasize that the Bible is like a library. For example, cover the Gospels in yellow to designate their grouping and the Psalms in green because they belong to the poetry section. Play games putting the books in order. Cut the tops off these boxes to keep an open end. The books can then become storage places for handouts and pictures about the specific books they represent.

● Use a small box of any shape as an ornament to be a gift for someone. Perhaps each child could decorate a box and keep it in class. Then on a birthday or special day, a treat would be inside.

● To celebrate the blessings that each person brings to our world, give a child a box. On the inside of this small box glue a mirror. Wrap the box beautifully. On the gift tag write: **To** *(person's name)* **from God.** Explain that his or her life is a gift from God. Then ask the person to open the box. On the inside is a second tag taped to the mirror. This tag reads: **To God from** *(person's name)*. Explain that what that person becomes is his or her gift to God. Celebrate the surprises that may be discovered and revealed when each of us opens ourselves to receive God's gifts.

Where Do I Find Boxes?

There are many free sources for cardboard boxes, only your initiative and wit are necessary to find them. Put a notice in your church newsletter in November requesting that people bring leftover Christmas boxes and deposit them in the attractive display box you have created. Be sure to get any needed approvals for this.

Think about the size and shape of the boxes you want, as well as their uses. Make a poster of all the shapes you can imagine and picture them on your display box. This may help others think creatively.
Try:
● medical facilities
● fast food places
● appliance stores
● manufacturers and other businesses

Look in the telephone directory for a box manufacturing company and ask for seconds or rejects. Be sure the vehicle you take is large enough to hold refrigerator boxes.

Boxes have potential for uses other than protecting or hiding. We can creatively use them in ministry!

Ginna Minasian Dalton is a consultant in Christian education Before her ministry as a consultant, Ginna was director of the Ecumenical Resource Center in Richmond, Virginia

Light From Seven Lanterns
by Sharilyn S. Adair

Light is an important image throughout the Old and New Testaments. Long before the time of Jesus, light became a symbol of goodness and deliverance to the Jewish people. They recalled the pillar of fire that led the Israelites through the wilderness by night during their escape from Egyptian bondage; they equated light with God in triumphant psalms such as Psalm 27: "The LORD is my light and my salvation; whom shall I fear?" The prophet Isaiah, in describing a coming deliverer, proclaimed, "The people who walked in darkness have seen a great light." As recorded in Matthew 5:14-16 Jesus challenged his hearers to *be* light, ending by saying, "Let your light shine before others, so that they may see your good works."

Because it's not difficult to find biblical references to light, you can supplement many lesson plans with activities and crafts using light. Try some of the following ideas. **For safety's sake those that involve the use of candles should not be used with children younger than eight or nine. When candles are used with a child of any age, be sure to have adequate adult supervision.**

Soup Can Lanterns

1. Clean enough soup cans for each child to have one. Remove the label and hammer flat any sharp edges around the top.
2. Two days before class, fill the cans with water and freeze them in a freezer as close as possible to your teaching space.
3. Give each child two sheets of paper as tall as the soup can labels but only half as wide, and have him or her follow these instructions:
   • Draw some simple object or word on each sheet (a cross, your name, the Christian fish symbol, a heart, the word *love*). Then draw large dots half an inch apart around the outline of the object or in the letters of the word.
   • Take a can from the freezer and cushion it on a pillow or towel folded several times.
   • Tape one of your patterns to a can and use a hammer and nail to pound holes in the can at the dots.
   • Repeat the process by using your second pattern on the opposite side of the can.
4. Give each child a votive candle to use in the can.
5. When the ice has melted enough, encourage the children to empty their cans and place the votive candles in them.
Warning: The cans may conduct the heat of the candles. If these lanterns are to be carried, each bearer *must* use a potholder or oven mitt and grasp the can firmly around its bottom.

Flashlight Crosses

1. Give each child a working flashlight and a piece of black construction paper.
2. Have the children place the flashlight lens-side down on the paper, trace around it with white chalk, and cut out the resulting circle.
3. Have the children draw the outline of a cross on the circle and then use a round, sharp toothpick; an awl; or a large needle to prick holes half an inch apart around the outline.
4. Let the children tape the circles over the lenses of their flashlights and project their crosses on walls, on the table, or on one another.

Stained Glass Lanterns

Give each child a jar that is short enough to easily secure a candle. Ask the children to follow these instructions:

1. Tear or cut several colors of tissue paper into pieces from dime-size to half-dollar-size.
2. Use a paintbrush to brush the jar with a solution of half white glue and half water.
3. Position pieces of tissue paper on the jar, overlapping some pieces and butting others together.
4. When the jar is covered with paper, paint a thin film of glue over the tissue paper and set the jar aside to dry.
5. When the jar is dry, insert a votive candle and light it.

Warning: If these jars are to be carried, be sure the bearer uses a potholder or oven mitt and grasps the bottom firmly.

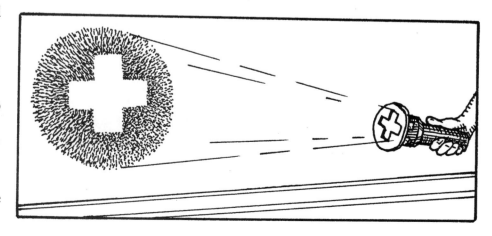

Colored Flares

Give each child a working flashlight, a cold-drink cup that is wider at the top than at the bottom and that is narrower than the head of the flashlight at the bottom; colored tissue paper or cellophane; and a rubber band. Have the children follow these instructions:

1. Carefully cut out the bottom of the cup.
2. Slide the flashlight, bottom first, into the top of the cup until the cup is snug around the flashlight head. Tape the cup to the flashlight.
3. Cut a circle of cellophane or tissue paper two to three inches wider than the top of the cup.
4. Secure the cellophane or tissue paper around the top of the cup with the rubber band. Turn on the flashlight.

Option: A small shape of a cross could be cut from black construction paper and glued in the center of the tissue paper or cellophane to cast the shadow of the cross when the colored light falls on the surface.

Glowworms

Give each child a working flashlight, a brown paper lunch bag, felt-tip markers, and a length of yarn or string. Have the children follow these instructions:

1. Lay the lunch bag flat so that the closed end of the bag is away from you and the open end is toward you.
2. Use markers to draw a face on one side of the bag close to the closed end.
3. Place the bag over the head of the flashlight.
4. Gather the bag around the flashlight and tie yarn or cord around the gathers.
5. Turn on the flashlight to see the glowworm glow.

Jar Candle Holders

Give each child two small glass jars the same size and that are clean and have the labels removed. Have available modeling clay and small decorative items such as seashells, dried flowers, and grasses. Have each child follow these instructions:

1. Remove the lids from both jars. Turn one lid upside down and place a lump of modeling clay in it. Make a pretty arrangement by sticking natural items into the clay.
2. Screw the lid onto one of the jars and turn the jar over so that it rests on the lid.
3. Put a lot of glue on the bottom of the jar (which is now the top). Press the bottom of the other jar onto the glue. Place a candle in the top jar and let an adult light it.

Option: Instead of making an arrangement in the bottom jar, one or both jars could be decorated with glue, glitter, and sequins before the jars are glued together.

Clam Shell Candle Holders

Give each child a clam shell or other large seashell with a similar shape, three beads or marbles, a piece of floral clay, and a votive candle. Have the children follow these instructions:

1. Turn the shell upside down. Squeeze three dabs of white glue in a large triangle on the shell bottom and let the glue dry partially but not completely. Place the beads or marbles in the glue and let them dry overnight.
2. Turn the shell onto its bead legs and place a dab of floral clay in the shell.
3. Secure the candle to the shell by sticking it onto the floral clay.

Sharilyn Adair does freelance writing and editing of children's materials. Sharilyn is a retired editor of children's curriculum of The United Methodist Publishing House in Nashville, Tennessee.

Celebrating Birthdays in Sunday School

by Barbara Bruce

Birthdays are important for all of us. Our birthday is the one day of the year that is just ours, when we are singled out and made to feel special. As a church family we can create special times for those having birthdays. We can also balance the celebration with the reality of limited time for covering lesson material during Sunday school. How can we find ways to make birthday persons feel special as a part of our ongoing lessons and activities? Let's explore several ways.

Let the Child Choose

Invite the birthday child to select an activity that he or she particularly enjoys from the lesson plan in the teacher book. The week before the child's birthday, offer options from the curriculum and have the child select a specific activity. Perhaps the child can take a leadership role in the activity he or she has selected. You can announce to the class that this learning activity was chosen by the birthday student.

Have a Birthday Bank

During opening exercises or any time that is appropriate, invite the birthday student to put in a coin for each year of his or her life. Decide as a church school where the money will go at the end of the year.

Your denomination may have a special fund that helps special children's projects. A local children's mission or a particular community need are other suggestions.

Contact your denomination's headquarters for information on your denomination's mission projects for children.

Have your church treasurer send the money through the proper channels for you, so that the money will be sure to go where you want to designate it to go.

Create a Bulletin Board

Create a monthly bulletin board entitled "Jesus Is Special—I Am Special—I Was Born in (fill in the appropriate month)." Names and pictures of each student born that month, along with their specific birth dates, would be a neat celebration in a church hallway. At the beginning of each church school year, you might ask parents to submit a picture of each child with his or her birth date printed clearly on the back. Teachers can take turns gathering the pictures and setting up the bulletin board for the month.

Celebrate Birthday Sunday

Select one Sunday each month to celebrate birthdays. Parents of children born that month can decide on a theme: for example, September's theme might be Back to School, while March's theme might be Lions and Lambs, reflecting the traditional saying about how the month begins and ends. Biblical or church year themes would also work well. Let April reflect Lent/Easter; October, All Saints' Day. Parents of those having birthdays can supply cookies or a cake decorated according to the theme as the snack for that Sunday. Birthday names can be displayed, and birthday persons can be allowed to receive first helpings or to help serve others.

Donated
in honor of
John Thompson
on his
tenth birthday
December 1, 1998

Donate a Book

Start a children's library in your church if one is not already in place. Donate a book to the church library or resource room with the birthday child's name and birth date inscribed in the inside cover. Select age-level-appropriate books from the "Recommended Resources" pages in Sunday school teacher books or choose from the "Books for Children" pages of book and curriculum catalogs available from Cokesbury and other religious publishers. Abingdon's Great Big Books are another good choice.

Match Children With Older Adults

Connect children with older adults who share the same birth month. In our transient society, where extended family is often miles away, pairing children and older adults who share a birth month might create special caring relationships across generations. Children need grandparent figures; older adults need child friends. Each has so much to share with the other. An ice cream sundae, a visit to the zoo, or a movie can be a unique birthday experience when shared with someone of a different generation who is not the parent.

Make a Worship Announcement

Mention the child's birthday in worship during the time the pastor is receiving announcements about joys and concerns. Children need to know how special they are. They need affirmations and reasons to feel good about themselves. Recognition in church and Sunday school is an important means of enhancing children's self-esteem and of helping them experience the love and grace of God that is talked about in our sermons.

Have Children Write Affirmations

Affirmation sheets for the birthday child can help children get into the habit of saying nice things about one another. Having classmates write a positive word or phrase on a bright sheet of paper during the class time, perhaps as a learning center activity, would be a special gift for both the classmates and the birthday child. My guess is that this affirmation sheet would be proudly displayed on the refrigerator at home or in the child's bedroom.

Serve Birthday Snacks

Have parents supply the snacks. Many churches have a snack time anyway. Giving snacks a birthday emphasis is another way of making the birthday child feel special.

As we strive to live out God's love by being God's hands, there are many ways to show children how each one of them is important to God and to the church. Celebrating birthdays is a neat way to say, "You are special. God loves you, and so do we."

Barbara Bruce is is a Christian educator in Rochester, New York. She has her own consulting firm called Process: Creativity *and helps churches and organizations across the country learn and use creative skills.*

Hosiery Games

Enliven your summer activities with creative use of old or irregular nylon stockings and pantyhose. These nylon lengths can be used for creative movement and dance, for catch and pitch games, for cooperative play, and for variations on familiar game themes. Using old or waste stockings allows your class or group a creative opportunity to recycle a familiar object into a new use.

Ask members of your church to save stockings that they would have discarded, wash them, and donate them to your class or group. Cut out the toe section of each stocking. If pantyhose have been donated, cut these in half and make the tops even. Scarves or even strips of fabric work with the following activities where noted, but nylon stockings work best.

Some nylon hose manufacturers are willing to sell stockings that do not pass inspection. One such company is Sara Lee Hosiery. For a box of approximately 300 waste hose, send a letter of request and a check or money order for $12.00 to

Peggy Oates
Sara Lee Hosiery-L'eggs Products
1901 North Irby Street
Florence, SC 29501

Make checks payable to Sara Lee Hosiery and mark them "for waste hose."

Creative Hosiery Movement

Play music on an audiocassette and give each child one nylon stocking or fabric strip. Encourage the children to make movements with the hose. Numbers and letters suggest delightful patterns. Have the children try making figure 8s, 6s, and 2s or writing their names. Have the children pretend to sweep the floor, wash a window, or bathe a dog while moving in time to the music.

After the children get used to movement with the stockings, have them join in pairs or trios to dance and move together to the music.

Attached Mirrors

Have pairs of children hold two stockings or scarves. While they maintain their holds on the stockings, one child will reflect the movements of the other child. After five minutes, the other child becomes the reflector.

Threaded Knots

Give each child a hose or fabric strip. Have the children stand in a circle, with each child holding one end of his or her hose in one hand and an end of another's hose in the other hand. Have the children play a game of Knots. The object of the game is to have everyone become tangled and then to untangle this human knot without any group members losing their grips on the hose.

Circle Dance

Have the children form groups of six. Give each child two hose, strips of fabric, or scarves. Have the children hold the ends of one another's hose. (They may hold the hose of the next person or the person opposite.) Standing in place, the children may move the hose in and out, around, under, or over to create different patterns.

Head Dance

Stuff the toe of a nylon stocking with a rolled-up sock. Have each child pull the stocking leg over his or her head. Have each child move his or her head to make the stocking swing in a circle. A variation on the Head Dance is to pair head dancers, who, through swinging movements, try to tangle and remove one another's hose.

ACTIVITY IDEAS

Wheelchair or Seated Square Dance

You may wish to use this form of dancing when your group visits a residential care institution. Put nylon hose on the hands of a person who is seated or nonambulatory and also on the hands of a person who is standing. The standing person moves his or her hands to music played on an audiocassette, enabling the seated person to dance. Children may also sit in chairs, forming squares of four. Using hose or scarves, the children can dance while remaining seated. Let the children use their own imaginations to create a dance movement of their own.

Saucers

Have children make a soaring saucer from stockings by putting an arm through one stocking and rolling the stocking down the arm to form a tight ring. Make six of these rings and tie them into a large disc, using stocking or fabric strips as ties.

Soft Stocking Ball

Tie two Saucers together with stocking or fabric strips. Insert a balloon in the center, then inflate and tie the balloon.

Use the stocking ball with young children for games of catch and throw. Older children may play volleyball with this ball. Groups may also play a version of indoor basketball, using wastebaskets as goals. Players should move around on their knees. No physical contact is allowed in this sport.

For further Hosiery Games ideas you can get a video by Glenn Bannerman called "Creative Nylon Hoseplay." Contact Celebration Services, P.O. Box 399, Montreat, NC 28757.

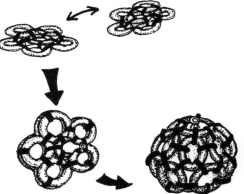

(Adapted from Great Games, in *Pathways to Discovery, Volume 2*, © 1993 Abingdon Press.)

Using Bulletin Boards as a Learning Tool

by Mary Alice Donovan Gran

There is that wall space in your classroom. You know it could be put to use to help students learn. Yes, it's time to do a bulletin board.

What do you do? Do you, like me, procrastinate, putting it off as long as you can? Do you, like me, feel you do not have artistic skills or aren't a fountain of creativity?

Don't despair. Read on. You can make wonderful bulletin boards. Put yourself into a positive frame of mind about the project. Be clear about what you want to accomplish. Set aside some time, gather basic materials, and start in. If you make a mistake, try again. If you aren't sure how to begin, ask someone to help you and plan together.

Bulletin boards bring color, cheerfulness, and interest to an otherwise drab area. Bulletin boards support the ongoing ministry of your Sunday school, and of your church. Bulletin boards become a fun way to learn, for you and for your students. Bulletin boards are worth the time, energy, and effort. Let's get started!

Ask Yourself These Four Questions to Get Started

Question 1:
"Why would I want to create a bulletin board?" Answering that question will help you focus on the purpose of a bulletin board. Don't just think about it; write down a simple statement in response.

Question 2:
Look at each item visible in your classroom and ask yourself, "Is this item relevant to what is currently happening in the classroom?" If you say no to any item, take that item down and put it away.

Question 3:
"Are there items on the walls that are as old as Methuselah?" If so, remove them promptly.

Question 4:
"How can the bulletin board space be used as a learning area for my students?" Ask that question each time you make a plan for your students. You have so little time with them. Make it all count.

> **Bulletin boards support the ongoing ministry of your Sunday school, and of your church.**

Before beginning, stand and look at the space you want to use. What colors will be visible? How much space will you use? What should the background be? Imagine the end product!

Gather supplies. (See "Tips.") What will you need? scissors? lettering stencils? pattern? pencil? yard or meter stick? stapler and staples? construction paper? masking tape? glue? markers? Think through each step of the preparation, making a list of all supplies needed; and gather them before starting. When working, use a large table or floor space. Take a deep breath and start.

Bulletin Boards in the Classroom

Make use of the walls in your classroom in ways that reinforce curriculum themes and emphasize the reasons you gather as a class. Will the bulletin board teach something from the lesson? Will it help students to know one another or to learn something about the church? A room that invites the student and says "You are important" creates an atmosphere conducive to learning.

Bulletin Boards for the Christian Year

March: "Jesus Loves Me, This I Know." Use photos of people from your class, your congregation, and from history who believe the statement.

April: "Flying High With _____." Kites (with long tails). Use bows on the tails for listing people from the early church, from curriculum, names of members of the class, and so on.

May: "We Are the Church." Make a large outline of a church with faces of students peeking from windows or pictures of people from around the world, cut out from magazines, and so on.

June: "In the Beginning, God Created the World" or "God Spangled the Night With Stars." On a dark blue background, paste white stars.

July: "Poppin' Prayers." Use three or five firecrackers (round tubes of colorful paper) with glittery sparklers (thin strips of metallic paper) coming out the tops. Attach slips of paper with sentence prayers.

August: "Sailing with Jesus." On the sails of sailboats, list ways and places we can be disciples of Jesus in our summertime activities.

September: "Our Special Class." Post photos of individual class members with their names. Frame each with colored paper.

October: "World Communion Sunday." Use pictures of people and churches from all over the world. Use symbols of bread and grape juice, or chalice (cup) and platen (plate), or grapes and wheat.

November: "Thankful for God . . . and People Too." Use pictures and words to illustrate fall Bible stories, people from your church, and others for whom the children can be thankful.

December: "The Road to the Manger." Use pictures from past *Class Paks* to illustrate the Christmas story. Connect the pictures with a winding road made of sandpaper strips. Put flannelgraph pictures of Mary, Joseph, and others on the road.

January: "Our Gifts for Jesus." Illustrate with pictures of various gifts and talents God gives us that we can share with others. Begin with the Magi and add talents of class members and others.

February: "Blooming Love," "Love One Another," "God is Love," or "God Loves Me, God Loves You." Make flower pots of construction paper (curved to add dimension). Make flowers using petals of hearts. On each heart write names of persons we love or Biblical heroes or disciples of Jesus.

Bulletin Boards for Interaction

Make bulletin boards that require persons to do something.
1. Have a door that opens to reveal an answer to a question.
2. Leave slips of paper and markers with directions for persons to add their thoughts ("What I am thankful for . . ." at Thanksgiving.)
3. Hang a voting box with attached ballots and pencil for readers to vote for the Bible person they most admire.
4. Put up a large birthday cake. Have lots of paper candles and paper flames in a box. Invite persons to place a candle and flame on the cake. On the candle they could write a reason to praise God.

For Mission Education

● "Be in Mission at Home." Illustrations or words to show a variety of projects or ways persons can be of help in the community.
● "Our Church Helps Others." A big church with loops of yarn leading to pictures labeled with names of projects of local or world mission projects.
● "God's Missionaries." Pictures of people identified by what they do to be missionaries (teacher, doctor, builder of wells, person who invites others to Sunday School, and so on.) Include children.

For Stewardship Education

● "Take Care of God's World." Use children's illustrations of ways we can take care of God's creation.
● "Give to God With Joy." Use a large picture of a coin. Surround the board with medium-sized smiling faces. Under each face indicate a specific example of something for which the offering is used.
● "God Gives Us Talents to Use." Use pictures from old curriculum or magazines to show a variety of talents people can use with others. Show a wide variety of activities and persons; the more diverse the better. Mount each picture on construction paper.
● "Your Presence Is a Present to God." Create gift-wrapped boxes of different shapes and sizes to hang on a bulletin board. On each box write an activity (worship, Sunday school, Kids Club, and so on) at your church that is appropriate for those who will be reading the bulletin board. [Option: To each box add a large gift tag with "To: God" "From: (Space for persons to sign their names)".]

Child-Created Boards

Nothing draws more continued interest than a bulletin board created by a group—the more the merrier!

Create a graffiti wall with a sentence starter and let people draw or write whatever they choose. Have lots of colored markers close by.)

Post student-created activities. (Make a huge crossword puzzle and invite persons to fill in the blanks.

For Teacher Education

If there is a common area for teachers to pick up supplies or attendance sheets, that is the place for an informational motivational bulletin board. Any size board will work. Just practice what you preach and change it often. Make the color bright, cheery, and attention getting. Keep the information current and relevant. Don't let your bulletin board become a place for regular sign-up sheets. Make it a place where teachers can quickly find information that is pertinent, and where they can read a cartoon or saying that encourages them.

In the Hallways

Communicating with all students, with parents, and with the church community is crucial today. Using one or more bulletin board areas strategically placed is an effective means of communicating within the church. Is there a place where people frequently wait? Put a bulletin board there. Is there an entry, corner, or hallway where most people pass? A good location. But remember, a bulletin board is only as effective as the information that is displayed on it. Other suggestions:

Introduce a new quarter's curriculum; introduce teachers with photos and names; display photos of recent church events; clip items from newspapers about congregation members; promote

> ## A bulletin board is only as effective as the information that is displayed on it.

upcoming events (encourage creativity or this could become a cluttered mess); introduce a "Class of the Month" with pictures (and names), examples of activities, Scripture studied, and notes from students to the congregation. Provide an opinion box with a question to spark a response. (Print some responses in the church newsletter.)

For Parents

Create a bulletin board for parents and guardians. On it place current articles, cartoons, notes, facts, or pictures. Include items for child and parent faith-building. Include articles from curriculum teachers' books. Use large titles, borders, and so on. Include the name of the publication and date for items clipped from magazines, curriculum, or newspapers. Make church announcements a primary part of the area. Change items frequently.

Tips for Creating Bulletin Boards

THEMES: Keep themes simple. Be clear about what you want to say or do. Persons who just walk by should be able to clearly understand what is being communicated.

COLORS: Use colors that attract attention (yellow on dark or medium blue, grass green on soft yellow). If in doubt about color combinations, hang samples up and move back several steps. What do you see? If still in doubt, ask someone else. If using a rainbow of colors, use a white or neutral background. If lettering doesn't stand out, outline with a dark color.

BACKGROUND: Change the background of the bulletin board frequently. Try fabric (a small print is a nice change of pace.) Use want-ad sections from the newspaper. Use gift-wrap paper. (I once used as a background a blue Christmas wrapping paper with a small white dove. Using an opaque projector, I made a large copy of a dove on heavy white paper and centered it on the background. No words were used. The board's simplicity was dramatic and drew lots of comments.)

LETTERING: Make letters simple for easy reading. Lettering stencils are helpful. Try making your own. Or, ask a school teacher friend if he or she has access to a letter cutter. Make two copies (of two coordinating colors) at the same time. Attach them just slightly offset, creating a shadow effect. Outline letters with a dark marker for accent.

LARGE PICTURES: Using an opaque projector makes it easy to make a large copy of a small picture. Overhead projectors also work well after you photocopy a small picture onto an acetate sheet. Simple pictures outlined with a black marker are very visible.

FASTENING: Thumb tacks, map tacks and push pins become a part of the design. Use with care. Straight pins are less obvious but add a bit of shine. (Use a thimble to protect your fingers.) Staples are the least obvious and are easy to use. Careful placement makes them almost invisible. Glue works well if you do not want to reuse any pieces. All-purpose white glue can wrinkle paper.

ADDING DIMENSION: Cut strips of firm paper and fold them like an accordion. Paste to the back of an item and then to the bulletin board to make a pop-out design. Use firm paper and fasten the middle of edge only, letting the rest of the figure stand out from the bulletin board. Design a part of the bulletin board to hang over the edge. Use layers, with the bottom layers getting progressively darker in color.

HELP!

Some people really enjoy the creativity of making bulletin boards. Find those persons. Recruit several persons who will take responsibility to help with bulletin boards. The look of the boards will be different with each person. Interest will increase. Provide training and supplies for the bulletin board volunteers. Be clear about a schedule.

Put together a kit or a shelf with scissors, stapler and staples, yard or meter stick, straight pins, and other requested supplies.

A step stool is helpful, as is a rolling cart or table from which to work. Rolls of colored background paper found at a school supply store are a much appreciated bonus. A few idea books on bulletin boards are always helpful (along with, of course, copies of this article).

One Last Word

Creating bulletin boards is a challenge. May you face the challenge of bulletin boards with renewed vigor and appreciation. Enjoy the finished products. (And change them often.)

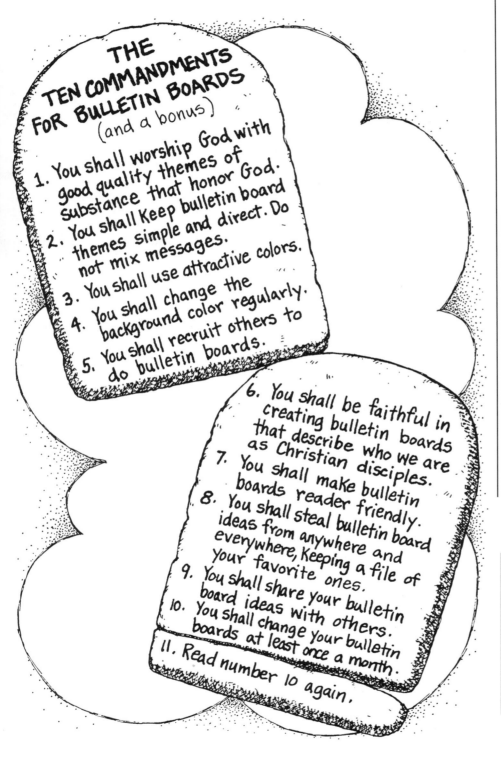

THE TEN COMMANDMENTS FOR BULLETIN BOARDS
(and a bonus)

1. You shall worship God with good quality themes of substance that honor God.
2. You shall keep bulletin board themes simple and direct. Do not mix messages.
3. You shall use attractive colors.
4. You shall change the background color regularly.
5. You shall recruit others to do bulletin boards.
6. You shall be faithful in creating bulletin boards that describe who we are as Christian disciples.
7. You shall make bulletin boards reader friendly.
8. You shall steal bulletin board ideas from anywhere and everywhere, keeping a file of your favorite ones.
9. You shall share your bulletin board ideas with others.
10. You shall change your bulletin boards at least once a month.
11. Read number 10 again.

Mary Alice Donovan Gran has worked for more than twenty-five years as a volunteer and professional Christian educator. Mary Alice came from Iowa to be the Director of Christian Education and Children's Ministries for the General Board of Discipleship and now lives in Nashville, Tennessee.

Splash, Paint, and Play Sunday

A "Messy Sunday" for All Ages

by Elizabeth Crocker

When Jesus taught his disciples that they must become like little children in order to enter the kingdom of heaven, he probably wasn't thinking about smudgy fingerprints or splashing in the nearest puddle. But Jesus was teaching his followers the value of childlike qualities: humility, curiosity, spontaneity, and wonder.

These attributes are vital to developing our faith at any age, and they are among the gifts children bring to their church community. Why not make the most of these with a special Sunday school session this summer?

Invite God's children of all ages to participate in a Splash, Paint, and Play Sunday. This event will be a change of pace from your regular Sunday school, but it could be held during the usual Sunday school hour.

Plan far enough in advance to allow for posters, fliers, and newsletter and bulletin announcements asking everyone to come to Sunday school in their play clothes. (Be sure to have paint shirts or smocks on hand for those who forget.) On this day, everyone will become as a little child to experience, explore, and celebrate God's good creation.

Splash, Paint, and Play Sunday can be developed by a team of children's Sunday school teachers or by your education work area or children's council. Involve your pastor and check with the board of trustees to address any concerns they might have. The more people you can involve in the planning and promotion, the more successful the event will be. If you decide to use the event as a culmination of summer Sunday school or vacation Bible school, you might ask the children's classes to help with planning.

You will need a large open area—outdoors if possible. For every one hundred people you expect, you will need ten to twelve activity centers with enough space for traffic flow. Think in terms of safety and weather when choosing a site. Decide on an alternative location or backup plan in case of rain.

Is there space indoors for activities that require an electrical outlet? If you use extension cords, be sure to tape them snugly against the floor. Allow drying space for projects involving paint or wet materials, and decide where participants will wash their hands.

Next select the activities. With the planning team, spend time in prayer and search the Scriptures for a theological basis for each activity.

Try using the suggested Scriptures from your children's summer Sunday school curriculum or VBS. For example, if the children are studying a unit on Creation, perhaps you will fill a dish with water and have participants breathe through a straw to blow air across the water, reminding us how God's spirit moved across the water in the beginning (Genesis 1:2). Older children through adults will be interested to know that the Hebrew word for *spirit* meant breath. Be clear about connecting the learning experiences to Scripture and to our Christian faith.

Choose activities that involve the five senses: taste, touch, smell, sight, and hearing. Add activities that encourage whole-body movement. This event would be a great time to try some of the suggestions from your children's Sunday school curriculum that you have not been able to use in your usual Sunday school setting.

Check to see that the activities are well-balanced in terms of their appropriateness for all age and ability levels. For instance, are the activities inviting for pre-readers? Are the activities environmentally sound?

Find a volunteer artist and ask him or her to make rebus posters with instructions for each activity so that the activities will be as self-directed as possible. Keep instructions simple and allow for individual creativity rather than cookie-cutter productions.

Arrange for Sunday school teachers or other volunteers to manage the centers. Decide who will be responsible for gathering the supplies and setting up. Be sure to have someone take photographs.

Twelve Activity Ideas to Spark Your Imagination

1. **Paint a tempera wash.** Have participants brush diluted blue tempera paint over a crayon drawing of God's wonderful world. Remember that water covered everything until God contained the water and created land (Genesis 1:6-10).

2. **Make solar prints.** Use solar paper, available through a school supply or nature store. Have each learner select from assorted natural objects—leaves, twigs, shells, or flowers—and follow the instructions that come with the paper. Recall how God separated light and darkness to make day and night. Thank God for the great light of the sun (Genesis 1:3-5, 16).

3. **Enjoy water play.** Fill a tub or children's wading pool with water. Provide seashells and pebbles (or aquarium gravel) for scooping. Talk about how the water feels and sounds. Give thanks to God for water (Genesis 1:10).

4. **Make clay people.** Let participants use play clay to shape their own creations. Recall that God formed a human being from the soil (Genesis 2:7).

5. **Paint a starry sky.** Have participants sponge paint or stencil yellow stars on dark blue or black paper. Or they can draw stars with glue and shake gold or silver glitter over it. (Be sure to use a glitter pan.) Thank God for the stars we see at night (Genesis 1:16-17).

6. **Mix some mud.** Provide a tub of potting soil or dirt and some small watering cans filled with water. Let participants use their hands to mix the earth and water together. Encourage them to explore the way the mud feels and smells. Talk about how we need both soil and water for living things to grow. Give thanks to God for planning for all things to grow (Genesis 1:24-30).

7. **Plant a grass garden.** Use an egg carton, milk carton, or other biodegradable container. Fill it two-thirds full with potting soil. Have participants sprinkle some grass seeds on top and add water. Use this to create a sense of wonder about God's gift of grass and other green, growing plants (Genesis 1:30).

8. **Make a handprint tree of your church family.** Hang a white sheet on a wall. Draw a simple tree outline with a laundry marker, indicating a trunk and branches. Place a protective covering (paint tarp, cardboard, or the like) on the wall and floor. Have several colors of tempera paint from which to choose. Invite the learners to dip their hands in tempera paint and to add their handprints to the tree. Have them first dab their paint-covered hands on absorbent paper such as newsprint to prevent running of the paint onto the fabric. Celebrate being part of God's creation (Genesis 1:27-28).

9. **Make a sand-art fish.** Cut out fish shapes from posterboard. Prepare colored sand in salt shakers by mixing powdered tempera with clean sand or with salt. Make several colors. Invite the learners to brush a fish shape with glue and then to shake colored sand over it. Let learners enjoy the colors of the sand, the patterns it makes, and the way it feels when it is dry. Recall how God made creatures to fill the sea (Genesis 1:20).

10. **Enjoy colorful toast.** You will need a toaster and an electrical outlet for this activity. Add food coloring to small amounts of milk to make paint for the bread. Have learners use cotton swabs to apply the colored milk to sliced bread. Let them make their own designs that remind them of God's good world (Genesis 1:31). Tell learners to be careful not to saturate the bread. It should not drip or be soggy. Toast the bread. Say a thank-you prayer before eating.

11. **Play Animal Charades.** Encourage learners to enjoy the fun of moving as their favorite animal does. Say a prayer to thank God for wildlife (Genesis 1:24-25).

12. **Trace people shapes.** Roll out long sheets of paper on the floor and have learners lie down on the paper. Use a crayon to trace the outlines of their bodies. The outlines can be cut out and decorated to make life-size paper dolls. Remind learners that we are God's handiwork, too (Genesis 1:26).

Do not expect that everyone will participate in every activity. If you want to be sure that they do, you will need to reduce the number of activities and plan timed rotations. It will be more fun, though, if you allow learners to fully enjoy the activities they choose and to work at their own pace. Stop the festivities in time to clean up, and ask everyone to help. After the event, send special thank-yous to volunteers who served on the planning team or managed an activity center. Display photos as a reminder that Sunday school is a place where all ages can grow in wisdom and faith and can have fun in the process.

Elizabeth Crocker says that she is an experienced messmaker, having learned from the children and youth in the local churches she has served as a diaconal minister of Christian education. She lives in Lugoff, South Carolina.

Snacks in the Classroom

by JoAnne Metz Chase

We are a people who gather around the table. In worship we are called to share bread and juice at the Lord's Table. Our special gatherings may include a potluck meal or coffee and desert. We have bake sales, and we bring meals to others as a sign of hospitality and comfort. The disciples recognized Jesus in the breaking of bread at Emmaus, and the disciples received instruction from Jesus over a breakfast of fish. Is it any wonder that many Sunday school lessons for children include a snack? Yet, too often food is limited to being a time filler or group pleaser when it could be so much more.

Snacks can reinforce the lesson focus, expand the learning by incorporating more of the five senses, build cooperation and community, and create a dramatic atmosphere. How can teachers use this ready-made enhancer to increase learning?

Three Steps

1. Decide what objective the snack should help accomplish. By identifying the objective, you will be better able to create a food experience that will fit the lesson. For example: an objective might be to visualize what being a shepherd was like in order to understand Psalm 23 in a new way.
2. Consider what foods would fulfill that function. You could choose to serve raisins and pita bread filled with cheese or warm bread with honey or homemade butter. For the beverage, serve chilled goat's milk or room temperature water poured from a leather flask.
3. Select ways to use the snacks to meet the objective. While the children are eating, discuss the life of a shepherd or read Psalm 23, adding comments that connect the words with the reality of a life spent caring for sheep. Tell younger children about David's childhood responsibility of watching the flock, or examine with older children ways that God cares for us like a shepherd watching a flock.

Some Ideas for Learning

In addition to enhancing learning, food can be a symbol of community, a way to increase class cohesiveness and identity. There are a variety of food possibilities. Try some of these:

> ## Snacks expand learning and build cooperation and community.

• Create a guessing game for younger children, smelling, tasting, or touching food that is hidden from view. Create a "crazy recipe" puzzle where groups of older children try to name the snack from a disguised list of ingredients.
• Use a "production line" to make snacks for the class or for visitors, to feed persons living in a shelter or family dealing with death or serious illness, or to send to college students far from home. Working together for a common cause is an excellent group-building experience.
• Tell the folk tale *Stone Soup* while making soup from vegetables or cans of soup brought by each child or while making a salad from everyone's favorite fruits.
• Many children do not have the opportunity to cook or bake with their fathers. Inviting several men from the congregation to help prepare food with the children can address stereotypical role models as the participants decorate cookies for distribution to others. Use large store-bought or homemade cookies, tubes of frosting, and sprinkles.
• Potlucks are a regular part of adult classes and gatherings. Adapt the potluck for use with children in class or on retreats by having a junk food potluck or "my favorite breakfast food" potluck, which could include cold pizza.
• Baking bread for communion can be a multi-layered experience set during a study of the sacraments or during Holy Week. Making grape juice can be a messy but interesting way to explore the Lord's Supper since it allows us to visualize the broken nature of the grapes used for wine and grain used for bread.
• A number of foods reflect life in biblical times and can add to the classroom experience and discussion. Glean corn or other vegetables in a field or nearby yard to learn about Ruth. Expand a simple mealtime menu of cheese, dates, figs, olives, lamb, bread, and honey to become a wedding feast at Cana. During the season of Easter, fish-shaped crackers or a cake shaped like a lamb can be the edible part of an exploration of some symbols for Jesus.
• One of the most helpful props in a simulation or drama, next to costumes, is food. Children are more willing to volunteer and find it easier to enter into a role when familiar things are part of the experience.

• A role play with teens about communication with parents over grades or car usage can be facilitated by seating the participants around a table at mealtime and providing food.

•A simulation where all students have been assigned a handicapping condition can become something more when a meal is shared. The discovery that by helping one another, all can be fed is a very deep learning experience in this setting.

•Think about the moment when Christ was discovered in the breaking of bread by the travelers who met him on the road to Emmaus. That dramatic moment when the loaf is torn in half could be relived again and again in the minds of children as bread is broken during communion.

Seasonal Suggestions

Sometimes the season of the year or the church calendar will suggest certain seasonal foods. A summer lesson on creation or the beauty of God's world might lead to an edible flower salad. Apples, pumpkin seeds, and cider are fall snacks. Epiphany lends itself to star-shaped cookies or to slicing apple rings to find the hidden star. Making butterfly-shaped snacks out of bread dough or cookie dough is a relatively non-messy activity for Easter, when many children are dressed up.

Final Warnings

Be aware of any food allergies or health problems that the children in your class might experience. Parents or guardians are more than willing to give this information when asked. Or it might already be on file in the Sunday school records. If foods such as chocolate, nuts, milk, dyes, and so forth are used in a food activity or snack, provide alternatives or allow the family to send a snack from home. When a child's food intake is monitored for timing or quantity, the parents or guardians can help work through this obstacle. Growing dietary awareness encourages teachers to use healthful food rather than high-fat or salty snacks. Food used as a reward or to make children feel better if feelings are hurt reinforces some negative eating behaviors.

Because food is so central to our sense of well being, it is important not to abuse the use of food. Always be willing to change, modify, or drop an activity rather than use it to manipulate or exclude any student.

Snacks in the classroom, with some creative planning and fore-thought, can be a useful learning device in any teacher's tool box.

> # Food used as a reward or to make children feel better reinforces some negative eating behaviors.

JoAnne is a diaconal minister of Christian education in Naperville, Illinois.

Drama in the Classroom

by Peggy Goochey

I had just arrived in a Middle Eastern country where I was planning to live for the next two years. As I climbed up the side stairs of my house and stood on the flat roof for the first time, I felt as if I had been here before! How strange!

And then I remembered. Yes! The house reminded me of those little box houses I made in Sunday school as a child. Did you also make the ones with a flat roof and stairs up the side? And suddenly the good feelings I had experienced in Sunday school came over me, and I began to feel good about this place too.

> # Feelings are a link between the "then" and "now" of a biblical narrative.

Does this seem a bit dramatic? Perhaps, but then, feelings can be very dramatic! And feelings are a key ingredient to good drama, whether it is on stage or in the classroom. Feelings are a link between the "then" and "now" of the biblical narrative.

Use It in Sunday School

Using drama in the classroom as a teaching tool enables children to get inside the feelings, thoughts, and words of the stories and make them their own. Drama in the classroom is not about performance. It is about using process as a learning experience. Process, not performance, is the product.

With younger children drama helps "tell" the story, and with older children drama provides a way for them to "get into" or "respond to" the story. Your role, as the leader, is to be the storyteller/director/guide, standing alongside, probing, nurturing, and giving the group guidance.

Pre-readers
Play the Story

Children learn through play. One way to use drama with pre-readers is "playing the story," or dramatic play. Pre-readers "play a story" in much the same way that they play house. The difference is that you, as the leader, narrate and sidecoach while the children act out the story (*Theater Games for the Classroom: A Teacher's Handbook,* by Viola Spolin; Northwestern University Press, 1986; page 5).

Sidecoaching is calling out words or phrases that help the players focus and create movement. It happens in the midst of the activity, without breaking the mood. In sidecoaching you say the phases spontaneously out of observing what is happening in the playing area.

Use this outline as a guide to "play a story" with pre-readers.

Moses in the Bulrushes

Invite the children into the story area.

Give the name of the story. Tell the characters in it: mother, sister, princess, attendants. Name the props and which props go with each character: mother-doll, sister-basket, princess-headdress.

Assign the parts, give out the props, and put the headdress on the princess.

Place the mother and sister on one side of you in the story area, with the princess and attendants on the other side. Identify the river as being in front of you. Other children are seated in the area, listening and watching the story unfold.

Instruct the children to stand up when they hear their character mentioned in the story, and to do exactly what the story says they do.

Tell the story in a simple, direct way, sidecoaching the action at the same time.

Let the children play the story more than once, changing parts if they want.

Props and Costumes

Using props and costumes helps children get into the story. Most three-year-olds through first-graders love to play "dress up." Take advantage of this and provide simple costumes and headgear.

A few props, such as a basket for Moses in the bulrushes and a doll for the baby, will help get the children into the story and further enhance their experiences.

Elementary-Age Children
Improvise Situations

Imagination is the key ingredient that enables children to believe that what they are playing is possible. A method involving both imagination and feelings is *improvisation,* and it is excellent for use with children in the first through sixth grades.

Art by John Ham

Do an improvisation before you tell the story. This activity is not used to tell the biblical story. It is used to tell an everyday experience that contains the same feelings as the biblical story. It enables the children to get inside the feelings of the characters, thus relating to the story in a believable way.

In preparing an improvisation for class, first identify the feelings present in the story. Then think of a situation common to an elementary-age child in which he or she might have experienced those feelings. Don't try to make the *situation* match; just make the *feelings* match.

The activity can be a group improvisation or consist of couples, trios, and so on. Divide the group into whatever patterns you need for the situation you are going to act out.

Suppose you were going to tell the story "Jesus and the Money Changers in the Temple." Divide the children into groups of four. Then give the following directions to the children:

"Each group needs a mother and three children. One of the children belongs to the mother. The other children are friends. Decide who will play which parts. When you have made these choices, I want the mother to raise her hand so I will know when we can move on. If you are playing a child, you will play your real age.

"The scene takes place in the home of the child whose mother is gone. If you are playing that child, imagine yourself in your house, expecting your friends. As the improvisation begins, your friends arrive. You are very impressed with them, and you want them to be impressed with you. Invite them to do whatever you want—play with your toys, eat a snack, watch TV, and so on.

"Improvising is putting yourself in the situation and allowing your feelings to come forth spontaneously as if it is really happening. Pantomime your actions, and speak to one another in character only. Each group continues in the situation until I say 'Cut.' Any questions?"

(Privately instruct the friends to take advantage of the situation, be rough in the house, and mess things up.) "Mothers leave the room now. Decide where you have gone and imagine you are there. This will help you get into character. I will come get you when it is time for you to come home. Friends get ready to arrive. Action."

All groups improvise at the same time. As leader, you circulate among the groups, sidecoaching the activity. After things get going with the friends, get the mothers and have them go to their houses. At this point (not before) tell the mothers the situation and what they

will each find at home. Call "Cut" after each mother has had an opportunity to be a part of and respond to the situation at home.

When the improvisation is over, invite the children to discuss what they experienced, asking them to tell you how they felt. Now you are ready to introduce the biblical story through some of the feelings they have just experienced.

Drama Brings a Sense of Realness to the Story

Drama in the classroom offers children the opportunity to imagine themselves in the life, time, and situation of the biblical story. They then act out their own version of that story through their experience and feelings. Thus, they are able to relate to the story according to their own levels of understanding.

Have you offered drama to your students? How about now?

Peggy Goochey lives in Menlo Park, California, and is a diaconal minister. She leads an elementary-age creative drama troupe, is a workshop leader and a consultant in religious drama.

Roundup Your Church
by Martha Coburn

Our children's council began its planning with families on our minds, thinking about a church family as a necessary extension for individuals in today's mobile society. Our goal was to include every member of the church in all of our programs and become an intergenerational church that showed love in all we did. We decided that we needed to implement an all-church event to succeed. Our main goal was to have 100 percent attendance.

The planning began for a Fall Roundup, and the date of October 3 was highlighted on the church calendar. Each council member selected an area of interest to start planning for. Each group worked independently, making contacts and putting details into place.

By the middle of August, the performers were scheduled, animals were reserved, and the building of booths and a stage was started. On the first of September, we gathered the leaders of all Sunday school classes to share our excitement. We asked the leaders to tell their classes about this event and to emphasize that the goal was to have an all-church event.

We knew that weekly announcements needed to be directed to all age groups and had to be announced from the pulpit during worship. Our associate pastor dressed in his western suit and used his best Texas drawl for the kickoff invitation. The Uncalled Four barbershop quartet sang during one service to give everyone a sample of what to expect at the event. We built excitement into each step of our planning.

The roundup was located outdoors behind the church and culminated with a chili supper and auction in the Chuck Wagon (our church gym). Events were scheduled so that people could move from each activity with something for all age groups. (See the schedule next to this article.)

After the chili supper, an auction of baked goods netted over $400. Many items were donated by local businesses. Many church people provided the labor to build booths and enjoyed the fellowship of working together. The profit exceeded our greatest expectations and went to our children's mission fund, which provided mittens, hats, and socks at Christmas for the

Denton City-County Day Nursery. Other money went into our Back-to-School project for children in the Denton area who need school supplies.

The real joy was to have other intergenerational events follow the success of this first roundup. Our children's summer Sunday school program started meeting as a "family" (kindergarten through 5th grade) with each of the adult classes assisting with the event on an assigned Sunday. Small groups for Bible study and prayer began during the week. Now many people participate in and enjoy our Wednesday night meal. The congregation is benefiting from the fellowship of this extended family known as the church.

Martha Coburn attends First United Methodist Church, Denton, Texas.

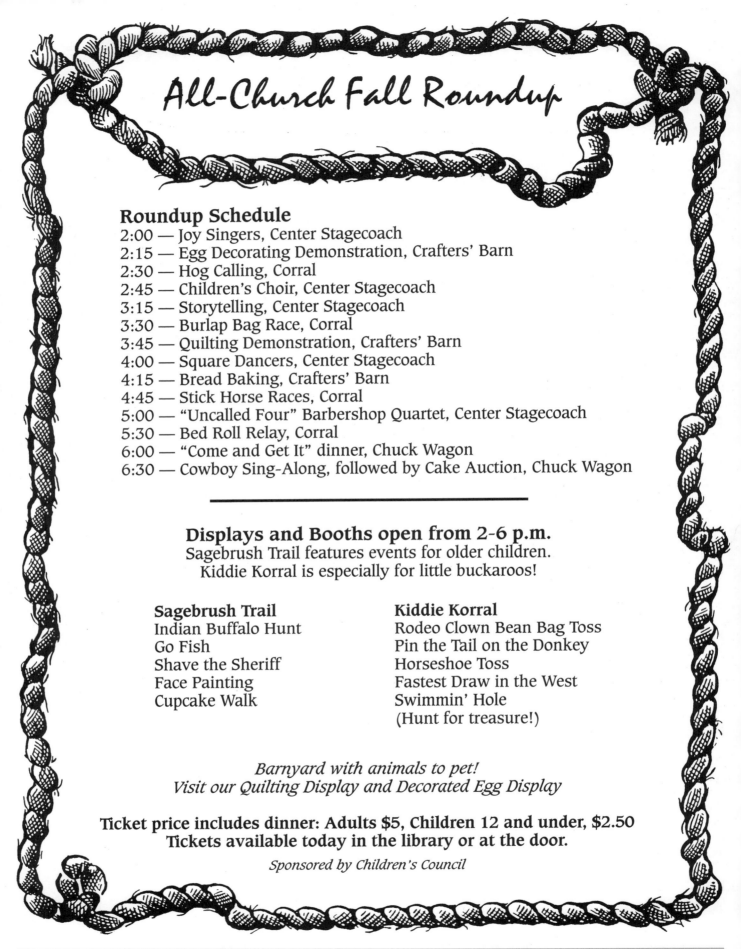

All-Church Fall Roundup

Roundup Schedule
2:00 — Joy Singers, Center Stagecoach
2:15 — Egg Decorating Demonstration, Crafters' Barn
2:30 — Hog Calling, Corral
2:45 — Children's Choir, Center Stagecoach
3:15 — Storytelling, Center Stagecoach
3:30 — Burlap Bag Race, Corral
3:45 — Quilting Demonstration, Crafters' Barn
4:00 — Square Dancers, Center Stagecoach
4:15 — Bread Baking, Crafters' Barn
4:45 — Stick Horse Races, Corral
5:00 — "Uncalled Four" Barbershop Quartet, Center Stagecoach
5:30 — Bed Roll Relay, Corral
6:00 — "Come and Get It" dinner, Chuck Wagon
6:30 — Cowboy Sing-Along, followed by Cake Auction, Chuck Wagon

---

Displays and Booths open from 2-6 p.m.
Sagebrush Trail features events for older children.
Kiddie Korral is especially for little buckaroos!

Sagebrush Trail
Indian Buffalo Hunt
Go Fish
Shave the Sheriff
Face Painting
Cupcake Walk

Kiddie Korral
Rodeo Clown Bean Bag Toss
Pin the Tail on the Donkey
Horseshoe Toss
Fastest Draw in the West
Swimmin' Hole
(Hunt for treasure!)

Barnyard with animals to pet!
Visit our Quilting Display and Decorated Egg Display

Ticket price includes dinner: Adults $5, Children 12 and under, $2.50
Tickets available today in the library or at the door.

Sponsored by Children's Council

Animals of the Bible

by Jean Gordon Wilcox and Branson Wilcox

Did you ever wonder about some of the animals that are mentioned in the Bible? How did Mary and Joseph get to Bethlehem? How did shepherds spend their time? What was a fatted calf? If you learn more about some of these animals, you may be able to help the Bible stories come alive for the children.

A Donkey in Every Stable

The donkey was the pickup truck or low-priced car of Bible days. It was small but strong. The donkey ate much less than a horse, so it was cheaper to own. Abraham and his family did their traveling with donkeys. Mary and Joseph would have taken a donkey to Bethlehem.

Travelers fastened their bundles and packages to the donkey's back. The family walked beside it. Small children or the old or sick or pregnant could ride instead of walking.

Every family that needed to haul heavy loads depended on a donkey. A carpenter would need one to carry building supplies. This meant that most homes needed a place to keep a donkey, just as homes now need a place for a car. Each courtyard house had a stable for the animals at one side of the courtyard. The manger, where the animals ate, was often a hollowed-out stone box, flat on the ground. Even one-room houses might have a small courtyard, with an animal shelter made of brush and poles. Or a donkey might be tied outside the house.

Some books about Bible lands show houses much like poor village houses of the nineteenth and twentieth centuries. These have one room, with a raised end for the

> **The donkey was the pickup truck or low-priced car of Bible days.**

family and a lower area for the animals. But so far archaeologists have not found evidence of this kind of house during Bible times. Village houses normally had courtyards. City people often lived in apartment complexes instead, but they wouldn't have needed a donkey as much.

Shopping Malls on Four Legs

Sheep and goats provided a main part of a family's supplies. Sheep provided meat and wool for clothing. Families also liked to keep a goat for milk and cheese. A goat and her kids (young goats) could share the donkey's shelter.

Even relatively poor families tried to find enough money to buy two lambs in the spring. One of the lambs was killed and eaten for the Passover celebration. The other would be raised as a pet during the summer, cared for by the children. Nathan's story in 2 Samuel 12:2-4 tells of such a lamb. In the fall it would be killed and the meat preserved in its fat for winter food. In most families meat was only eaten on special occasions.

Some herders owned large flocks of sheep and goats. A young man of the owner's family might be in charge of several hired shepherds. Owners of large herds also sold their best lambs and kids for Temple offerings.

Cloth and leather were the main products of large flocks. The black or brown goat hair made good tents. Goat skins were used to make bottles for wine and water. Skins were tanned for leather for strong tents and for sandals.

Village shepherds had to lead the flocks carefully to good grass. They had to find still, fresh water that the sheep could reach, or pour well water into drinking troughs. The shepherds might take care of sheep and goats for several owners during the day, and return them to their houses at night. Large flocks usually stayed in folds or stone pens outside the town at night, so that all but one guard could go home.

The shepherds protected the sheep and goats from dangerous animals. (There were bears, lions, leopards, and wolves in Israel in Old Testament times. Most were later killed off.) The shepherds had to pull, prod, or hook wandering animals back on safe ground. Shepherds also treated the wounds of injured animals.

What About Cattle?

We don't read much in the Bible about cow's milk or cheese, or eating beef. Perhaps these animals were just too expensive compared with goats and sheep. Young bulls or calves were sometimes sacrificed to God by the rich. Calves were used as food for special occasions. A prize calf might be kept its whole life in a stall and fed by hand so that it was fat and tender. The father of the prodigal son gave such a calf for his son's homecoming feast (Luke 15:23).

Think of oxen as tractors. Farmers liked to use oxen to pull plows or threshing sleds.

Ships of the Desert and Weapons of War

The Arabian camel was rare in Israel until the time of David. Even after that, camels were used mostly in long-distance and desert hauling to Arab lands. The Persians, including the Magi, were mostly horse riders.

Horses were used almost entirely to pull war chariots in Old Testament times. In New Testament times, powerful Romans and the rich used horses. Jesus chose to ride into Jerusalem on Palm Sunday on an ordinary donkey.

Animals and the classroom

How can you use all this information in your teaching? There are several ways to include animals in classroom drama. You can use imaginary animals, students can play the parts of animals, or you can use prop animals. You can make a stick donkey with a stuffed cloth head. Wires inside the ears will help stiffen them. Or make donkey masks out of brown paper sacks joined together (Fig. 1). Fasten the masks to chairs or a sawhorses. Include caring for animals as part of your roleplay of daily life in the Bible.

You might make models or scenes of stories that include stables and animals. Small animals can be cut from folded heavy paper (Fig. 2).

Make a small sheep from a cotton ball. Tie a string around a corner of the ball to create a neck and head (Fig. 3). Glue in chenille stem (pipe-cleaner) legs.

Suggest that the children include animals when they use art to illustrate Bible stories. For young children, white packing foam pellets make a great flock of sheep to glue to paper.

As you study the Bible stories you teach, reflect on how each story fits into a whole way of living. Animals were almost certainly a part of Bible-times life. Including them will help the children understand how real the Bible stories are.

Jean Gordon Wilcox and her son Branson have many years of Christian education experience between them. They reside in Concordia, Kansas.

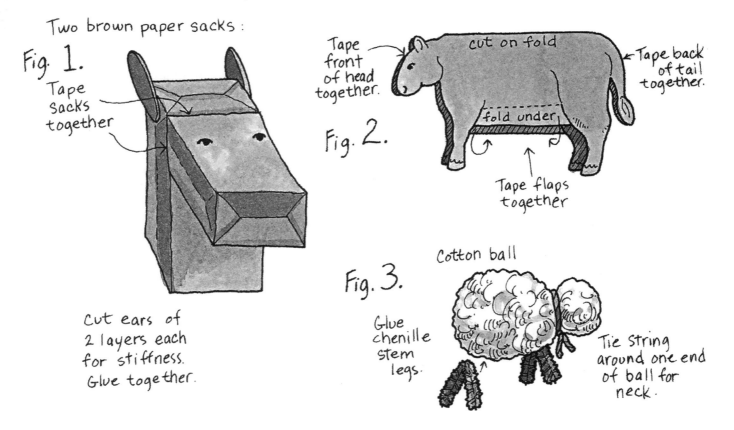

Two brown paper sacks:

Fig. 1.
Tape sacks together

cut ears of 2 layers each for stiffness. Glue together.

Tape front of head together.

cut on fold

Tape back of tail together.

fold under

Fig. 2.

Tape flaps together

Cotton ball

Fig. 3.

Glue chenille stem legs.

Tie string around one end of ball for neck.

Living in a Working-Class Home

by Jean Gordon Wilcox and Branson Wilcox

How did Bible people live? If you understand the cultural background of the Bible stories you tell, you will be able to help your children see Bible people as real people like themselves.

In Jesus' time different people lived in different kinds of houses, just as we do today. Because of the warm dry climate of Israel, a house usually had a flat roof and a courtyard.

In the rocky hills most houses were built of uncut rocks from the fields. Rocks were chosen that a man could carry by himself, and they were held together with mud. In the plains, where there were fewer stones, cheaper houses could be made of sun-dried mudbricks.

Since field stone was cheap and mudbricks could be made even by the children, the size of a family's house was limited mainly by the space they had available and by the availability of the help of friends and relatives.

The typical house was really a cluster of rooms around a central courtyard. In towns, where space was precious, families might have lived in one or more rooms in a kind of apartment complex.

Who Were the Poor People?

Many different groups of people were poor. The poorest were the slaves housed by their owners. The independent poor included widows and fatherless children who had very few ways to earn a living and no help available to build or repair their houses.

Other poor people included those who farmed small pieces of land and the many laborers who worked for farmers, fishermen, or shepherds by the day or who worked for wages in shops and small businesses.

Skilled craftpersons, such as carpenters, often struggled to make ends meet, but they would not have been considered poor.

Houses of the Poor

We do not have reliable information about the houses of the poor because the flimsiest and lightest structures of Bible times were not preserved well enough over the centuries for us to learn much about them through the digging of today's archaeologists. In some villages and in the lower city of Jerusalem archaeologists have found what may have been the remains of adjoining one-room houses. Such stone houses probably had flat roofs made of beams, branches, and mats, topped with hard-packed mud.

With a sun-shade or a small upper room built over one end, this kind of roof could have served the same function as a courtyard, where cooking, eating, napping, and most work could be done.

Thin-walled stone or mudbrick one-room houses probably were too flimsy for the weight of such a roof. Houses with lighter branch and straw roofs were often clustered around a common courtyard. If a poor family was lucky enough to own a goat or other animal, these animals were sheltered inside the house at night.

The family lived on a raised platform at one end, and the animals occupied the lower section of the floor.

A Day in the Life of a Hired Worker's Family

Now we will reconstruct what it might have been like to live in the home of a typical family in Bible times. This typical family consists of a husband, a wife, several sons and daughters, and perhaps a grandmother.

The small pottery oil lamp burns all night as a night light and a source of fire. If the lamp goes out, the wife gets a light from a neighbor. Before dawn the members of the family are up. They have slept in their clothes. The wife immediately

adds oil to the lamp from a small jug and adjusts the wick. She lights a second lamp from the first one while her family gets ready for the day. She sets each lamp on a small shelf carved into the wall.

Each family member pours water into a bowl to wash hands and face. Breakfast consists of bread saved from the evening before.

The husband and his older sons put on their sandals and comb their hair with carved wooden combs. They take their outer cloaks from pegs on the wall and walk to work if they have work that day. If not, they go to the place where employers come looking for day laborers and wait.

In the villages the men and boys probably take with them a lunch of bread and cheese and perhaps dried fish and a small juglet of watered wine. In a town or city, if they can afford it, the men and boys may buy a bowl of soup or hot cereal at one of the many food stands along the streets.

The woman of the house leaves her baby in the charge of an older daughter or grandmother and begins her day's work. First, she hangs the blankets and sleeping mats where air will blow through them to freshen. Then she empties the washbasin out a window and carries the family's chamber pot to the village dump or a city sewer to empty it.

Next she hurries to the market, where the local farmers and fishermen bring their foods to sell. Since there is no way to keep fresh foods, the wife has to shop every day. She has only a little money, so she finds some cucumbers and some grapes that she can afford. Then she looks for bargains in dried fish, dried fruit, olives, olive oil, wine, and ground grain. When she has finished shopping, the wife carries her purchases home.

Then the wife picks up a large clay water jug and walks to the village well or public fountain. She balances the heavy jar of water on a pad of cloth on her shoulder or head to carry it home. Like her husband and sons, the wife may buy hot soup and fresh bread for lunch, or she may just eat cold food at home.

While the wife is out, a daughter sweeps the hard-packed dirt floor with a twig broom and tidies up by returning the family's possessions to the boxes, shelves, or pegs where they belong. The baby's cradle is a piece of heavy cloth hanging by its four corners from a ceiling beam. The older daughter has tried to keep clean cloths wrapped around the baby. And she has washed out the soiled ones, probably muttering to herself that she always gets the dirty jobs.

The rest of the women's day is spent in food preparation and crafts that might earn some money. The wife or the grandmother might spin thread from flax or goat hair. The thread can be sold to the dyer or weaver, since the family doesn't have a loom of its own. The women may also sew or embroider clothes for others or make small crafts.

Cooking for the Family

If the family has a courtyard or roof, it will have a small stone-lined fire area. The wife uses dried animal dung or dried olive waste, after the oil is removed, for fuel. There is never enough wood available to burn.

The wife lights the fire with a wick lit from the lamp. She balances a round-bottomed clay cooking pot on three rocks over the fire. Into the pot she puts water, grain, lentils, and salt to cook for the family's evening meal.

While this stew is cooking, the wife mixes flour, oil, and water and shapes flat circles of bread. One way to cook the bread is to wait until after the fire has burned for a while. Then the wife scrapes the coals away from an area of the fire circle and bakes the bread directly on the hot rocks.

Another way is to use a flat clay frying pan. Kneeling beside the fire, the wife uses cloth pads to move the stew pot off the tall rocks. She puts the flat pan there instead. When the pan is hot, she bakes the circles of flat bread, one at a time, in the pan. Then she puts a wooden handle into the short hollow clay handle of the pan, lifts it off the fire, and puts the stew pot back on.

On a rainy day the wife can cook on a flat stone inside the house, but that makes the place very smoky. Nearby a neighbor owns a short clay cookstove, in which she builds a fire. She cooks with her pots on top.

An Evening at Home

When the men come home, the wife sets the stew, bread, olive oil, fruit, and vegetables out on a mat on the roof or courtyard (or inside in bad weather). She lights the lamps to give light for the meal, and the family members wash their hands.

The men come to sit around the mat first. The husband asks God's blessing and gives thanks for the bread. The wife serves the stew in small clay bowls, and it is eaten with wooden spoons. When the men finish eating, the wife pours wine into their cups. She then fills the cups with water so the wine won't be too strong. The husband lifts his cup and gives thanks before drinking.

When the men have finished eating, the women and small children eat. Then they wash all the bowls and pots and stack them in a corner of the room.

After supper the family may sit and talk, play games, or listen to a neighbor tell stories of the experiences of the early Hebrews. Later the family members spread out their sleeping mats and fall asleep. It is the end of a busy day, and the tired housewife puts out all the lamps except one before she too goes to sleep.

Jean Gordon Wilcox and her son Branson have many years of Christian Education experience between them. They reside in Concordia, Kansas.

Living in a Middle-Class Jewish Home

by Jean Gordon Wilcox and Branson Wilcox

BIBLE TEACHING HELPS

This is the second of two articles on life in the time of Jesus.

Your Bible stories will be more successful if you can create word pictures that help children know what it was like to live in Bible times. For instance, how did people live in a typical middle-class Jewish home in a small town in Galilee during the time of Roman occupation?

The building itself, because it was in the rocky hills, was probably made of stone. One part had two stories, the other part one story. A woven reed awning shaded the flat rooftop terrace. The only windows were high up, and from the main street the only entrance to be seen opened into a shop.

In the Shop

Most small business owners had their shops in or near their houses. Some worked with leather, while others made metal goods. Some dyed textiles; others prepared olive oil or perfumes. Let's look inside a carpenter's shop.

Here we smell the fresh wood stacked against the walls. A modern carpenter would recognize many of the simple iron and wooden tools hanging on pegs around the room—planes, saws, and hammers. Pieces of wooden wheels, a door, and a bed frame wait to be worked on. An older boy is smoothing a bench leg with a piece of sandstone. On the small workbench the carpenter is building the frame for a three-legged table.

Entering the Home

If we take the path or street at the side of the building, we see the entrance to the family quarters. This doorway is made of more carefully squared stones than in the rest of the house, and a small mezuzah at the doorway holds a Bible verse.

The heavy wooden door pivots on pins that extend into sockets below and above the door. A bar on the inside locks the door. From the entryway we can see straight ahead into the family room, or at the side into the courtyard. Several small rooms open off each side of the courtyard, including the shop we saw earlier. Today the weather is good, so everyone is in the courtyard.

In the Courtyard

In one corner of the courtyard a half-wall of pillars and feed troughs, as well as a barnyard smell, marks the home of the donkey that provides the family's transportation. A goat shares the donkey's stall and also provides milk for the family. Also in the courtyard a small mudbrick dome marks the home of a family of chickens.

A small kitchen garden in the courtyard includes a couple of grapevines and a small fig tree. A shelter in a corner hides the toilet, a wooden seat over a deep pit. Young children are playing games in the center of the court.

In another corner, two women and an older girl are sitting by a low, round clay oven. The fire in the oven is nearly out, but the walls are still hot. As two of the women pat lumps of unleavened dough into flat circles, the third slaps the circles against the hot inside wall of the oven, where they stick and bake.

If the women choose to make risen loaves instead of flat bread, they add to the mixture some fermented dough from a previous baking as leaven. Then they shape loaves, let them rise, and place them on a pottery tray to bake in the oven.

Next to the oven are round flat mill stones. The women turn the top stone around and around by a handle, grinding the grain into flour between the two stones.

Also in the courtyard is a fire-ring with pottery stands that hold cooking pots above the fire. Dried dung and dried olive paste—left when all the oil has been pressed out of the olives—are stored in baskets as fuel for the oven and fire-ring.

In a bowl nearby are wool fibers and a spindle. It takes every free minute a woman has to twist enough thread between her finger and the spinning spindle to make thread to be woven into cloth for the family's clothing. Older women may spend all their time spinning and weaving as they watch the children, so the younger women can do the harder work of the household.

Fortunately, several women can usually work together. Grandparents, married sons, and unmarried daughters usually share one or more connected courtyards. Each family has its own family room and sleeping area, but much of the housework is shared.

Inside the House

The inside room closest to where the women are working in the courtyard is the tiny kitchen. This middle-class kitchen has an indoor fireplace containing another small oven, a real convenience on a cold day. Next to the fireplace is a stack of clay serving and cooking bowls and pots that reaches nearly to the ceiling. A large brass basin that hangs on the wall is large enough to wash clothes or children. Soap is not yet known in the Holy Land, so fine scouring sand helps clean the dishes. Standing in a tall pot are wooden and metal cooking spoons and spatulas and knives. On a peg by the fireplace are large iron fire tongs for handling hot fuel. The floor in the kitchen is plaster over stone, kept clean by the wig broom in the corner. This floor is a contrast to the floor in the animal stall and the shop, where cracks between the stones let liquids soak through.

The kitchen opens into the main family room, where guests are entertained and where the family eats and works when the weather is bad. The walls here are high, and some high windows let in light. These walls and floors are smoothly plastered and painted. The bottom part of the walls is brown, the top is white. And a brown stripe outlines each doorway. This is a simple paint job compared with the elaborately painted walls and mosaic floors of the rich, but it marks the family as substantial in their town.

Pegs on the wall near the main door hold the family's outer wraps. A large stone jar holds water drawn from the cistern under the house; and a dipping cup, basin, and cloth nearby are used for washing hands and dusty feet before eating.

Niches or small built-in shelves in the walls hold oil lamps. Because this is a patriotic Jewish family, they do not use the fancy Roman-style molded lamps. Instead, the lamps are the plain wheel-made local lamps with a flat spout.

Three wooden benches are covered with cushions. A smooth wood tray sits on a three-legged frame to form a small table. A pile of cushions and rolled mats is stacked in a corner.

The benches and small table allow the carpenter, his oldest son, and a guest to eat Roman style if they wish, lying down with one elbow propped on cushions and their heads facing the table. The women serve the men of the house first and then wait behind the men's feet to be sure they have everything they need. After the men are finished, the rest of the family eats, probably sitting on cushions on the floor around a mat that serves as a table.

On one side of the room is a door to a low storage area and above that a curtained door to a tiny second-floor sleeping room. In the storage room, pottery jars hold grain, wine, olive oil, salt, lentils, fava beans, dried dates, and dried and pickled fish. Onions and dried herbs hang in bunches from the ceiling. The loom for weaving cloth is stored here too, along with other things the family will need during the year.

Upstairs

Back in the family room we climb a wooden ladder to one of the small sleeping rooms. A wooden bed frame on short legs has a rope platform and a wool mattress. Clothes hang on pegs or are stored in wooden boxes. One shelf holds a carved comb with large teeth on one side and fine teeth on the other as well as a box containing decorative pins to hold clothes together. The housewife's sewing kit is here also, with pins and needles made of bone.

This sleeping loft has a door onto a rooftop terrace over the kitchen. The roof is made of wooden beams topped with reed mats and a layer of hard-packed clay, a good floor for both the upper rooms and the outdoor rooftop terrace. A low stone wall keeps children from falling off the roof.

The rooftop, which is cooler than the courtyard in hot weather, is used for many of the same activities —eating, reading, working, or relaxing. A lightweight shade of branches and mats covers part of the roof area, and an outdoor stairway connects the courtyard with the roof and the other upstairs rooms.

Because this is an extended family compound, there are other family rooms and additional small sleeping and storage rooms around the court. Each family unit makes its own private quarters unique, and the entire family lives a happy life together.

Jean Gordon Wilcox and her son Branson have many years of Christian Education experience between them. They reside in Concordia, Kansas.

Wrap Your Children in the Story

by Ardis L. Letey

The Bible is too important to be studied only as history. You need to provide opportunities for children to gain a deeper and more personal understanding of the Bible.

One way to meet a Bible story is to "wrap yourself in the story," that is, to dress up and act it out. This approach is useful with children in Sunday school, in after-school programs, and in weekday young children's programs.

You may use the designs for biblical costumes suggested here along with whatever curriculum you are using in your group. The patterns are adjustable to the various sizes of your children, and the materials are easily available and inexpensive. You can hem the garments or leave the edges raw. Involve your children as much as possible, both in the creative stage and in the embellishment stage. This helps them feel they are part of the process.

These biblical costumes are sure to enliven your children's learning experiences at church. The designs honor your own gifts of imagination, so use them as a starting point. In biblical times the people who made clothing were no more creative than you are. So trust your ability and have fun!

BIBLE TEACHING HELPS

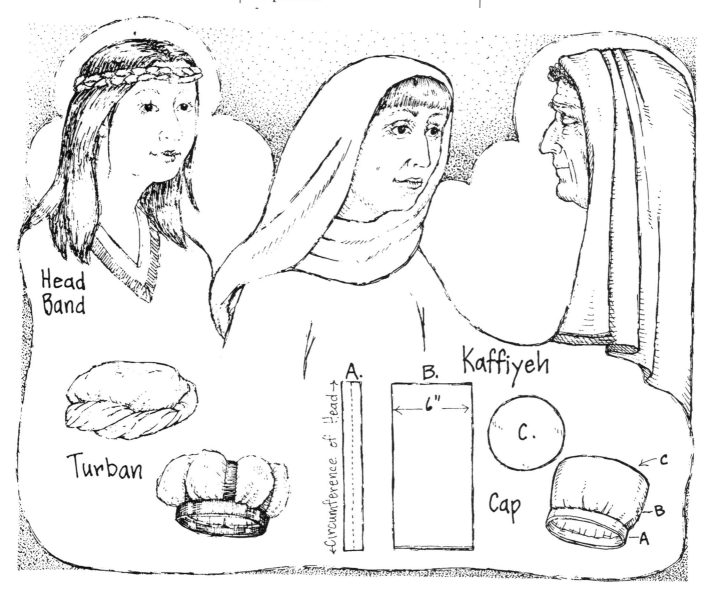

Head Band

Turban

A.

Circumference of Head

B.

6"

Kaffiyeh

C.

Cap

c

B

A

Materials

The Bible has many references to linen, a fabric woven from a plant called flax. Linen cloth was used for everyday clothing as well as for holy vestments. Fabric for clothing was also woven from cotton and wool. The economic status of people in Bible times had a direct influence on the fabric their clothes were made from. The wealthy had fine, smooth fabrics; the poor had coarse, rough fabrics.

While linen fabric is expensive today, cotton is an inexpensive alternative for your use. Some coarse weaves of cotton look like linen.

Colors and patterns were limited in biblical times. Fabric was usually woven in one color or with stripes. Embroidery was often used as a decoration on tunic tops for women or on the clothing of the rich. The colors most often mentioned in the Bible are white (unbleached), blue, purple, and scarlet. Other colors like brown, yellow, and black could be created by combining dyes.

Age Level Guidelines

At each age level, children discover meaning from the Bible for their own lives. Dressing up in biblical costumes helps set the stage for your children to use their imaginations.

With your help children will interact with the biblical stories, relating them to their own pain, joys, and discoveries. Dressing the parts will make the stories more real as your children mime, dramatize in their own words, or read directly from the text. Have the children help create the costumes at levels appropriate for their abilities. The more involved your children are, the more they will remember.

Ages 3–5—Tell the biblical stories in a way that relates directly to what the children will understand. This is a good time to hear about and act out the stories of people who lived as God wanted them to live. Allow the children to have time to play in the costumes.

Ages 6–7—At this age children are ready to study in more depth. They can dramatize stories about people different from themselves. Dressing in clothing of the biblical period will enliven the investigation and exploration.

Ages 8–12—This is the stage to really get involved with the stories through drama, music, and mime. At this stage your children develop a sense of belonging to the faith community. Making the stories personal will strengthen each child's foundations for a lifelong faith journey.

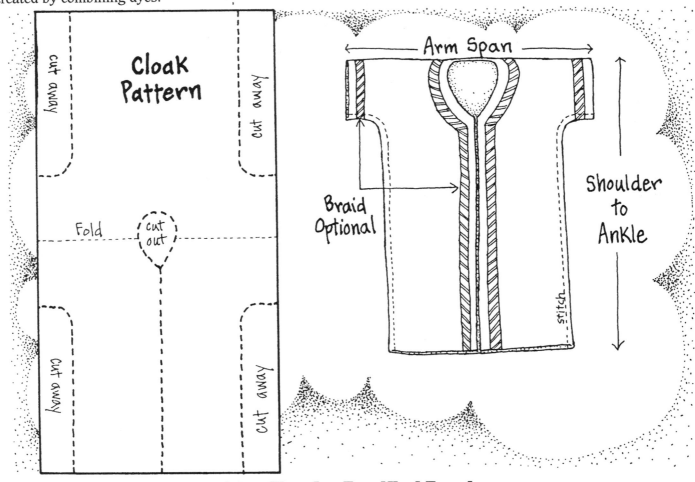

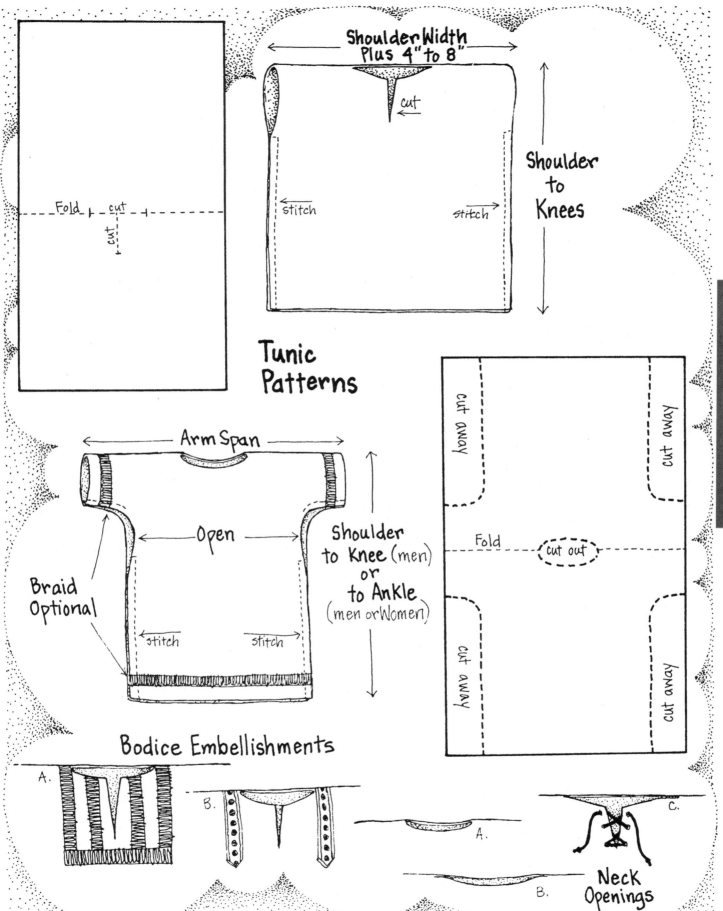

Shoulder Width
Plus 4" to 8"

cut

Shoulder
to
Knees

Fold | cut

cut

stitch

stitch

Tunic
Patterns

Arm Span

Open

Braid
Optional

stitch   stitch

Shoulder
to Knee (men)
or
to Ankle
(men or Women)

cut away   cut away

Fold   cut out

cut away   cut away

Bodice Embellishments

A.

B.

A.

B.

C.

Neck
Openings

Basic Biblical Costumes

Local fabric stores and the shelves of those who sew will yield fabrics that will represent those that were available in biblical times. If you don't sew, this is a wonderful time to enlist the help of others in your congregation who want to make a contribution without having to teach children regularly.

Headdresses

In Bible times each woman wore a kaffiyeh (scarf). These can be of varying lengths, from shoulder to ankle length. The kaffiyeh hangs loosely over the head or is fastened behind the neck. A small Velcro closure attached to the edge of the cloth makes it possible to secure the kaffiyeh quickly and easily as your girls are donning their headdresses.

Men wore a variety of head gear in Old Testament and New Testament times. The head gear indicated their economic status. Men of poorer circumstances sometimes wore brimless caps. Those of higher status wore turbans. Men also wore head scarves sometimes, mainly for warmth. These were draped loosely over the head and held in place by a headband of twisted narrow strips of fabric wound around the head.

You can create a headband for your boys by cutting nylon stockings into one-inch wide sections and stretching the nylon over a square of fabric to keep the child's head scarf in place.

Girdle

Both men and women wore a girdle (a large belt wrapped around their waist with the ends hanging down). The women's girdles may be of rainbow colors.

Wrap Yourselves Up

So wrap up your children! Wrap up yourself! Make biblical costumes your children can wear. Make a biblical costume you can wear each time you tell a Bible story.

See illustrations in your old curriculum resources for additional ideas. A wealth of ideas exists from which you can borrow. Adapt other people's ideas to make them your own. Use your own creativity.

Use costumes to help make Bible stories come alive for your children. Get into the story together so that the children will feel they are actually there living the experience. And above all, have fun!

Ardis L. Letey is a diaconal minister appointed to the University of Oregon Wesley Foundation as artist in residence, and director of the Spirituality and Arts Project.

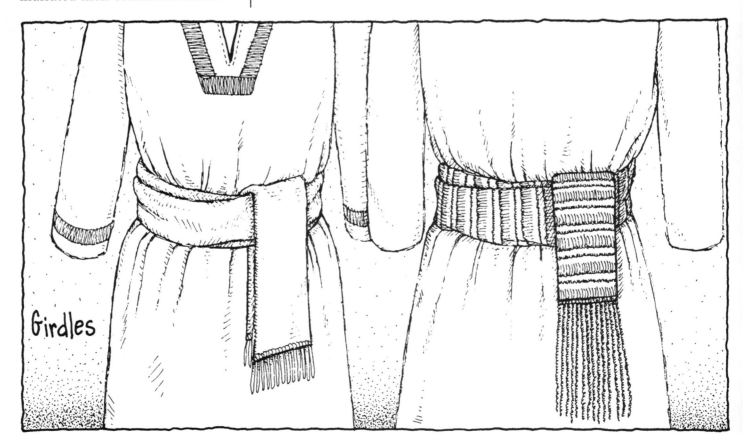

Girdles

Creating Bible Settings

by Dorlis Glass

A View of the Holy Land

I stood in the bow of an excursion boat as it pulled away from the shore at Tiberius, a modern city on the shore of the Sea of Galilee. At a distance I saw men in fishing boats casting their nets as they have done for thousands of years. After a while our guide pointed to the distant shore where Jesus taught his disciples and preached to multitudes.

Still later we stood at the site where tradition says Jesus fed the crowds with two loaves and five fishes. We admired a field of red, poppy-like wildflowers, the "lilies of the field" about which Jesus spoke in the Sermon on the Mount. In those moments I remembered familiar Bible stories and felt I was a part of them.

Since my own visit to the Holy Land, I have tried to involve children in Scripture by creating settings in which they become part of the stories they hear and tell.

Sometimes I use a prop. Sometimes I build a setting. Sometimes I encourage boys and girls to help create the setting.

Each time, the setting helps children become participants in the Bible passage. The purpose of this article is to encourage and to assist you as you focus on the creation of Bible settings.

Create Quick and Easy Settings With Simple Props

Use a Storyteller's Candle (YE, OE)*

Children love stories. Choose an open space where you can gather together. Place a candle in a jar of sand, and set it on the floor in the center of your space. Bring the children to the area.

Establish rules. The candle is for your use only. You will light it, and you will blow it out. When the candle is lit, you will tell a story. Once the fire is extinguished, you want the children to share their thoughts and questions. Ask someone to turn off overhead lights. Light the candle and tell the story. Extinguish the candle and turn on the lights. Ask questions; encourage discussion.

> *Additional suggestions:* Encourage older children to become the storytellers. Use the candle when quoting long passages of Scripture—a psalm, the Nativity story of the shepherds, the Ten Commandments, and so on. Use a candle as a setting for music and informal worship.

Help Children Become the Props (YC, YE)

Help the children become a part of the story. For example, if the focus of the story is a shepherd and his flock, tell the story as if you were a shepherd. Where are your flocks? Before class, attach tape loops to small fuzzy fabric squares or cotton balls. Then, before you tell the story, stick a fuzzy on each child and say, "You're a sheep" or "You're a lamb." Then gather your flock and ask them to make sounds like the sheep they are pretending to be. Then tell the story.

> *Additional suggestions:* Wear a robe; carry a shepherd's crook; play and sing to an autoharp.

Use Common Seasonal Objects (YC, YE)

Close to Christmas, bring a basket of small candy canes—enough to provide a treat for each child later in the hour. But first, examine the shape of the candy cane. Compare it with pictures of the shepherd's crook. Talk about why shepherds might carry crooks.

> *Additional suggestion:* Bring a real cane and a stuffed animal, preferably a lamb. Let the children rescue a fallen animal in the crook of the cane.

Use Symbols of Jewish Worship

Well before you need them, prepare an assortment of materials and articles used by various Hebrew and Jewish groups in Bible times and today. For example:

Construct a scroll. Wet and crinkle a piece of brown butcher paper. Spread it flat and press it with your hands. When dry, it will resemble an animal skin called parchment. On it write Old Testament verses. Attach each end to a dowel and roll it to make a scroll.

Make a yarmulke. Cut a ten-inch circle of black paper or felt. Fold into fourths and trim as shown in the diagram.

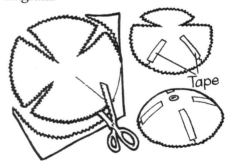

Tape each "seam" closed to form a small cap. Optional: Glue a small button in the center.

Find a small, temple menorah or a picture of one. A menorah is a seven-branched candelabrum used in Jewish worship and is the symbol of the modern state of Israel.

---

*Age levels are suggested as follows: YC (young children), YE (younger elementary), and OE (older elementary).

Make a Hanukkah menorah.

Drill nine holes, each large enough to hold a candle, into a strip of wood. Do not drill the center hole as deep as the other eight so that the center candle will be higher than the others. Use the center candle to light the others on specific days during Hanukkah.

Additional suggestions: Make a star of David (a six-pointed star), a lamp, a loaf of hallah (twisted bread used during certain Jewish holidays), a chalice or cup for wine (used in ceremonies at home and at worship), or a prayer shawl fringed at each end. Use one or more of these symbols when studying Hebrew worship and Jewish holidays.

Young children will enjoy knowing that Jesus used many of the articles similar to these at school and at home. Younger elementary children will understand that Jesus was a Jewish boy who read from the Torah at the synagogue school and participated in Jewish holidays. Older elementary children will understand the symbols and their relevance to Jewish life and worship today.

Use Food as the Prop

Prepare a pot of red pottage (see recipe below). (YE, OE) Tell the story of Jacob and Esau and the selling of the birthright. Serve each child a small cup of pottage.

Purchase a box of matzos or unsalted crackers. (YE, OE) Serve with haroseth, a Hebrew Passover food (see recipe below) or a cup of grape juice and talk about Passover.

Provide a loaf of unsliced bread, cheese, juice, or grapes. (YC, YE, OE) Eat the food when you study the way Bible people lived. Tear the bread. Expand the meal with older elementary children to experience a "house church," a congregation of New Testament Christians who met in homes to eat, share stories and news, and participate in a reenactment of the Lord's Supper.

Red Pottage

In a meat broth, boil dry lentils as directed on the package. Add a minced onion and salt and pepper to taste. Before serving, let the children add a can of tomato juice.

Haroseth

Finely dice or grind peeled apples, raisins, and a few nuts. Add a spoonful of honey, some cinnamon, and a dash of grape or apple juice. Stir. Serve on matzos or crackers. This food reminds the Jewish people of the mortar with which their ancestors made mud bricks in Egypt.

Use a Puppet as Storyteller

(YC, YE)

The puppet might be a furry little critter (lamb or dog) or a person dressed in Bible costume. Use commercial fun puppets who in the process of talking with one another tell a story.

Explore What Life Was Like

Additional suggestions: Display rocks, seashells, a tray of flowers, or a bowl of fish. Tell creation stories or read a psalm of praise for God's gifts.

Use appropriate costumes while telling a story. Carry and swaddle a doll as you tell of Jesus' birth.

Boys and girls may better appreciate a story when they understand the geography and history surrounding its origin. Help children reach these understandings by simulating the setting.

Nomadic Life

Background: Many faith stories originated in the desert wilderness of Mesopotamia, Canaan, and Egypt where people lived in tents, cooked over campfires, tended flocks, and built altars.

The campfire. Drape a blanket over chairs or a table. Stack logs to make a campfire; or, if the area must be cleared each week, simulate logs using paper towel tubes. Lay the fire and stuff a piece of crinkled red paper between the "logs." Bury a small flashlight in the pile. There you have it! A campfire fit for Abraham, Isaac, Jacob, or a gathering of Jesus and his disciples.

Bring the children to the campfire. Dim the lights, turn on the flashlight, and tell a story. Later invite the boys and girls to share their favorite stories. Use the campfire as a stage on which to act out the life of a Bible person.

Additional suggestions: Enjoy a "meal" of unsliced bread, a cup of grape or apple juice, grapes, raisins, or dried figs. Add costumes. Use the campfire setting for singing and games. Add to the setting by including stuffed animals: a dog, a lamb, a goat, or a wild animal.

Choose an age-appropriate story and use the setting with children of all ages.

Older elementary curriculum resources often focus on how our Bible came to us and on oral tradition, the passing of stories by word of mouth from one generation to another. Such sharing predated by many generations the writing down of stories, laws, and traditions. Quiet evenings around the campfire were often the times and places for sharing information.

Use the campfire when talking about these times. Share especially the Genesis stories. Invite children to retell them.

Near the River, Lake, or Sea

Background: Many Bible stories had their settings near bodies of water. For example:
- Moses led the Israelites across the sea.
- Joshua and the Israelites carried the ark of the covenant across the Jordan River into the Promised Land.
- Jesus chose four fishermen to be his disciples. He preached from a boat on the Sea of Galilee; he also preached on the hillside by the sea. After his resurrection, Jesus found some of his disciples fishing there.
- John baptized Jesus in the Jordan River.
- Paul sailed from a Mediterranean seaport.
- Jonah had a remarkable encounter with a great fish while sailing to Ninevah.
- Noah protected his family and the animals from a great flood.

How might we create these settings?

Spread a bedspread, a piece of green carpet, or a sheet on the floor. Simulate water by using a crumpled sheet or strips of blue crepe paper. Add a boat—a cardboard box draped with a (citrus-fruit bag) net.

Place rocks and shells along the shoreline and paper fish in the water. Sprinkle flowers on the hillside.

Hang a long piece of butcher paper behind the seaside scene. As time permits, have children draw or paint trees, clouds, birds, people, and animals. Add cutout pictures of people and animals.

Use the setting to tell stories and to involve children in storytelling. Invite groups of elementary children to choose and to act out their favorite stories. Young children may simply explore the seaside area with you as their guide, or go fishing in a sea of fish made with paper-clip noses, using a line or net fitted with magnet lures. Younger elementary children will hear and act out stories and present puppet shows. Older elementary children will use the setting as a backdrop for drama and the entire area for recalling favorite stories. All children will enjoy helping to create the mural backdrop and playing quiet games.

Home Settings

Build a Palestinian home.

Learning about a Palestinian home with its flat roof and outside stairway has been a treat for generations of children.

Bring a large cardboard carton. Lay the carton with its open side to the floor. Tape a "railing" around the perimeter of the roof and outside steps leading to the roof. Use a smaller box to add a small "room" at one end of the roof. Cut or draw doors and windows on the lower level. Add baskets and jars around the outside of the house and bedrolls on the roof. If space permits, make several houses and group them around a common courtyard.

Encourage young children and younger elementary children to examine and play with the house. Add dolls to the setting. Snack on bread and cheese or fresh fruit in the courtyard. Older elementary children may use it as a drama stage and story area.

Additional suggestions: Build the house as you talk about a Palestinian home. Prepare all materials in advance, marking where each will go. Gather the children, and assemble the house using a hot glue gun.

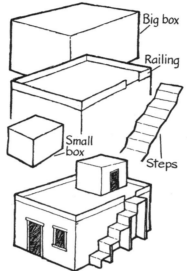

Build a miniature Palestinian village. Encourage older elementary children to construct a miniature village. Provide them with an assortment of small boxes (children's shoeboxes, jewelry boxes, and so on). By taping or gluing the lid (open side up) to the inverted box, they will create the wall that surrounded the rooftop of the homes. Add an outside oven and a village well, trees, animals, and people. In the fall of the year add Succoth booths to the scene.

Assemble the village on a tabletop, a window ledge, or a bookcase. Use it as a focus for studying how Bible persons lived or as a stage for small puppets. Invite other classes or parents to visit the village.

Store the set for use at other times of the year.

The Village Well

Background: Much of Palestine (Israel today) is arid, and many

Additional suggestions: Look for opportunities to live and work in the village: sing to the accompaniment of an autoharp or guitar; use home-made rhythm instruments with young children. Introduce weaving, pottery making, and food preparation with elementary children.

Bible stories took place in oasis communities near a well. Abraham's servant found Rebekah there and chose her to be Isaac's wife. Jacob slept near the well at Samaria and had a dream. Jesus met the woman at the well in Samaria. Jericho existed then and exists today because of natural springs that turn the wilderness into an oasis city.

To build a well, make a large circle of cardboard 18 to 24 inches high; the overall size will be determined by the space available. Secure with staples.

Draw rocks to simulate the outside of a well or let the children glue paper stones to the cardboard walls. Secure a stick across the top of the well and twist a rope around and over it. Tie a small bucket to one end of the rope, and you have a simple well that can be used in storytelling and as a setting for drama by elementary children. Young children will enjoy "filling" the bucket and bringing it to the surface. Provide a scoop for them to fill their pretend cups.

Places of Study and Worship

Background: In early Old Testament times, God's people worshiped at simple altars built in the wilderness. After receiving the tablets containing the Ten Commandments, the Hebrews built an ark (a simple wooden chest) in which to carry them.

In the time of Solomon, the Israelites built and worshiped in the great Temple in Jerusalem. This Temple was later destroyed, and a new one built. Jesus worshiped in the Jerusalem Temple at twelve years of age and at other times in his life.

The early Christians met and

worshiped in the catacombs, underground tunnels where Christians were buried. Sometimes they hid there from the Romans who were persecuting them.

At appropriate times in your studies create areas of worship to represent these places and times.

Ask early-arrivals to fill brown paper grocery bags with newspapers. Staple closed. When the story says that Abraham built altars in the wilderness, stack the "stones" to make an altar.

Prepare an ark of the covenant using a large box with poles running through it lengthwise. Young children will hoist the poles on their shoulders and carry the box (ark) just as people did in Old Testament times. Elementary children may want to decorate the ark. Provide pictures for them to simulate. Take the class for an imaginary pilgrimage, across an imaginary Jordan River, and into the Promised Land.

The Temple at Jerusalem

Preparation. Instructions for preparing some of these religious items are in the section above on using simple props.

Prepare an altar using a box or table covered with a white cloth. Place on it a lamp or candle and a scroll. Obtain or make a fringed prayer shawl and a yarmulke. Later temples and Jewish temples today have a temple menorah.

If the children are learning about Hanukkah, the temple menorah described would be replaced by a Hanukkah menorah, a candelabrum with nine candles. The center candle is higher than the others and is the one used to light the others.

When using this setting with young children, focus on the scrolls, the Jewish Bible that Jesus read. Younger elementary boys and girls might read a verse from the scroll or from their Bibles while wearing the yarmulke and shawl. They will also be interested in the menorah. Older elementary children should understand the words *Torah, temple menorah, Hanukkah menorah,* and *yarmulke.*

The Synagogue— A Place of Worship and Study

A similar setting of the Torah and lamp on an altar is appropriate when discussing synagogues, community places of worship and study. Include a clay or wax tablet on which the children might write, as well as a pointed stick or stylus to use for writing on the tablet.

Encourage young children to "play" Hebrew school. Elementary children may read from the Torah scroll, which was written in Hebrew and is read from back to front.

Older elementary children might read from their own Bibles portions of the Torah (Genesis through Deuteronomy) and portions of the Psalms, all of which were available to Jesus.

Additional suggestions: Introduce older elementary children to the apocryphal books First and Second Maccabees, the original stories related to Hanukkah. Check your library for other activities related to the celebration of Hanukkah. Teachers, read The Wisdom of Jesus Son of Sirach (sometimes called Ecclesiaticus) in the Apocrypha for insights into the lives and education of Hebrew boys.

The Catacombs (OE)

Lay two or more long tables on their sides about 5 feet apart, tops facing inward. Cover with paper. The paper-covered tabletops represent

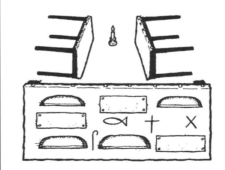

the walls of the catacombs. Draw burial "niches" (see diagram), which were graves chipped out of the soft stone walls. The niches were sealed with slabs of alabaster or other stone when a body was interred. Provide a basket of markers and pictures of the catacombs. As the children arrive, ask them to draw Christian symbols on the walls between the burial niches. Later use this area for telling the stories of the early church, perhaps on the day of Pentecost. Darken the room and use the candle to light the area.

The Outdoors

Background: Nature provides wonderful settings for a variety of activities: storytelling, nature walks, scavenger hunts, games, and living a story. Scout the area and dream of what might happen. Provide a blanket for quiet times and a jug of water in hot weather.

I remember one summer morning when four first- and second-grade children lifted the ark containing the scrolls and began the long trek toward Canaan with Joshua leading the way. Our class followed, and when we reached a small stream with large stones forming a bridge, we picked up stones from the stream and took them to a place where we then built a memorial. We lived the Joshua story!

Help Children Experience the Bible

Creating settings for teaching the Bible is a combination of recollection and experimentation. When children encounter the story in a special setting, they are learning not only by word but through experience. When used as one of many creative teaching activities, these settings will become keys that will unlock vast treasures.

Enjoy!

Dorlis Glass is a laboratory leader and trainer of teachers. She and her husband, Verne, have been to the Holy Land twice.

What Bible Resources Can Do for You

by Dana M. Bunn

How far did Jesus have to walk to get from Bethlehem to Jerusalem?

What is the difference between Hebrews, Israelites, and Jews?

When should you say Canaan instead of Palestine, Judah, Judea, or Israel?

What Bible resource would you use to locate the source of the Golden Rule or the Lord's Prayer?

Use a Bible Dictionary

A Bible dictionary is probably one of your most important resources as a Sunday school teacher.

Use a Bible dictionary when you need to define or describe people, places, or things in the Bible. If you're not sure of the difference between a Pharisee and a Sadducee, or if you need more information about the Passover, use a Bible dictionary.

The Harper Collins Bible Dictionary, Paul J. Achtemeier, general editor (Harper, 1996); $45.00.

This Bible dictionary is an up-to-date teacher resource that can be used with any translation of the Bible. It explains words, beliefs, theology, insights about God and humanity, archaeological discoveries, Dead Sea Scrolls, and more. It is accurate, thorough, and technical.

Nelson's New Illustrated Bible Dictionary, Ronald Youngblood editor (Thomas Nelson Publishing, 1986); $39.99.

This is probably the easiest to use of all the Bible dictionaries. It takes a very practical approach and offers biblical information at a layperson's level of understanding. It has an unusual approach in its pronunciation guide (example: Elijah [ee LIE juh]).

The Revell Bible Dictionary, Lawrence O. Richards, general editor (Fleming H. Revell Company, 1994); $39.99.

Based on the New International Version Bible, Revell is probably the most fun to use. It includes phonetic spellings, Greek and Hebrew names and meanings, timelines, photographs, biblical art, maps, and a summary of each book in the Bible.

Use a Bible Atlas

You are a more effective Sunday school teacher if you know whether Jesus ever went to the Golan Heights or if the Garden of Gethsemane is controlled by Palestine or Israel.

Use a Bible atlas when you need to locate places on a map of the Holy Land. Usually a Bible atlas will include maps of Babylon, Egypt, the Sinai, Asia Minor, Greece, and Italy. Middle and older elementary children can use a Bible atlas to compare modern countries in the Near East with ancient Bible lands. A Bible atlas helps children find the places where Bible events and stories took place. Choose Old Testament maps and New Testament maps for appropriate stories.

Nelson's 3-D Bible Mapbook, by Simon Jenkins (Thomas Nelson, Inc., 1995); $9.99.

Children are fascinated by the computerized graphics and 3-D color graphic maps. Bible references make it easy for teachers to use.

Use Bible Maps

Bible maps help children see where cities, lands, and seas were located and their relationships to one another.

Bible maps are good for classroom purposes because they are larger and can be seen by all the children at the same time.

Bible Teacher's Map Set, Basic Set, $189.95. Available from Cokesbury.

Eighteen large maps that mount on wall, bulletin board, or tripod. In addition to Old Testament and New Testament maps, clear overlays of modern Jerusalem, Israel, and other countries help students relate our modern world to Bible lands and places.

Nelson's Complete Book of Bible Maps and Charts: Old and New Testaments (Thomas Nelson Publishers); $19.99.

Use a Bible Handbook

A Bible handbook will give you and your children much important factual information about the Bible.

Use a Bible handbook when you need a basic manual on the Bible or a how-to book that contains facts, charts, and graphs. Use a Bible handbook when you need to know the who, what, where, why, and the possible meanings behind the stories and people. For example, use a Bible handbook if you are teaching children about people and stories found in the Acts of the Apostles. You will discover that Acts is really volume 2 of the Gospel of Luke, that it is Christianity's Hall of Fame with stories of the heroes of our faith, that chapters 1–12 could be called "The Acts of Peter," and that chapters 13–28 could be called "The Acts of Paul."

Holman Bible Handbook (Broadman and Holman Publishers); $26.99.

Nelson's Illustrated Wonders and Discoveries of the Bible (Thomas Nelson Publisher); $29.99.

Illustrated Bible Handbook, edited by Lawrence O. Richards, (Thomas Nelson Publishers), $29.99.

The Lion Encyclopedia of the Bible, edited by Pat Alexander (BMH); $29.95.

England's greatest Bible scholars have come together to produce this incredibly helpful Bible resource. It is colorful, easy to use, and is designed for Sunday school teachers. It includes such subjects as Bible lands and archaeology; understanding the history and story of the Bible; key Bible words, people, places; and a special section on the nations and people of the Bible.

Use a Bible Commentary

A Bible commentary is really a gift from biblical scholars who have gone before you so that your journey in the Scripture will be more meaningful and powerful.

Use a Bible commentary when you need verse-by-verse explanations, notes, remarks, and observations about the books of the Bible. This information will help you understand better the real meaning of the passage you are teaching. Some commentaries focus on what the message to the original audience was, while others focus on what the message is for us today.

Harper's Bible Commentary, James L. Mays, general editor

(Harper San Francisco, 1988); $45.00. This commentary covers all of the Bible and the Apocrypha and contains helpful cross references to its companion book, *Harper Colins Bible Dictionary.*

Use a Bible Concordance

A Bible concordance will help you track down a Scripture passage if you remember just one word in the passage.

Use a Bible concordance when you can think of a word or phrase from a Bible verse but you cannot remember what verse or what book it is found in. For example, if you want to look up the Golden Rule but cannot remember where it is located in the Bible, look up *others* in a Bible concordance. You will see a long list of verses where the word *others* is found. There you see ". . . do unto *others,* as you would have them . . ." (Matthew 7:12).

The Concise Concordance to the New Revised Standard Version, edited by John R. Kohlenberger III (Oxford, 1993); $14.95.

An index to the most important words in the NRSV Bible.

Use Children's Bible Storybooks

Use a children's Bible storybook along with your curriculum resources to make the Bible message come alive for children.

Use a children's Bible storybook as a supplement to the Bible story found in your curriculum's student resource. Bible storybooks take many important stories in the Bible and retell them at a child's level of understanding, providing a paraphrase of the Bible stories.

The Bible: The Greatest Stories, by Blandine Marchon (Abingdon Press); $6.98.

Use this children's Bible storybook when you want the Bible stories retold at the children's level. The language and the pictures make this volume useable by children who have developed good reading skills and appreciate reading. It can also be used by the teachers or parents to read to children.

The Family Story Bible, by Ralph Milton (Word Lake Publishers); $19.00.

This Bible storybook includes stories from parts of the Bible often ignored by other children's storybooks such as the prophets and the letters of the early church.

Why Use Bible Resources in Your Classroom?

Make use of good Bible resources in your teaching. Treat them as your friends.

One goal of the ministry of Christian education is to help you become the best teacher you can possibly be. To be a good Sunday school teacher you need love, compassion, patience, and insight, among other things. But you also need a spiritual willingness to rely on experts who have gone before you and who have provided biblical resources that you could not possibly have developed for yourself.

Availability and prices of resources are subject to change without notice.

Dana M. Bunn serves as a pastor in North Carolina. He is a certified Christian educator and a certified church business administrator.

Using Our Bibles

by Mary Jane Pierce Norton

While Tim, a soon-to-be third-grader, was helping me straighten classrooms one day, he suddenly asked, "When will we get our Bibles?"

"The first Sunday in September," I answered.

"What kind are we getting?" he asked.

"What do you mean?" I responded.

"Are we getting the big ones with pictures or the red holy ones?"

That conversation enlightened me in several ways. I realized that the children who receive Bibles look forward to receiving them. I also realized that children form impressions of the Bibles they receive based on appearance. And I realized how important it is to help our children know how to use their Bibles.

What Do We Give?

A common question is what Bibles do we give children? For Tim, the red-covered Bibles seemed more "holy" or important. However, the large Bibles were much easier for the children to read. In selecting a Bible to give, ask these questions.

1. What translation of the Bible is most used in our curriculum? If children are reading Scripture in class, then it is less confusing to also be reading from the same translation in their personal Bibles.

2. What translation of the Bible is most understandable by children? As adults, we may have used many translations. Each may be meaningful for us in different translations. Most of the Psalms I memorized were from the King James Version. Many of the stories that I remember I learned in the Revised Standard Version. When I am studying at home, I use the

Good News Bible. When I am teaching Sunday school, I use the New Revised Standard Version. But I didn't begin learning to use my Bible by using several translations. I grew in the ability to use different translations for different times. As children grow, they will learn to use a variety of translations, but it is much easier to begin with one. The New Revised Standard Version and the *Good News Bible* are both somewhat easier for children to understand.

3. Is what we are considering a translation or a paraphrase? A translation of the Bible is done when scholars go back to the original Greek and Hebrew manuscripts and to the best of their abilities translate the words into other languages. A paraphrase is made by starting with a translation and changing the words to update them into current language. The translation will be much more accurate.

4. What Bibles do we already have in our classroom? It can be expensive to change from one translation to another. Children may

forget their Bibles. If we have classroom Bibles of the same translation, the children can more easily keep increasing their Bible skills. Last year my church began buying new classroom Bibles. We decided to do this slowly and change first those in the classroom with the children who would receive their Bibles that fall. We are a small congregation, and this makes it easier for us to manage financially. It also helps those children who are new at reading the Bible.

How Do We Teach Bible Skills?

Do you remember what it was like to be new at reading the Bible? For me, that's more than a few years in the past. As a teacher, you may be aware of the many questions children have when they first begin using a Bible. Some of those questions you've probably heard are:

- "What are the big numbers for?"
- "Why do we have all the little numbers?"
- "What do you mean when you say Old Testament and New Testament?"
- "I thought the Bible was a book. What do you mean by turning to a book in the Bible?"
- "How can I find what you're asking me to find? I don't understand this book!"

Learning to use the Bible is as important a skill as learning verses and stories from the Bible. as children learn how to use their Bibles, they will be more likely to read and study at home. They will be more likely to volunteer to read in class. They will be more willing to read in worship. We give children a lifelong skill when we teach them how to use their Bibles. We start them on a personal journey of study and reading, learning God's message to Bible people and to us today.

It's important to allow time, either in Sunday school or in special sessions, for children to explore their Bibles and build Bible skills.

> # Learning to use the Bible is as important a skill as learning verses and stories from the Bible.

Consider the following:

● Take the first four weeks of the fall to concentrate on building Bible skills. Use the curriculum, but make sure your plans include three or four activities each week to help children increase their knowledge of how to use the Bible. Ideas include:
- Asking parents to help children remember to bring their Bibles each week;
- Starting your story time with everyone finding the Bible verse and story in his or her Bible;
- Choosing to use all activities in the curriculum that build Bible skills;
- Setting up a "Getting to Know Your Bible" table with games for finding Scripture verses, different books in the Bible, maps, the

index, and other special features in the children's Bible. You could also use the book *Finding Your Way Through the Bible.* This is a self-instruction book that teaches children how to find books, chapters, and verses, and lets them practice these skills. It is available from Cokesbury.

● Invite another adult to come each week and share his or her favorite Bible story. The person could tell why the Bible is important to him or her.

● Set up special "using your Bible sessions" for four weeks, one afternoon each week. If you have a children's choir program that meets during the week, see if you can add time before or after choir for the sessions. Use activities from the curriculum or use the special materials "Learning to Use My Bible: New Edition." This material can be ordered from Cokesbury by calling 800-672-1789.

● Have an after-church Bible skills afternoon at the church. Eat lunch together, then spend one to two hours playing Bible games, looking up passages in the Bible, and discovering all the special features in the children's Bibles.

● Plan an overnight retreat. Start on Friday evening. Include Bible skills activities, food, and fellowship. Sleep over at the church or at a nearby camp.

● Ask a youth or adult class to meet with you either during Sunday school or on a Sunday afternoon to help children gain Bible skills. Invite the adults or youth to plan some games and activities that will help the children learn more about their Bibles. Make sure the youth or adults bring their own Bibles and ask them to be prepared to tell the children why reading the Bible is important to them.

Starting a Lifelong Practice

We have the perfect opportunity to start children on a lifelong practice of reading and studying the Bible. They are eager and ready for this when they receive their Bibles,

> # We have the opportunity to start children on a life long practice of reading and studying the Bible.

particularly if the Bibles are given at the third or fourth grade when the children have better reading skills. By intentionally using Bibles in the classroom, emphasizing the importance of bringing Bibles to Sunday school and church, and helping children gain the skills they need to find stories and verses in the Bible, we help them begin this journey of study and Christian growth.

Mary Jane Pierce Norton is a diaconal minister in the North Carolina Annual Conference. She teaches the older elementary class at a church in Nashville, Tennessee.

Cooperative Learning—Is This What Jesus Meant?

by Ginna Minasian Dalton

"Donna, it's time for breakfast. I've made pancakes," announces Thea Lopez. She'd do anything to entice Donna to get up and go to Sunday school. Before she could turn around, Donna was at the table dressed and ready with a smile.

> # Cooperative learning results in higher achievement.

"I can't wait to see what Mr. Stein has planned for us today." With shock and amazement the Lopez family arrives at church on time.

Mrs. Lopez recalls the difficult times Donna has had in learning situations because of dyslexia. Now she sees her daughter involved and excited about her faith while working alongside children, such as Vilma, who are in the talented and gifted programs in their public schools. How are these very different children all energized by learning at church about their faith?

What Is Cooperative Learning?

Mr. Stein, Donna's teacher, discovered that cooperative learning is designed to create an interdependence of each person with others to accomplish a goal. To do this, everyone in the group comes to know that they can benefit only when each person in the group can obtain their goals too.

Why Is Cooperative Learning a Good Idea?

Jesus called us into community by the way he organized his disciples. Christ called us into community through the gift of the church. Both circumstances brought different people together with one common thread. They believed in the truth in the message of Jesus, about God, and for life. Each person was probably very different from the next, not only from his or her cultural roots, but in the way he or she learned and the things he or she knew—a tax collector, a fisherman, a Zealot. Jesus challenged the men and women around him to work together.

Cooperative learning results in higher achievement, positive relationships between students, positive attitudes toward the lessons of Scripture, and higher self-esteem of the learners.

Cooperative learning strategies offer you ways to:

♥ allow the children to move around;
♥ show consideration toward others;
♥ promote decision-making;
♥ give a sense of belonging;
♥ provide opportunities for children to be sensitive to others' abilities and talents;
♥ encourage independence from the teacher;
♥ keep excitement and energy flowing.

Cooperative learning gives you a way to inspire the development of the values of the church and becomes an instrument for creating the realm of God on earth.

Ten Steps to a Cooperative Learning Experience

1. Involve the children in a whole group discussion that gets their curiosity juices flowing. Try "what if" questions. Have the children play out the scenarios in their minds.
   "What if the wise men had never found Jesus?"
   "What if you lived where it was not possible to have a Bible?"
   "What if Samuel had not listened to Eli?"
2. Organize small groups to vary the gifts of the children. Bring together a person who thinks internally and pair him or her with a person who thinks out loud or pair an artist with an athlete.
3. Do an ice-breaking activity to get things going. Have the group sit in a circle. Let one child begin by asking a question to the person on his or her right. That person must answer with a brief sentence. For example: "What if the wise men had never found Jesus?" (Answers might range from "We would never know that Jesus was known by many people" to "We would never have Christmas vacation from school.")
4. Give each group only one part of a topic to deal with so that their fuller understanding is related to the work of the other groups. If you are teaching the Epiphany story, give one group the Bible references to read, another group a Bible dictionary, still another group a children's book about Epiphany and Christmas customs around the world, and still another group art books that display classical presentations of the Christmas and Epiphany stories.

5. Encourage each child to pick part of the topic that the child wants to explore or think about. Someone in the Bible group may list the sequence of events in the story, while another may identify the wise men and where they came from.

6. Have each child gather her or his own material about a topic. Then have the group pull together a presentation.

7. Let each child present to the group what he or she has discovered. Then have the group discuss the material and raise further questions for that child to think about. After the group discussion, have each child return to his or her private task to polish the answer.

8. Let the small groups re-form. Ask each group to put together a presentation of the material they have uncovered.

9. Encourage each group to present their material to the whole class.

10. The whole group talks about the things that were most helpful to them to learn and the questions that still remain. How can you help the children get on board?

Try This Exercise

Corners: Each child moves to a corner of the room representing one of the following alternatives you will give them:

♥ If the wise men had not found Jesus, the wise women would have.

♥ If the wise men had not found Jesus, the star in the East would still be burning and the wise men would still be wandering around.

♥ If the wise men had not found Jesus, there would be no gifts at Christmas.

♥ If the wise men had not found Jesus, Mary and Joseph would have never understood who their child actually was.

Have the children move to the corner that they agree upon to discuss the impact of the alternative within their group. Then ask the children to listen to and to paraphrase ideas from other children. After that, have them return to the whole group and report their thinking.

Then have the children process the experience by listing all of the things necessary for this to work. The children will probably mention the following:

♥ Everybody needs to help and can help.

♥ Listening is important.

♥ Everyone should share the work.

♥ Following direction is necessary.

♥ All should use quiet voices.

♥ Everyone should stay on task.

♥ All should respond appropriately.

♥ Each person should be respectful of others.

♥ Good explanations are needed.

♥ Groups should ask good questions.

♥ Everyone should praise one another.

This exercise will help them understand the value of cooperative learning.

Some Other Cooperative Learning Exercises

Roundrobin: Each child in turn shares something with his or her teammates.

Pairs Check: Children work in pairs within groups of four. Within pairs children alternate—one solves a problem while the other coaches. After every two problems the pair checks to see if they have the same answer as the other pair. For example, the problems could be: What do you do if someone hits you? makes a face at you? or calls you a name you do not like?

Three-Step Interview: Children interview each other in pairs. Children share with the group information they learned in the interview.

Team Word Webbing: Older children write simultaneously on a piece of chart paper, drawing main concepts, supporting elements, and bridges representing the relation of ideas in a concept. Discuss what each contributed and how one person's ideas help another draw a conclusion or bridge.

Turn to Your Neighbor: Ask the children to turn to a neighbor and ask him or her something about the lesson; to explain a concept you've just taught; to summarize the story; or whatever fits the lesson.

Use your own community of teachers to develop a list of exciting ways children can learn cooperatively!

Ginna Minasian Dalton is a Christian education consultant and writer of curriculum and educational articles. She is a graduate of Presbyterian School of Christian Education and a member of the United Church of Christ.

Using Maps With Children

by Youtha Hardman-Cromwell

Using maps to supplement your Sunday school lessons can help make the Bible story come alive, can give your students a better perspective on distances, and can increase your students' understanding of modes of travel in Bible times and of the difficulties Bible-times travelers faced. A study of Paul is particularly suitable for map use because he traveled over a larger area and more frequently than most other biblical figures.

The detail of a map should be determined by the purposes for which it is to be used and the age of the students. If possible, use maps that limit the detail to the places and geographical features in your lessons.

The younger the student, the simpler the map should be. Use maps sparingly, if at all, with preschoolers. Limit the time the class spends on the map and make the map simple for grades 1–3; add more detail to the map and increase the complexity of the activities for grades 4–6.

From session to session as the story, missionary journey, or event unfolds, represent movement with a figure, pointer, star, or the like that follows the journey on a map. Let children trace with their fingers, pencils, or crayons the path or route to places you want them to remember. Have each one assume the role of a character who lives or travels in that place.

One way to help children assume the role of a biblical character is to let them take turns moving a paper cutout of the character along a route on a large map. Make smaller versions of the same figure so that each student can mark the information or travel route on his or her individual map.

If the study is a series of lessons, have each child create a map folder to take home at the completion of the study. Since students often do not attend every Sunday, retracing and reviewing as students bring their individual maps up to date provides continuity to the study.

Sources for Maps

If you need maps to supplement the ones that may be included in the class kit or packet that is part of the curriculum you are using, large commercial maps are available from Bible bookstores. These maps depict geography as it was in particular biblical periods. Having a map for the specific period you are studying is important because names, locations of cities, and boundary lines changed over time. One source is Cokesbury (800-672-1789), which has sets ranging from a master set of eighteen maps that are 27-by-39 inches in size for $189.95 to tear-off pads of maps, twenty-five of a kind, for $2.25. Call or consult the Cokesbury catalog. If your church owns an opaque projector, another possibility is to project a map from a Bible or other book onto the wall.

If you buy paper maps, preserve them by covering them with clear self-adhesive vinyl before you use them. Doing so will allow you to use wipe-off markers on them and to fold them repeatedly; they will then have even more durability.

Having a world map or globe available in the classroom is useful to help students understand where the biblical events occurred in relationship to where your students live. Do not assume that students of any age have geographical knowledge, map skills, or an understanding of direction on a map or globe. Ask questions to find out what they already know and what help they need from you.

If necessary, take your students outside and help them learn how to use the sun's location to determine north, south, east, and west. Then show them how these directions on the map help them to know which way they are moving in relationship to specific areas on the map.

Creating Maps

You can make your own maps. In a Bible, Bible Atlas, Bible Dictionary, encyclopedia, or other source, find a map of the area and time period you are studying. Draw an enlarged copy on posterboard. You can do so by putting tissue paper or tracing paper over the map and drawing a grid on the paper with horizontal lines and vertical lines an equal distance apart. Draw a similar grid, but with larger squares, on your posterboard. Next, draw what you see in each small square on the original grid onto the corresponding large square on the posterboard. Eliminate as much excess detail as possible, however. Remember that the purpose of the map is to help students gain an understanding of relative position of places and the geographical elements in the area that are pertinent to your study. Include other details only if they help to orient students.

Display this map on a flannel-board, wall, bulletin board, or large piece of cardboard. Or you can have a transparency burned at a copy store and use an overhead projector to project it on a wall.

Think through and experiment with how you will display your map so that it will stay where you want it and will be visible to all class members. If you are conducting your class in a sanctuary, mount your map on cardboard from an appliance box and use an easel to display it. An ineffective display will compromise any use you had planned. Try what you have planned before using it with your students.

You can also create a flannelboard or tabletop map. Use several colors of felt or other fabric for fields, water, roads, and mountains. Use markers and pictures of cities, towns, or other geographic features on a flannelboard map. Use toy buildings and trees or ones you create from branches, moss, and cardboard on a tabletop map.

Scale is an important element of maps, but for your purposes some sense of relative distance is sufficient. You can give your students a sense of scale by creating an outdoor map in which you designate existing parts of the landscape as the elements of the biblical map you are trying to create in your students' imaginations. Use signs and pushpins or tape to designate a tree as Jerusalem, the azalea bush as Joppa, and the parking lot as the Mediterranean Sea, for example. The children can then act out the story in this setting.

A simple way to give expression to scale is to use construction paper feet to represent one mile. Talk about how many of the feet you would need to represent the distance between the places on the map.

A diorama is a type of three-dimensional map that can become a creative project that expands your students' understanding. Third-graders and above can use a shoebox to express their understanding of such things as a Judean town, the synagogue, or the setting for the biblical story. Students can use clay dough, clay, construction paper, twigs, moss, small plants, and pâpier maché to create the elements of the scene.

Such a project should follow the learning experience and cannot substitute for other teaching strategies, of course. Creating the diorama can be a group activity during class (it will take at least one full class period). It can also be one large tabletop display on which the entire class works.

If you have insufficient space for such a project, trade with another class that has tables, use the picnic shelter, or set up card tables out of doors. Display whatever the students create where church members can see it and get some sense of what is happening in your Sunday school program.

Making Pâpier Maché

Here is an easy recipe for pâpier maché: Soak ¼-by-2 newspaper strips in water overnight. Drain off excess water by placing the strips in a sieve, kneading, and pressing. This action will create a pulp. Add paste (wallpaper paste works nicely, but children's paste for ordinary artwork works equally well) and shape the mixture as you would clay. The pulp can be mixed with sand, clay, lime, salt, or borax to give it body. Be sure to experiment before you use it with your class. Ask your children or neighbor children to help you see how it will work.

Another method of creating pâpier maché is to soak the newspaper strips for 15 minutes and then to layer strips over crumpled paper or over a form you have created with chicken wire. Cover each layer with paste.

Making an Easel

An inexpensive and versatile easel can be made from cardboard from a large appliance box. Cut two matching pieces, punch matching holes along the top of each, and lace them together with twine. You can cover the resulting easel with felt (in this case it will double for a flannelboard), other material, or self-adhesive vinyl. The easel can be placed on a chair, small table, or the floor to use.

Dr. Youtha Hardman-Cromwell works in Washington, D.C., as a ministerial consultant for congregation revitalization, administrative services, and spiritual formation. She frequently is involved in retreat leadership, training, teaching, and preaching.

How Children Can Participate in Mission

by Jacqulyn Thorpe

Amazing things happen when children reach out and touch the communities in which they live. Follow these three steps to meet mission needs in your community:

1. Assess the needs of people and ways to respond to those needs;
2. Become aware of the nature of God's call to care for others;
3. Act.

Become familiar with your church's mission priorities by asking
- the coordinator of mission
- the youth group
- organized men's or women's mission units
- the pastor
- area or national church leaders about projects they support.

Ask what is being done locally, regionally, and globally. Ask, "How can our children support this project and learn more about mission?"

A Non-Meal Ticket?

Here is a Bible study activity with missional ties: older elementary children can personalize and embody the parable of the talents (Matthew 25:14-30). Give the participants $2.00 each and instruct them to increase the money by using their own talents. Suggest that they may draw or paint, wash cars, walk dogs, rake leaves, or clean windows. When they bring their earnings to class, pool the monies collected to support a mission project. Tell others about the gifts through your church's newsletter or bulletin.

Raise money for mission projects by selling one of the following:

- homemade cookies
- homemade candies
- home-baked desserts
- tickets for a non-meal

What's a non-meal ticket? It is a coupon that says, "This non-meal ticket supports (____) mission project. $2.00" Younger children can decorate the tickets.

Be sure to promote the sale of tickets. Don't overlook church and community channels such as newsletters, public service radio and television spots, and newspaper columns.

Plan a Saturday "Muffins for Missions" night in which participants spend Saturday night making different kinds of muffins and enjoying creative activities and Bible studies. Sell the muffins before and after worship the next day.

Some Starter Strategies

Plan one class mission project each quarter and one cooperative mission involving several classes per quarter. Include younger and older children. Maintain a balance between hands-on mission and events that raise money for mission.

Here are some ideas for all ages:
- Make a "Mitten Tree" for Advent. Put the outline of a Christmas tree on a bulletin board or anchor a tree branch (one that has fallen down) in a bucket filled with gravel. Put up a sign explaining that your class is collecting mittens and gloves, either new or old. Ask for all sizes. Use push pins to attach the gloves to the board or tie the mittens with string to the tree limb. Give the items to a local clothes closet.
- If not mittens, how about socks? They are needed year-round.
- Make handmade cards, decorate paper place mats, or make napkin rings for a local hospital.
- Establish "Operation Stork," a project to supply clothing for newborn babies to wear home from the hospital. Attach a note saying that the clothing is a gift from your church. Include the church address.
- Collect a "Mile of Pennies" (or quarters) for mission.
- Invite a missionary on furlough to talk with the children.
- Help the local animal shelter.
- Make simple bird feeders (pine cones spread with a peanut butter and corn meal mixture and hung from trees) and distribute these around a neighborhood. Making these feeders can be a great cooperative activity during a Parent's Night Out program.
- Have a "Saint Nicholas Gift Day" early in December, during which children make gifts for others.
- Adopt a grandparent.
- Collect toys or eyeglasses.
- Go Christmas caroling where no one else goes.
- Hold a free car wash.
- Stock a food bank.

If your church has a Sunday fellowship time with refreshments, encourage the children to work with the coordinator. Encourage children to serve as church greeters, ushers, acolytes, and liturgists.

"WELCOME to our first annual St. Nicholas Gift Day."

Make Friendship Boxes

A friendship box shows care and concern. Boxes may be decorated by children and filled by children and adults. Here are some different kinds of friendship boxes:

● Child in a hospital: crayons, activity and coloring books, cards, small puzzles, writing or drawing paper, a pen, stickers, *Pockets* magazine;

● Adult in a hospital: stationery, pens, books, a magazine such as *Alive Now;*

● New to the neighborhood: map of the neighborhood, special events calendar, homemade cookies, list of fun and free places to go and see;

● Invite children to bring small tubes of toothpaste, toothbrushes, soap, and deodorant to make personal hygiene bags for persons in need. Use small plastic bags with twist ties or a zip-type closure to the package. Distribute these through a local feeding program or food bank.

Children of all ages can support a local food ministry with canned food collections. If possible, let the children collect the food near the altar in the sanctuary.

Think Globally

The Children's Fund for Christian Mission offers many ideas for mission education. Request an information packet from The General Board of Discipleship, P.O. Box 840, Nashville, TN 37202-0840. The free packet is updated annually.

Heifer Project International helps hungry families feed themselves and care for the earth. Your money can buy baby chicks, a cow, a sheep, or a goat. Call 1-800-422-0474 to learn more.

Red Bird Mission, HC69-Box 700, Beverly, KY 40913, is in the heart of Appalachia, and there are many needs here. Write or call 606-598-3155 to learn what your children can do to support this outreach.

Your church may send out short-term mission teams to build new churches or health centers in other parts of the world. Ask a team leader how the children can support their work. Some items that could be collected and donated are paint brushes, carpenter's tools, or disposable products.

Whatever you decide to do as a children's teacher, please coordinate your plans with your mission work area or other church leader if you plan a service project or fundraiser.

Jacqulyn Thorpe is a Diaconal Minister of Christian Education in the Washington-Baltimore area.

Called to Share God's Love

by Melanie C. Reuter

The Saturday afternoon before Christmas, three-year-old Philip and his mother traveled to the downtown area of our city to pick up a Christmas gift at a specialty store. As they walked toward the store, a homeless man approached them and asked for money. Philip's mother grasped her small son's hand a little tighter and hurried past. "Mommy, wait," Philip wailed. "That man needs our help!"

With the excitement of shopping for Christmas gifts, Philip's mother diverted her son's attention. "We weren't in a safe area of town," she later told me. "Our church had done a lot for needy people during the holidays. Besides, three-year-olds don't understand what it means to be homeless, do they?"

I didn't think so, but I decided to visit a Sunday school class of three- and four-year-olds to find out. "What does *homeless* mean?" I asked. To my surprise, each child had an answer: "Not enough to eat . . . nowhere to sleep . . . being cold . . . no Mommy and Daddy to take care of them . . . no house."

"What should we do about it?" I asked. The children answered: "Pray . . . make food . . . give them clothes . . . love them . . . be friends."

Fishing for Disciples

After Christmas our church planned to help all of our children continue to reach out in love. On the Sundays in February and March, we went "Fishing for Disciples." We used this basic plan:

1. Read aloud the story of Jesus calling Peter, James, and John (Luke 5:1-11). Explore these questions with your children: What does it mean to be a disciple? What do you need to be a disciple?

One way to examine these questions is with a brown-bag lesson. Before your lesson, cut from construction paper two hands, a heart, and a smile. Place the cutouts in a brown lunch sack. Tell the children that in your sack you have everything they need to be disciples. Pull out the cutouts one at a time, explaining how hands help, hearts love, and smiles touch others.

2. On another day follow up with the story of loaves and fishes (Matthew 14:13-21). Explore these questions: What does it mean to be welcome at God's table? What are some things we take for granted?

3. Make individual offering boxes shaped like fish. Encourage the children to put a few coins into their boxes each week for a local shelter or food bank. Make a display in your classroom with a fishing net. On a designated Sunday, bring the offering boxes and place them in the net. See how many fish you've caught.

4. Take the children fishing. Go on a fishing trip. Older children and middle schoolers especially enjoy this activity. With younger children, have a fishing game, such as those at carnivals. Attach a string and clothespin to the end of a stick. Let the children cast their lines over a curtain or behind a large box. Have an adult behind the curtain or box to help the children make a good catch. Attach stickers or some other small prize to their lines.

Other Ways to Share God's Love

The children's excitement was contagious, and soon our entire church was inspired to continue mission participation throughout the year. Here are some activities generated by our teachers:

1. Make a mitten or sock tree. Use a small artificial Christmas tree, or have the children draw a large tree for the wall. Designate a Sunday to bring in a pair of mittens or socks (new or used in good condition) for the tree. Photograph the children with their tree and put the photo on the church bulletin board. Donate the mittens or socks to a shelter or clothing closet.

2. Make refrigerator magnets or lapel pins in the shape of houses. Give the magnets and pins as gifts to members of the congregation to heighten awareness, or sell them and donate the money to Habitat for Humanity or another mission project.

3. Sell framing material, windows, concrete blocks, and so forth for Habitat for Humanity. Find out how much each item costs, raise money for that item, then visit the Habitat work site to see your donation installed. Or arrange to have children make lunches for Habitat volunteers on a Saturday workday. Your church can build a Habitat house with older children, youth, and adults working together.

4. Make place mats for a homeless shelter. Use low-cost white paper place mats for artwork, then laminate them. Or make handmade centerpieces for the shelter's tables. Any artwork is welcome at your local shelter and will provide a different sort of warmth from the cold.

5. Collect money. No amount of money is too small. One group of children collected quarters for an area program that helps homeless people wash their clothes. The children were so earnest about the importance of their work that teenagers and adults asked to participate.

6. Bake cookies or bread for a shelter. Older children and teenagers may deliver the food to the shelter. Youth groups may visit youth shelters or runaway centers.

7. Have a missionary visit the class. Or have persons in the church explain to your children why they support missions.

8. Have the children study another country and learn about the Christian witness there. Young children will learn something by making native foods. Older children and youth may explore economic development and family life. All can learn about ways the church supports other Christians across national boundaries.

9. Make a prayer garland from construction paper. Learn about a missionary or mission project, then let children add a link every day that they pray for that person or project. After a designated time, place the garlands in the narthex or fellowship hall and tell the congregation about this activity. Encourage the children to express to the congregation their feelings about the prayer garland.

10. Sing at a local retirement center or residential care facility. This activity becomes a mission of relationship, especially during the months of January and February. Your group need not be a choir to bring cheer to the residents.

11. Learn about your denomination's heritage. Discover the mission projects supported by your offerings. Help the children see the difference your church's witness is making in the world.

The Church's Mission

Three-year-old Philip and his Sunday school class remind us that the church's mission is to share God's love and that we need to share that mission with our children. Here are two great resources to help you get started:

• *I Caught a Little, Big Fish: Fishing for Faith in the Heart of Your Child,* by Jill Briscoe and Judy Golz (Servant Publications, 1994)
• *Helping Children Care for God's People: 200 Ideas for Teaching Stewardship and Mission,* by Delia Halverson (Abingdon Press, 1994).

It's never too soon to show others the love of God. In fact, the time is right.

Melanie C. Reuter has worked as a volunteer and professional Christian educator in the church for more than fifteen years. She lives in Beaverdam, Virginia.

A Reason and a Season for Service

by Kel Groseclose*

The Advent/Christmas season is a wonderful time to encourage spiritual growth in children, especially through service to others. Children are receptive to acts of compassion and deeds of love as at no other time of the year. In the midst of a materialistic Christmas advertising blitz and an over-emphasis on gift-getting, you can share with children the wonder of giving and communicate the deep satisfaction of serving others.

Most children understand the value of preparation, so Advent can be a rich experience of learning about getting ready for something special, much more than a time of impatient waiting until the big day arrives. One good way to enhance this awareness is through creative classroom service projects that help children discover the joy of sharing.

The following are Advent/Christmas service projects that others have used successfully. Adapt any of these ideas to your particular setting. Remember the point behind the projects: to help children learn that giving can be just as enjoyable as receiving.

Christmas Letters to Missionaries

Purpose: to help children develop a global perspective of the Church and to appreciate how various cultures observe and celebrate Christmas

Age levels: younger and older elementary

Begin planning in early fall. Lists of missionaries are available from your denomination's mission office, or from someone in your local church who works with missions. Ask not only for names and addresses but also for information about the countries where the missionaries serve.

Then talk with the children about the culture and customs of the people in those countries. Encourage children to do independent study and report back to the class. If any members of your congregation have lived or traveled in the areas involved, invite them to visit your class and to share their experiences. Be sure to suggest guidelines and a time limit.

In October have the children begin their letters. Give them the freedom to write poetry, to draw illustrations, to tell about themselves and their plans for Christmas, and so forth. They might decorate their letters with designs cut from old Christmas cards and include a recent photo of themselves. Provide large envelopes in which the letters can be mailed.

The letters should be mailed by the first of November to allow time for delivery and for possible replies from the mission field before Christmas. Check with the post office regarding mailing costs.

Invite Another Class to an Advent Celebration

Purpose: to teach children the satisfaction of sharing; to bring together people of different ages

Age level: all children

Plan an "Advent Event" using personnel and resources available. Suggestions include lighting candles on an Advent wreath, singing familiar carols or songs, reading a brief Advent Scripture, and praying a closing prayer. Older children should help with the planning, and simple refreshments might be served.

Any class could invite any other class. For example, older children might invite an adult class; or the kindergarten class could host the youth group. Make the length of the celebration appropriate for the age levels involved.

A variation of this project would be to invite parents and families of the children rather than another class. Invitations would need to be sent in plenty of time to allow families to make the necessary arrangements.

Ye Olde Christmas Cookie Shoppe

Purpose: to help children have positive contacts with older adults and experience the joy of completing a group project

Age levels: younger and older elementary

Select a convenient meeting time, perhaps the first Saturday of Christmas vacation. Ask each child to bring enough dough to make two dozen of his or her favorite cookies. Gather in a kitchen large enough to accommodate the class comfortably. Provide baking sheets, cookie cutters, and decorations for the cookies (sprinkles, chocolate chips, peppermint candy, and so on), plus attractive paper plates to hold the finished products.

Explain to the children that the cookies are to be given to nursing home patients or to people of the congregation who are homebound. (Get a list of names from the pastor or church office and prearrange the visits.)

While the cookies are baking, plan what you'll do when making the deliveries (sing carols, share any musical talents the children have, read or tell a special Christmas story). If possible, make the deliveries that same day, involving several parents in the transportation of the class.

Share the Season on Videotape

Purpose: to use a contemporary medium to reach out to those who are ill

Age level: older elementary

Locate a camcorder and a knowledgeable operator, possibly a

responsible child in the class. Provide a blank videocassette tape.

Decide together with your children in advance of the actual filming what the content will be. Develop a script or at least fairly detailed notes. Use the group's imagination.

Some ideas: singing Christmas carols as a group; acting out a play based on the birth of Jesus; doing a choral reading of biblical material relating to the Advent season; or showing scenes of the church building decorated for Christmas.

Have the children preview the production so they can admire their work. If needed, make copies of the original video and circulate them among the church's members who are unable to leave home or who live in nursing homes.

Make an Advent Booklet

Purpose: to help children articulate what Advent and Christmas mean to them; to enable children to put their thoughts and memories about this season in writing to share with their families and with the congregation

Age levels: younger and older elementary

Explain this project to the children in advance, and give them several weeks to think and reflect on the project. Help the children think through who will receive their Advent/Christmas booklets. Begin this project early enough (at the beginning of November) that the booklets can be distributed by the first Sunday in Advent.

Let the children contribute their Advent/Christmas ideas as they are led and according to their various gifts—in prose, poetry, or music; a short play; an illustration; a Christmas memory; or a recipe. Solicit help from the class in designing a cover.

Encourage the children's creativity. Make no boundaries other than the general theme of Advent and Christmas.

Set two or more deadlines for the contributions to be completed, the first one being a week earlier than when you actually want it. Do a minimum of editing. And do not make comparisons among the various contributions. This project has nothing to do with grades and everything to do with children's marvelous insights.

Supply the paper for the final copy so that the booklet will be uniform in appearance and easily duplicated.

When all the pages have been copied, have the children help collate and assemble the booklets. Let the children help in distributing the booklets to the intended recipients.

This project could also be turned into a money-raising project for a worthy cause, such as a local mission concern of your choice.

A Special Kind of Food Drive

Purpose: to assist people in need while helping children learn about the customs of one or more ethnic groups

Age level: all children

Food drives are rather common activities in churches and church schools during Advent and Christmas. They are badly needed and are worthy endeavors. Children of all ages can participate and feel good about making a difference.

But a food drive can be an opportunity for significant learning as well. Depending upon the residents of your particular community, choose to help someone from an ethnic background different from that of the majority of your children.

Find out all you can about the food preferences and eating habits of the nationality or culture of the persons you are helping. Then explain these to the class. You might also decide to study the Christmas customs of that ethnic group.

Make a shopping list of foods to send home with each child, and suggest that food be brought that is in harmony with the ethnic group you are helping. Arrange a time for the children to help pack the food for each person or family.

If possible, deliver the food gift yourself with several class members; or make arrangements to take it to the Salvation Army, a food bank, the public school system, or other agency.

Praying Hands for Advent

Purpose: To help children know they are loved and are a vital part of a larger caring community; to help them know that serving can be done quietly within our hearts and minds.

Age level: all children

Step 1. Recruit a group in the congregation (a Bible study group, men's or women's organization, the youth group) to be partners in this project. The members of this group will agree to pray daily for a child, using one child's handprint as a tangible reminder of that particular child's life. Set a certain length of time as part of the original agreement; two weeks during the Advent season might be adequate.

Help each child trace the outline of his or her hand on a bright piece of colored construction paper. Include the child's name on the sheet. When the handprints are done, deliver them to the other class or group.

Step 2. Suggest to the other class or group that this procedure be reversed and that they trace outlines of their hands to give to your children. Ask your children to offer silent or spoken prayers during the class session that day and to pray for their partner each day during the week. One week is long enough to expect the children to continue this part of the project.

Step 3. Conclude "Praying Hands" by having the two groups meet together, asking the individual prayer partners to shake hands and to wish one another a wonderful Advent and a joyous Christmas.

For preschool or younger elementary children, a brief explanation of this project should be sent home.

You might wish to have a few duplicate handprints available in case any are misplaced or lost.

*(*Bio info in author index)*

Project Ideas to Earn Money for Missions

by Raney K. Good

One evening at dinner Jack listened as his mother and father talked about a mission trip to Haiti that a group of adults from his church were planning. Although Jack's parents were not going on the trip, they expressed their support for the trip and spoke of plans to support the work of Grace Children's Hospital in Haiti. Jack heard about the children, the poverty in that country, and the illnesses that some children endure.

"I think that the kids in our church should buy toys to send to the kids in Haiti," said Jack. His mother answered, "Jack, you should talk to Mr. Cunningham, the trip leader, about that idea."

Jack's mother wondered if Jack would pursue the idea. *After all, he's only a first grader,* she thought to herself. Imagine her surprise the next day at church when Jack found Mr. Cunningham and told him the idea. Jack also told his Sunday school teachers and Mrs. Szabo, the director of Christian education. Together they developed a plan to collect small toys, school supplies, barrettes, and hair ribbons for the children in Haiti. A letter was sent out through the Sunday school classes, and collection boxes were decorated.

From this experience Jack is learning that although he will not travel to Haiti, he is still a missionary. He is living out the message found in Matthew 25:40, "Truly I tell you, just as you did it to one of the least of these who are members of my family, you did it to me."

Many projects offer opportunities for involving children as missionaries. How do you select one? Consider these questions:

1. What are the projects your church is supporting or has supported in the past?

2. Are mission projects suggested in your Sunday school curriculum? The United Methodist Children's Fund for Christian Mission highlights six projects each year that relate specifically to ministries involving children. Does your denomination have a similar type of program?

3. What has your class been studying that might lend an idea? The story of Jesus feeding five thousand people from five loaves of bread and two fish might suggest a food pantry or soup kitchen project. Hearing the story of Jesus healing the blind man might encourage supporting an overseas medical clinic.

4. Will you choose more than one project over the course of the year? You may want to alternate between projects close to home and projects far away. Doing so helps children develop a broader understanding of mission.

5. Would your class enjoy developing a relationship with a missionary? Choosing a particular missionary can be exciting, as children learn about a specific mission and the people who are involved in the project. Contact your denomination's headquarters for a listing of missionaries.

Raising Money

Once you have chosen a mission to support, the next step is to raise funds or to collect goods to offer the project.

1. **Make Children's Artwork Note Cards**—Have children draw or paint pictures of Bible story scenes using bright colors. Work with a print shop to put the pictures on note cards. Sell the note cards and use the proceeds for missions. Or try making a calendar. Talk to the printer about your project and about a possible discount on the cost of printing.

2. **Sponsor a Carnival**—Have games such as beanbag toss, fishing, and a basketball free-throw with small prizes such as stickers or bookmarks. Sell tickets and refreshments. Children could run the booths themselves.

3. **Deliver Christmas Cards**—With the help of adults, children can deliver Christmas cards to local addresses for members of the congregation. Charge a fee for delivery. Persons pay for the delivery service instead of for postage for mailing.

Art by Susan Harrison

Teaching Tips for Terrified Teachers

4. **Fill a Container**—If your project has a focus, use a related item to fill with money. Include the entire congregation by putting the containers around the church along with posters the children have made to explain the project. Examples: Fill baby food jars or baby bottles for a child-development project. Fill vitamin jars for a medical clinic.

5. **Have a Sidewalk Art Show**—Have children draw pictures on the sidewalk or parking lot of the church. Use Scripture stories for inspiration or depict the mission project your class has chosen. Charge admission or take a freewill offering.

6. **Do You Measure Up? or We're Big on Missions**—Ask each child to give a penny for every inch of his or her height. Extend this opportunity to other church members by offering to measure people during a fellowship hour.

7. **Put on a Talent Show**—Give children an opportunity to share their gifts and talents to benefit mission. Take time during the show to talk about the mission project the children are supporting. Take an offering or charge admission.

8. **Challenge Giving**—Challenge children to give as they explore their own lifestyle compared to the lifestyles of persons in other countries. Have children count the number of faucets in their homes and give ten cents for each faucet. Challenge them to give a quarter for each television in their home or for each soft drink they drink in a week. Talk with children about necessities in life, such as shelter and clean water. Talk about things that are not needed to live, such as televisions and soft drinks.

9. **Give a Penny Per Mile**—If your project is far from home, find out how many miles away it is. Invite children to collect a penny for each mile. Use a map to chart your progress.

Giving Goods

Understanding the connection between money given and a particular mission project can be hard for some children, especially young children. You may choose to give supplies rather than money. If you decide to mail supplies to a mission away from your community, consider the postage costs. You will want to ask for goods that are light in weight and, therefore, less expensive to ship. Contact agencies first for a list of items they use and need for their missions. Be specific in requesting these items as an offering.

Children have fun shopping and choosing items to give. Encourage older children to use some of their allowance to purchase something for a mission project. Talk with them about how it feels to give their own money.

Here are some examples of goods and supplies you can collect:

1. A homeless shelter may need small-size toiletries (soap, shaving cream, toothpaste, shampoo, deodorant) and towels.

2. A medical clinic may need vitamins, adhesive bandages, gauze pads, cotton balls, and cloth tape.

3. A food pantry may be in special need of baby items such as baby food, cereal, formula, and diapers.

4. A soup kitchen may need donations of food or help in preparing and serving food. Get busy as a class and cut vegetables for soup, wash fruit, or make cupcakes and cookies.

One church chose a different local project to support each year during vacation Bible school and asked children to bring in a different item each day for the offering. When they chose the homeless shelter, the schedule of offering looked like this:
Monday—toothpaste or toothbrush
Tuesday—soap or powder
Wednesday—shampoo
Thursday—shaving cream or deodorant
Friday—towel or washcloth

A tally was kept of the items brought in and was posted for everyone to see each day. After vacation Bible school concluded, a group from the sixth grade class helped deliver the supplies to the shelter.

Whether your class chooses to raise money or to give goods and supplies, you can rejoice in the giving. Your goal is not raising the money but sharing it.

When talking with the children in your class, do not make children feel guilty about those in need. Help them instead to understand and feel the joy of giving in response to God's love. Loving God and loving their neighbor (Matthew 22:37-40) becomes a reality as children become involved as missionaries.

Resources and Projects

CROP
Church World Service
P.O. Box 968
Elkhart, IN 46515

Heifer Project International
P.O. Box 808
Little Rock, AR 72203

United Methodist Children's Fund for Christian Mission
P.O. Box 840
Nashville, TN 37202

Raney K. Good is a Christian Education consultant in Northern Illinois.

Pennies From Heaven

by Sue Downing

Oh! People like to find a dollar,
quarter, or dime,
But a penny is overlooked
practically every time.
When a bright, shiny penny
comes our way,
We look at the penny briefly, and
then usually turn away.
But suppose we found a penny,
and began by giving that one,
As an offering to Jesus, to share
with everyone.
Could it be a single penny with
little worth to our eyes,
When placed in the hands of
Jesus would be greatly
multiplied?
For if Jesus could take the gift of
a small boy's lunch
And feed 5,000 people, which is
really quite a bunch!
Just think what Jesus could do
with the offering of a penny.
He would take and increase it, so
God's love could be felt by many!

Susan Harrison

What a wonderful message Jesus gives to us through the Bible story of the loaves and fishes (John 6:1-13). In this familiar story Jesus uses a boy's gift of five loaves and two fish to feed a multitude of people. In the same way Jesus can use our smallest offering, given out of love, and do great things.

You can help the children in your class experience the joy of giving by involving them in a Penny Project. Penny Projects are mission projects in which children gather pennies for a specific cause or group. Penny Projects can benefit local or global causes. To make your Penny Project a success, follow these simple guidelines.

* Select a theme or title for your project. This sets the tone, gives direction, and makes the project more fun.
* Determine what group or cause will benefit from the pennies you collect.
* Decide how the pennies will be collected and who will be included in the collecting. Will the pennies be collected in Sunday school, church, or both? Where will the pennies be collected? Will youth and adults be invited to participate?
* Create or gather containers for collecting the pennies.
* Update the class or congregation periodically regarding the progress of the collection.
* Give the project a definite beginning and end.
* Have fun!

Theme Ideas

Here are some Penny Project theme ideas. Use the ideas as they are or adapt them to your own situation. In either case anticipate great things happening when you work together to share your pennies!

Biblical Themes

● Theme: Sharing Pennies With Jesus
Place a picnic basket or other large basket in your Sunday School classroom, on your church altar, or in some other spot to collect the pennies. Introduce the project with the poem at the beginning of this article.
Beneficiary: Hungry children

● Theme: Have a Penny Flood!
Invite your children to "make it rain pennies" for forty days and forty nights. Create a cardboard box replica of the ark as a container for the pennies and place it under a big rainbow mural made by the children's handprints.
Beneficiary: Flood and hurricane relief

● Theme: Lost and Found Mission
Ask everyone participating to search for all the "lost pennies" they can find. Put the discovered pennies in a large clear jar for all to see. Children could be encouraged to share all the places they found their pennies (under a cushion, corner of a drawer, or in a pocket).

Beneficiary: Homeless children and families
● Theme: Fishing For Pennies!
Create a boat from a large cardboard box for children to place their pennies in, or let children make their own boats using shoeboxes. Hang a fish net on the wall and invite the children to place a paper fish in the net for each dollar's worth of pennies brought in.
Beneficiary: School supplies for needy children

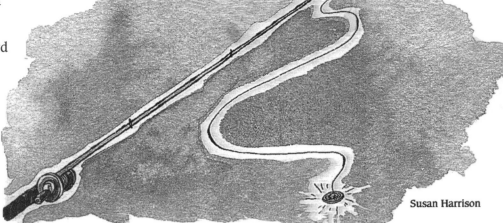

Susan Harrison

Anytime Themes

● Theme: Watch Our Pennies Grow!
Challenge children to gather their height in pennies. Mark a child's height on a wall or mural with a taped penny. Write the child's name and height in inches by his or her penny. Ask the children to bring a penny for each inch.
Beneficiary: Local adoption or foster care facility
● Theme: Going Places for Missions!
Have the children lead the congregation in collecting a mile of pennies. Figure how many inches are in a mile and attempt to get one penny per inch. Use an opened suitcase to display the pennies.
Beneficiary: Local charity.

Seasonal Themes

● Theme: Pennies Shine Bright for Missions
Set up a Christmas tree in a prominent place in your church. For every dollar's worth of pennies received, let a child place a paper or other type of star on the tree. Another option would be to have a night sky mural behind your manger scene and try to fill the sky with shining stars!
Beneficiary: Local shelter for women and children
● Theme: Penny Stockings
Ask each child to fill one pair of heavy socks with pennies. The socks and pennies can both be donated to help those in need! If they are heavy enough, mittens could also be used.

Beneficiary: Any local charity
● Theme: Hatching Pennies for Missions
Encourage your children to fill one or more large plastic eggs with pennies. When they bring their eggs, have a big Easter basket for them to put the eggs in!
Beneficiary: Any local charity
● Theme: Planting Penny Seeds of Love!
Have each child try to fill some type of small flower pot with pennies, and/or have a large flower pot near the worship center in your room for children to "plant" their pennies in. Encourage the children to decorate their flower pots in some way (stickers, paint, colored markers). Make use of these pots later on for the children to plant flowers in and give as gifts.
Beneficiary: Any local charity

Collection Ideas

Here are some ideas for collecting the pennies that can be adapted for a chosen theme.
● Help children create Penny Pockets using two 8" square pieces of colored felt, cloth, heavy paper, or other materials. Ask them to put their names on their pockets and decorate them. Say: "Let's fill our pockets with pennies to help others!"
● Plan for groups of children to carry baskets and collect pennies from the congregation as they enter the sanctuary for Sunday worship.

Or have the children collect pennies as the offering is taken and then place the baskets of pennies close to the altar.
● Ask the children to select a favorite hat and attempt to fill it with pennies. At the close of the project have a "Penny Party" to celebrate and give thanks for all the pennies collected. Let the children wear their emptied hats, share a treat together, and have a special time of worship!
● Pair children together, or pair children with members of an adult class to gather pennies. Let each pair decide on the kind of container(s) they wish to use. Have a joint worship celebration at the close of the project.

Now, are your thoughts filled with pennies, pennies to share?
Look, there are pennies everywhere!
So let's not delay, our mission is clear.
Make pennies a priority all through the year!

Sue Downing teaches preschoolers at Brentwood United Methodist Preschool in Nashville, TN. She is a freelance writer and author of "The Seasons of Life."

Involving Children in Stewardship

by Susan Patterson-Sumwalt

*f*all is here. Your congregation will probably be in the midst of its annual financial stewardship campaign soon. This is a good time to involve children in one of the major annual projects of the congregation.

It is an even better time to think about your own understanding of stewardship and the ideas you convey to your children about stewardship. As a teacher of children you should plan carefully the messages and understandings you want to pass on to them this year. Decide now how you will guide your children to see themselves as Christian stewards.

What Is Stewardship?

When most adults hear the word *stewardship,* they hear only the word *money*. Is that the limited concept you want to give your children? Stewardship, understood more fully, is about an attitude toward life. The attitude a Christian steward has about life is one of joy and response. It is knowing that God is good, that creation is good, and that we are good. As we come to know these things, each of us has an opportunity to respond by sharing our prayers, our gifts and graces, our presence, and our possessions.

Helping Children Grow

Children seem to have an innate sense about trusting and responding. Their curious minds, open imaginations, and sense of wonder help them develop this sense.

As a teacher you will want to help develop this sense. Then your children will know they are loved and can trust. And they will then be gracious and generous in their responses.

Using Scripture

One of the most important ways you can help children develop their sense of trust and response is by sharing Scripture. In the church we have both the responsibility and the opportunity to share what is uniquely ours to share. In the sharing of Scripture children can open themselves to the wonder of God's love for them. As children experience God's love, they come to understand that what they have to offer God is very important.

As your congregation's financial stewardship campaign gets underway, find out what the theme is going to be. Also ask what the scriptural base will be for the campaign. How can you use the theme and passages of Scripture in your own classroom?

Use the Scripture verses and stories in a way that will make sense to the age level you teach. Help the children respond to the stories through art or drama. Talk together about what the stories or passages mean. Work with the children to list ways they might apply the story or passage to their own worlds. Then help the children make specific plans to carry the meaning of the story or passage into their everyday lives.

Involving the Children

Now try to find ways the children can be involved in the congregation's campaign. The following ideas will probably suggest others you might try.

• Could your children design a bulletin board display for your classroom or for some other visible place in your church building? The design for the bulletin board should come out of the children's understanding of the theme. Help them list various possibilities and then decide on one design to implement.

• Could your children share their understanding of the theme and Scripture by designing a worship bulletin cover or a bulletin insert for use by the entire congregation in worship? You will have to coordinate with both the worship planners and the stewardship campaign committee to carry out this idea.

• Will there be an all-church meal or a leadership team meal connected with the campaign? If so, your children could interpret the theme or Scripture by making place mats for the meal. Use white place mats or 11-by-17-inch pieces of paper, let the children draw, paint, or make collages to express their ideas.

• Invite a member of the stewardship campaign committee, the finance committee, the council on ministries, or the administrative board to visit your class to talk about your church's budget. Ask this person to bring pictures or posters to illustrate how the congregation's money is being used. Ask this person to share "people" stories, such as the mission projects the congregation supports. Help the children list questions they would like to ask your visitor about the use of the church's money. Try to make the church's budget come alive for your children in concrete terms.

• Design a pledge card for older children. Talk about what it means to make a promise. Help the children see that a pledge card is a promise we make about our money. Keep your children's parents involved and informed as you carry out this project.

• Hand out children's offering envelopes to all children. Talk together in your class about allowances. If your children get allowances, talk about the idea of saving part of "their" money to give to the church. Help children understand that we give our money in response to the love God has already given to us.

• Be sure to take an offering each week in your class. Make the offering an important part of your session plan. Pass an offering basket around if that is appropriate for your age level. After the money or envelopes are collected, show them to the children. Stress the fact that this is their money, their response to God's love. Talk together about where the money goes and what is done with it when it leaves your Sunday school room.

• Help the children share other kinds of responses besides putting money into an offering. Ask children to share one way they will be helpful to someone during the week. Ask them to think of something they can do for someone who is sick this week. Ask them to think of ways they can help care for our environment during the coming week.

Expanding the Meaning

As the children become more aware of the congregation's financial stewardship campaign, begin to broaden their understanding of the concept of stewardship.

Build in a time of prayer in your class session. This may vary from praying structured prayers, such as the Lord's Prayer, to a prayer before food, to more informal prayers. Encourage children to talk with God. Let them know it is OK to thank God for something or to ask God for something, to think and pray about people they know or about people they don't know, and to be concerned about the whole world. Help children develop a relationship with God through prayer.

Use a portion of your Sunday school time to encourage and to affirm each child. Take time to learn their interests and concerns. Talk together about the church as the Body of Christ made up of many parts. Explain this metaphor in words your children will understand. Then share with them that they are part of the Body of Christ and that what they have to offer is important. Remind them that they have important tasks to do, like caring for a pet, sharing crayons with another child, or comforting someone who was hurt on the playground.

Model God's unconditional love for your children. As your children realize that you value who they are and what they can do, they will learn to value who others are and what they can do. They also will learn the importance of respect for abilities and differences.

Snack time in your class session can even impart a message about stewardship. Do you pray a prayer before the snack? Are you helping your children be thankful for what they have received? Are your snacks healthy? As Christian stewards we must learn to make wise choices in caring for our bodies and keeping them healthy.

Find ways to expand your children's understandings of and concerns for the stewardship of all of God's creation. Concerns about our environment are very much in the news these days, so you will find lots of information available in magazines, newspapers, and

television reports. But you must add the perspective of Christian stewardship by helping your children see their concerns and actions as a direct response to the gifts God has graciously given to us in our beautiful world and our own healthy bodies. Talk about specific ways the children can be involved in caring for animals, preserving the beauty of our world, and using wisely our world's precious resources. Suggest that your children tell others why they should do the same things.

The Importance of Stewardship

Stewardship is about our relationship with God and with one another. At the beginning of a church school year you have an opportunity to begin again, whether you have the same children or a new class.

As you teach, you are always sending to your children messages about God's love and messages about how you and your class will live and learn together as God's children. These are really messages of stewardship that you can share throughout the entire year.

But take some time during your congregation's financial campaign to highlight these ideas of stewardship. Use the theme along with Scriptures to focus the campaign in your classroom.

Plan ahead carefully. Help your children know they are Christian stewards when they know the love of God and want to pass that love on.

Susan Patterson-Sumwalt is an ordained elder and serves as a minister of Christian education in Denver, Colorado.

Children and Natural Disaster

by Evelyn M. Andre

We're all affected by disaster. There are floods, tornadoes, hurricanes, mud slides, and bombings. Not one of us can escape knowing about them or maybe being personally affected.

And what about children? They see disasters on television, and hear parents and other children talk about these events. How can we guide children to experience empathy and ministry in action? How can they, even in small ways, let others know they care and that the sufferers are not alone?

Children who know disaster first hand: How can we ease their anxiety and help them cope with losses of loved ones, pets, possessions, and significant toys, as well as the inconvenience and trauma of being displaced without shelter and permanence?

Know About Your Denomination's Disaster Response

The Disaster Relief arm of The United Methodist Committee on Relief (known as UMCOR) provides supplies and funds to help those most vulnerable, and personnel to implement the process. A recent UMCOR leaflet (#3495) states "approximately every four days, UMCOR responds to a disaster. . . . Your gifts help activate a network throughout the United States and the world to help relieve the pain."

The UMC, as have many other denominations, has national and local organizations who know where the needs are and are instantly able to respond effectively. More of what you give actually gets to the victims through these denominational agencies than by any other means.

Information is available in these new leaflets:
- United Methodists in Disaster Response #3495
- Emergency Response and UMCOR #5333

Both leaflets are free except for postage and handling; so for $2.50 you can receive fifty copies or less of each leaflet from the Service Center, P.O. Box 691328, Cincinnati, OH 45269-1328. If you are a teacher of another denomination, contact your church's outreach or mission agency.

Many denominations have plans already in place to respond to disaster. Check with your pastor about the ways your denomination responds to disasters and how your children can participate. She or he will know how you can get more specific information.

Help Children Respond to Disasters

Older children will be more aware than younger children of the disasters that occur beyond their community, but be assured that children sense the anxiety of adults and will look for opportunities to process that tension. Give them as many facts as are appropriate for their ages. Help them understand how others hurt even though they may be unknown and far away, by relating stories of children struggling with disaster—make the tragedies personal. Talk with the children about the feelings they would have in that situation. What would they need? Next, give the children opportunities to respond to these needs. Local churches and/or community groups organize to supply food, clothing, toys, and money to help rebuild people's lives. Plan ways to involve the children in your class.
- Make contributions from their own money and belongings.
- Make posters to inform others of the projects.
- Help collect money and appropriate goods from church members and neighbors.
- Assemble "Kits of Comfort" to send to children who are disaster victims.

Teaching Tips for Terrified Teachers

- Write letters to those children. (The message might be "My name is Karen. My Sunday school class at Christ Church, Madison, is praying for you. We send you our concern and God's love.")

Help Children Cope With Disaster

Children personally affected by disaster will react in many different ways. Consider several kinds of disaster:

— An individual house fire, leaving the family without possessions, clothes, food, and shelter. Will that child come to Sunday school next week? Will you as the teacher visit and comfort that child? Can you be a calm and stabilizing influence in the midst of chaos and traumatized adults?

— An area-wide flood or tornado, leaving many children displaced. You, too, as teacher, may also be a victim. Is your church and classroom intact, or also in ruin? What are the messages of comfort? How can you speak for God and demonstrate God's love?

— A well-known family in your church and community has been killed in a car wreck. How can your class grieve? How will you answer the question, "Why did God let this happen?"

In response to any disaster, some children will exhibit fear, or some may "act out" with unpleasant and unnatural behavior, or some may revert to earlier childish ways such as losing bladder control, sucking thumbs, clinging, crying, or needing to be held. Some may become sullen, moody, or silent; while others may be overly aggressive. These responses may be seen in children of all ages.

Here are suggestions for responding when disaster strikes or affects children:

- Let children know they are loved. Call each child by name. Let each child know he or she is special to you. A hug is especially welcome.
- Listen to what they say. Take time to hear them tell their stories.

(This may mean having some extra teachers so that each child has someone to listen to him or her individually.)

- Don't smooth over or minimize the experience. Avoid giving a theological discourse on why such tragedies happen. Refrain from using pat phrases such as "Everything will be all right." Assure children that you know they hurt and you are sorry for the tragedy.
- Give many opportunities for creative expression. Play dough, finger paints, and easel paints provide ways through which children can express their feelings physically and emotionally even though there may not be words to describe what they feel. Let them tell you about their picture or objects if they want to, but don't verbalize your interpretation by saying, "Oh, that looks like a big tornado" or "that must be the flood waters rushing into your home." Instead, say, "Paul, that's an interesting picture (or object). Do you feel like telling me about it?" Sometimes the answer will be "no" because it wasn't anything. It just felt good to experience the medium.
- Provide for physical activity. Children who have been through trauma may need extra ways to move their bodies. Music for dance or creative expression may be meaningful. Streamers (crepe paper or scarves) to be twirled about freely may be the wind. Hands and arms moving up and down may simulate rain and storms. Jumping could imply earth movement. Helping children recall traumatic experiences through the use of fun music and movement will be a soothing and healing experience.
- Water play will relieve some stress. Therapists use water play as an effective calming tool. Go outside with tubs and utensils for filling and pouring, boats for floating, and pails and paint brushes for water painting walls and sidewalks.

- Include a rocking chair and an extra grandma- or grandpa-type loving person in your classroom for several weeks. Traumatized children may need extra attention and a loving set of arms.
- Respect the needs of some children to sit and watch. While it is important to keep some routines and structure available to your class, be prepared for the child who just wants to sit on the sidelines rather than being physically involved. Respect the child who will only be involved if she or he can be close to that one special adult or older sibling with whom a bond is felt.
- Move beyond the classroom. Let affected families of your children know you care about them—beyond the classroom. Be of help to your children's families in whatever way is possible.
- Plan time for special out-of-class time together. It may be a visit to your home, to the park, to the playground, or to a restaurant. Extra caring from a Sunday school teacher can make a lasting impression on a tramatized child and her or his family. You represent the caring of Christ.

Evelyn M. Andre is a retired editor of young children's curriculum. She has been involved in child care at disaster sites in Ohio, Kentucky, South Carolina, and Florida. She has helped train other adults to be caregivers. She resides in Nashville, Tennessee.

Children and the Environment

by Genie Stoker

Recycling is a circle of giving. God gives to us, and we give back to God. Some materials we put back into nature. Others we pass on to people in need.

The projects suggested here enable children to recycle common materials in ways that say "thanks" to God. Ideas are included that help children conserve food, plastic, aluminum, and lumber, while helping others at the same time. Most activities are appropriate for children ages four through ten, unless otherwise specified.

Food: Using Every Bit

Bible Lesson

In the story of the feeding of the five thousand (John 6:1-14) Jesus encourages conservation of food "Gather up the fragments left over, so that nothing may be lost" (John 6:12).

Preschool and kindergarten children will enjoy a visual account with a Bible picture book, a flannelboard, or puppets. Elementary children who have some familiarity with the Bible can participate in a dramatic narration. No props are necessary except for a basket, some food representing fish and loaves, and a receptacle for scraps. Ask for volunteers to portray the boy sharing his lunch, Jesus, and the disciples. The remaining children will be the people being fed.

Lesson Application

Have Ready: Several fruits with inedible parts (seeds, rind, core, or stem), such as a section of cantaloupe, an apple, a banana, or a few grapes. Also have ready two table knives to chop the fruit, a salad bowl and serving spoon, dishes and utensils for the students, a garden trowel, and a container for transporting the inedible parts outside.

How To: Invite the children to wash the grapes or berries, spoon melon chunks into the serving dish, or peel and slice a banana or an apple with a dull knife. Set the fruit salad aside for later in the hour.

Ask the children to gather the seeds, peels, and cores to fertilize a plant on your church grounds. Take the class outdoors to select a tree or bush to "feed." Let the children take turns with the trowel, burying the fruit peels. When they have finished, they can return to the classroom, wash their hands, and get ready to eat the fruit salad.

Discussion and Prayer: As the children sit together, discuss items to include in a prayer before the snack. These could include foods for which they are thankful, the tree they are helping to grow, people who provide them with food, or people who need food.

As the children eat, discuss ways of conserving food while sharing with others. Some children may be eager to tell how their own families are already conserving food. Each child can learn from the others. Perhaps one family shares extra garden produce with a neighbor. Another family may put vegetable peelings on a compost heap or bread crumbs in a bird feeder. Another may donate cans to a community food bank. This is a good time to make plans with your children to participate in a food collection drive or to start one.

Plastic Presents and Drink-Can Parties

Bible Lesson

God has given us a unique responsibility: dominion over all the other species (Genesis 1:26). We can help all God's creatures have a safer, cleaner world.

Older elementary children may share what they've learned about animals being harmed by litter.

Preschool and early elementary children would enjoy learning from an animal puppet. The puppet could tell how pollution affects its life. The animal might illustrate the point with a pop-can ring that needs to be taken from its neck.

Lesson Application

Below are a variety of projects to utilize containers that otherwise crowd landfills and litter beaches, forests, and rivers.

Festive Garlands

Have Ready: Plastic soft-drink-can rings, colored glue (or plain glue and colored glitter), clear cellophane tape, and a few newspapers. Prepare the drink-can rings by cutting them into two separate rows of three rings each. You can make colored glue with white liquid glue and a few drops of food coloring. Have ready paintbrushes and water to rinse them.

How To: Cover the work area with newspapers. Early arrivals can help with this. After the Bible lesson give the children soft-drink-can rings to color with glue or glitter. When they are dry, the rings can be taped together into garlands for home or church.

User-Friendly Containers

Have Ready: Plastic containers with handles (milk or juice cartons, vinegar or bleach bottles), adhesive materials for decorating the bottles (scraps of contact paper, leftover stickers, labels or colored tape scraps), and scissors. Rinse the containers thoroughly. Cut a large opening in the tops; remove the pouring spouts but leave the handles.

How To: Give each child a prepared container. Set the decorative items on the table so that each child can choose his or her own. The children can take the containers home for toy or crayon storage. They can give them as presents to Mom for use in the kitchen or bathroom. Older children may want to give the containers to younger children rather than use them themselves. A preschool class may welcome the gift of containers.

Suncatchers

Have Ready: Flat clear plastic (from bakery food containers or large blister packs), colored glue and brushes, scissors and black permanent felt-tip markers for the older elementary children. For the younger children, prepare the plastic by cutting it into shapes. These could be Christian symbols such as fish or church window shapes. Have ready newspapers and towels for covering and cleanup.

How To: Cover the work area with newspaper. Let each child pick the plastic shapes and colors he or she wants. Preschoolers will enjoy covering their shapes with many colors. Older children can use felt-tip markers and scissors to design their own suncatchers or small church windows. Place the projects on folded squares of newspaper for the trip home.

Discussion: As the children work, ask them what they might have made at home from tin cans, plastic containers, or lids; and encourage them to involve their families in recycling these items.

Pop-Can Smash Bash

Have Ready: Bags of empty pop cans. Pick an area outdoors where the children can flatten cans without disrupting worshipers.

How To: After the Bible lesson take the children outside to stomp the pop cans flat for recycling. The easiest way for small people to flatten the cans is to lay the cans on their sides and step on the easily crushable middle. Then step on each end to flatten that also. If you are working in an open outdoor area, be sure to have plenty of helpers.

Discussion and Prayer: As you talk with the children after the cans have been flattened, try to find out how they feel about the following questions: How can we help God's creatures have a safer world? What has God made that you would especially like to thank God for?

End your discussion with prayer, encouraging the children to offer their own prayers.

Carpenter's Workshop

Bible Lesson

Genesis 1:11-12 celebrates the creation of vegetation.

Invite the children to name some of their favorite uses for trees. Younger children would enjoy a visual lesson with a potted seedling, flannelboard or puppet trees, or even a person in a tree costume. Older elementary children can understand God's plan for trees in the oxygen cycle.

Lesson Application

Have Ready: A bathroom scale, a cardboard box that will fit on the scale, a pencil and paper, a thick stack of newspapers, boxes of wood scraps, and plenty of glue. Ahead of time advertise your need for wood scraps in your church newsletter, indicating where people will find a collection box.

How To: A simple demonstration shows how much wood it takes to make newspaper. Place the cardboard box on the scale. Have the children put the newspapers in the box. Read the total weight and write the number down. Take out the newspapers and ask the children to add wood to the empty box. Keep adding wood until the weight reading is the same as it was for the newspaper. Those who may be too young to understand the numbers will understand the visual comparison of the two piles.

Put all the wood scraps in a work area. Cover the table with newspaper, if necessary. Encourage the children to select scraps of wood to glue together. Some may need a few project ideas, such as creating a wood collage, building a miniature city or town, or framing a favorite picture.

Discussion and Prayer: Talk together about our need to save our forests. Ask questions like those that follow. What can you do to save on paper? cardboard? Do you think Jesus made things with wood scraps when he was young? What should we tell God we like about trees? Pray together for the future of our forests.

Why Do It?

The reasons behind recycling are so complex that even adults find it complicated because of constantly changing information. As you prepare these activities, plan how and what you can explain appropriately to the age level in your class. It's OK if your children cannot yet understand a lot about the environment.

Hands-on activities like these are excellent for involving children who may not respond to more traditional teaching methods. What all children learn and remember most is what they do. And best of all, with activities like these all your children will really be in ministry to others and to God's creation.

Genie Stoker is a Sunday school teacher in Tucson, Arizona. The ideas in this article were developed and used in a summer Sunday school program for a multigrade one-room class.

Worship Through a Child's Eyes

by Martha L. Neebes

You are peeling an orange; you hold it in your hand; you feel the roundness and bumpy peel. You smell the orange and look at the color. Then you tear the segments and the juice spills out onto your hand. The seeds are removed and you may recognize God's plan through the orange. If you are exploring this orange with a child, you might examine the individual parts: the peel, the core, and the seeds. And you would notice the smell of the orange, the taste of its juice, the feel of the peel.

The time a child spends with you eating the orange will become a memory triggered by the sight, smell, color, taste, or touch of an orange. A different experience comes with the juice in the bottle that sits in your refrigerator and is poured in the morning glass. The juice becomes, in the child's mind, a necessary nutrient and part of the morning routine. Both the orange and the juice are good for you, but which experience is more meaningful? Worshiping God can become an experience triggered by sensual (sight, smell, taste, touch, hearing) memory when children more fully participate in worship, and when the entire setting is designed to proclaim both to and through the senses.

Sunday school teachers and Christian educators have the responsibility to guide parents and children in worshipping God through hymns, liturgy, prayers, Scripture, the sermon, baptism, and Communion within the faith community.

To help parents prepare children for worship, invite children and their parents to a special time in the sanctuary. This might last one week or several. Or you might choose to plan individual sessions lasting several months. Using the orange description, help parents understand the importance of worship for young children, and of families worshiping together. Let's take apart the four components just like you did with the orange.

Adoration

God is worthy of being adored or loved very much.

* At the front of the sanctuary look around. Ask children and parents to point out the symbols that demonstrate adoration: the cross, Bible, statues, pictures, windows, flowers, and colors. Encourage touching, lifting, holding, and smelling.
* Next, sit in a pew and listen to the silence. Explain that when we are quiet, we may hear God. You may hear air blowing, or voices in another room: All of those sounds are God. We also hear God through music. Demonstrate the different instruments used in your worship service.
* Open a hymnal and show how words and music work together to express love for God. Which hymns praise God? Sing one hymn of praise and adoration.
* Look at the baptismal font. Has anyone been baptized at church recently? Describe baptism. Talk about Jesus' baptism, different modes of baptism, and ways water is part of Bible stories.
* Encourage parents to express adoration of God at home. Remind parents and children that we adore God because of evidences of creation, God's constant presence, and for the precious gift of Jesus Christ.

Teaching Tips for Terrified Teachers

Proclamation

What is *proclamation*? It is telling the Word of God through preaching, and also through reading Scripture, through hymns, through anthems, and through the children's message.
* Show children where proclamation happens in the bulletin.
* Let children stand in the pulpit, at the lectern, or in the choir loft.
* Ask your minister to describe her or his robe and the colors of her or his stole. Also ask the minister to tell how she or he chooses what to say in the sermon.
* Explain that the minister speaks about the Bible verses, and by listening carefully, we can learn how to live in God's plan. It is all right to say that sometimes a sermon is long and hard to understand! But it will get easier!
* Invite children to kneel at the Communion rail Describe Holy Communion to them. Explain that Jesus used bread and juice to create a holy moment at supper with his disciples. We have a special time with Jesus every time we kneel like this and take bread (or wafers or crackers) and juice. We can be happy that Jesus loves us and is present even now.

Confession and Intercession

Define the words. To confess is to tell what you did that was wrong. What we do wrong is *sin*. God doesn't want us to sin, and when we do, God says we must confess, and we do that as a part of our prayers. Intercession is praying for ourselves or for someone else. Confession and intercession are part of our worship service.
* Point to the prayer of confession in the bulletin. Talk with children about their actions or thoughts or words that were wrong or sinful. Lead children in a guided prayer that helps them silently confess to God. Remind them how fortunate we are that Jesus says God always loves us, not just when we do good.

* At bedtime, who do the children pray for? That is intercession. Who prays for them? Assure them that grandparents and parents, Sunday school teachers and pastors, all pray for them. Invite both parents and children to the Communion rail to pray for each other.

RESPONSE:

How do we respond to the proclamation of God's Word? What do we do? Look again at the bulletin: what clues are there? Our offering, the words of the last hymn, and our participation in Communion are all a response to God. How do we remember what has seen said and sung? You can give these suggestions to parents even as you demonstrate them with the children.

Before the service begins:

* help children put markers in the pages of the hymnal for the Psalter, affirmation, and the hymns;
* help children to follow the service in the bulletin;
* be sure children stand for singing and put their own offering in the plates.

When the service is over:

* talk about what was said or sung. What did your child hear? Clarify and interpret;
* sing one or more of the hymns or choruses again;
* review the children's message.

Respond through the week by:

* inviting neighbors to worship with you;
* preparing a meal for the homeless;
* gathering mittens for children;
* praying daily;
* repeating (and memorizing) weekly Scripture;
* setting aside money for Sunday's offering, or for special mission projects;
* reminding children that we respond this way because of God's love for us.

Don't stop with the parents.

Meet with your worship and/or education committees. How could your worship be more meaningful to children? Consider these questions: What draws the eye? Can you see stained glass windows? Are there banners? Chrismons? Are there memorable phrases or lines of music that will remain during the week? Are there smells (flowers, candles, incense, bread, juice) that will later recall the awe of worship? Can the water of baptism be heard and felt? Will God's presence be experienced by a child?

Remember the orange. Peel worship as you did the orange, and help a child worship.

Martha L. Neebes is director of Children's Ministries at Church of the Savior, Cleveland Heights, Ohio. She has a Bachelor's degree in Child Development and Teaching from Michigan State University and a Master's from Ashland Theological Seminary, Ashland, Ohio.

Teaching Children to Pray: A Sacred Trust

by Betty Shannon Cloyd

Have you ever felt overwhelmed with your responsibility to help children grow in their prayer lives? Don't feel alone—almost every Sunday school teacher has felt this way. Actually, it is not such an awesome task. Since children are spiritual beings, with very little prompting they will pray quickly and naturally. An old adage says that children and God speak the same language. Those of us who share time with children know that this is true. As a mother, grandmother, teacher, and diaconal minister of Christian education, let me share with you what I have gleaned about teaching children to pray.

What Is Prayer?

Children need a user-friendly definition of prayer, one in language that they can understand. I often tell children this: *Prayer is using our own words to talk with and listen to God, at any time, in any place, and about anything.* Let's look at the components of this definition.

"Using our own words"—Children want to know that their own words are adequate. They do not have to use flowery, complicated words or sentences for God to hear their prayers. Whatever their age or verbal abilities, their own language is sufficient and pleasing to God. Young children can begin with short prayers of praise and thanksgiving and as they get older can add prayers for forgiveness and guidance, blessing, intercession, and petition. Of course, the great prayers of our faith, especially the "Lord's Prayer,"are important for children, but spontaneous prayers in their own words are acceptable to God.

"Talk with and listen to"—We often talk to God in prayer, but we must also be silent and listen for what God wants to say to us as well. Sometimes we think that children can't or won't be still for times of silence. But some say that because the world of most children is filled with constant noise, times of silence are welcomed by and are meaningful to them. You can first help children experience silence by asking them to find a special place within the classroom where they can be alone with God. Even if there are others in the room, children can learn that they have a "portable sanctuary" within. (Make sure that the children understand that this is not a time of punishment, as asking them to be quiet sometimes is, but it is a special time to listen to God.)

Another way to introduce silence is to take the class outside on a "prayer walk." Ask the children to walk by themselves and to refrain from talking. Direct them to notice signs of God's presence in our world (such as birds, butterflies, flowers, and so forth) and to listen for God's thoughts. When they return, ask several students to share ideas and feelings they experienced on the prayer walk.

"At any time"—Established times of prayer such as mealtime, bedtime, or worship are very important; but we can also live in constant, ongoing conversation with God. I have a dear friend in a nursing home who says she no longer adds "Amen" to her prayers. When I asked her why, she said, "I might want to add something as the day goes on. I just leave my prayer open so I can do that." Ongoing communication is the goal of prayer. "Pray without ceasing," we are admonished in 1 Thessalonians 5:17, and as teachers, we want to nurture this spiritual act in children.

"In any place"—We want children to know that they can pray on the school bus, on the play-

Prayer Walk Checklist

- ☐ bird eggs hatching
- ☐ butterfly
- ☐ trees budding
- ☐ flowers blooming
- ☐ grass sprouting
- ☐ baby animals

CHILDREN IN WORSHIP

ground, in their classrooms, or in the backyard. God is not confined by the church walls! But we also want to encourage children to have their own special places of prayer at home. (It might be helpful for you to send a note home saying that you have made this suggestion to your class.) This special place might be behind a door, under the child's bed, or in the closet; but it should be a spot that is meaningful to the child. You may encourage children to gather items there like a bird's egg shell, a feather, a pretty rock, a flower, a mustard seed, or a picture of Jesus in order to make this a "sacred space."

"About anything"— Sometimes children have serious issues that they are afraid to discuss with anyone. Children need to know that they can share everything with God. The psalmists brought many emotions to God, even anger, and God was big enough to understand. God is a loving friend with whom everyone can be completely honest. It is comforting to know that God is always ready and willing to hear, especially the prayers of a child!

A Teacher's Prayers

Let me say a personal word to you, the teacher. Praying for the children in your class is important! We do not know how intercessory prayer works, but we have enough evidence to say that prayers bring results. When we pray, things happen; when we don't pray, they don't! I encourage you to have a list of your children at home in your special place of prayer and I urge you to pray for them every day. Both because we want our children to grow to know Christ, and because our culture is influencing them in so many negative ways; our children urgently need continuous prayers.

God Surrounds Us

I remember a story told to me by a young mother. She wanted her four-year-old son and two-year-old daughter to have an experience of God. One rainy day she and the children were tired of being in the house. Seeing that the rain had stopped, the mother looked out across the lawn and in the distance she saw a beautiful rainbow. Sensing that this could be a meaningful experience for the children, she rushed to help them put on their rain boots and coats so they could go for a walk. She hoped that in the process, they would discover the rainbow and that it would be a moment of worship and inspiration.

Much to her dismay, the children dawdled. They were distracted by their scattered toys and were frustrated as they finally made it down the steps and into the yard. To the mother's disappointment, the rainbow had vanished and her good intentions seemed lost. She decided to make the best of the situation and allowed the children to splash in the puddles and the water trickling down the driveway. They had a wonderful time!

Later, when they started to go into the house, the children's eyes caught a spider web sparkling with raindrops in the sunshine, displaying an array of beautiful colors. An exquisite butterfly was nearby, spreading its wings in glorious splendor. Stopping suddenly, the little boy said quietly to his little sister, "You know, don't you, that God made this butterfly and the spider and the rain and everything in the world?" There was a hushed silence and then his sister whispered in her small voice, "Yes, I know." The mother said that she could not have orchestrated a more spiritual moment if she had tried.

Your Challenge

Lest I have made it seem that the whole burden of a child's prayer life is your responsibility, let me hasten to say that you are not alone in this endeavor. God is with you and in many ways you are simply the gate-opener of God's Holy Spirit. You can introduce a child to God, by you cannot force a relationship. That relationship is God's work: you need to be faithful by providing sacred time and space.

You, as the teacher, do not need to do it all. God is with you as you make time and space in the child's life for the Holy Spirit to work. The prayer life of children is truly sacred territory and you have the wonderful opportunity of standing with them on this holy ground.

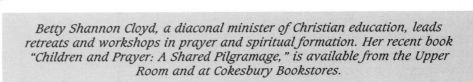

Betty Shannon Cloyd, a diaconal minister of Christian education, leads retreats and workshops in prayer and spiritual formation. Her recent book "Children and Prayer: A Shared Pilgramage," is available from the Upper Room and at Cokesbury Bookstores.

Eight Ways to Involve Children in Communion

by Zachary C. Beasley

*C*hildren are some of the most inquisitive creatures on God's green earth. They ask millions of questions and demand an astonishing amount of time from adults to help them develop into moral and responsible human beings. Often they do not understand the full meaning of the church activities they observe or participate in. But they are willing to seek information, and you are one of the persons they trust to give them good answers.

Holy Communion is one of those rituals that even many adults do not understand. It is full of symbolism that has been celebrated for centuries in the life of the Christian church. Children experiencing this sacrament have many questions about its meaning.

Children may ask: Why do we drink grape juice and call it wine? (Many Protestant denominations do so to support their stance on temperance.) Why do we call bread the body of Christ? Why does the minister say such things as "the blood shed for you"?

When adults are not sure of the answers themselves, the temptation is to feel that children are not yet ready for participation in or information about Communion rituals. But whether you belong to a denomination that includes children or one that excludes children from participation, you have a responsibility to help children learn as much as they can about the sacraments they may participate in currently or in the future.

Personally, I feel that children have an advantage in coming to Communion. They come to the table with a childlike spirit that reflects trust, faith, and expectation. Their participation is not a routine act but rather an opportunity to receive, without bias or criticism, what God has to offer. It would be wonderful if all Christians would come to the table with this childlike spirit, knowing that what God gives us in Communion is far greater than anything we can understand or convey in words.

Following are eight ideas Sunday school teachers can use to involve children in experiencing Communion at some level. Use as many of them as your denominational guidelines allow.

1. Consult With the Pastor

Before starting this project, find out what ideas your pastor may have about involving children in Communion. If your church is fortunate enough to have a children's minister, this person could be a great asset both to you and to the children. Invite the pastor to visit your classroom sometime during the quarter to tell the children what happens during Communion.

There are several methods of administering the sacraments. Have your pastor explain which methods are being used by your church and why. However, caution him or her to be aware of the attention span of the children. Suggest that two short sessions might be better than one longer one.

2. Encourage Observation

If your church serves Communion on a given Sunday, give the children an assignment at the end of your class session. Ask them to observe what happens in the upcoming service. On the next Sunday in class, ask the children to tell you what they saw and ask what questions they have about what they saw.

3. Explain What Holy Communion Is

Now that you have set the stage, explore the following points with the children in language appropriate to their level of understanding:

a. Communion is a covenant with God, a promise on God's part that God will always be with us, a pledge on our part of our faith in God's grace.

b. Communion is when we remember and celebrate Jesus' death on the cross. Here you may need to recount the story of Easter with special emphasis on Good Friday (Luke 9:21-23; 23:26-43).

c. Communion is a time to give thanks to God, who has given us victory in the resurrection of Christ. Here again the story of Easter is important. Give emphasis to the happenings of Easter Sunday morning (Luke 24:1-12).

4. Explain the Symbolism of the Wine and Bread

Many adults have problems understanding the symbolism of the elements of bread and wine or grape juice at the Communion table. Children, who are primarily concrete thinkers, can be even more confused. The simpler the words you use to explain to children, the better. Use as much action in your

explanations as possible. Take some time in study to make sure that you have a good concept of Communion yourself.

The wine represents, or is a symbol of, the blood of Christ; and the bread represents, or is a symbol of, the body of Christ. According to 1 Corinthians 11:24, Jesus took bread and broke it and said, "This is my body that is for you." In verse 25 Jesus continues with reference to the wine: "This cup is the new covenant in my blood." As we receive the elements, we are one in Christ, one with one another, and one with Christians around the world.

Children should know that Communion is *something we do* together in response to *something God does* for us. It is *what we do* as a result of God's grace to renew our commitment to God and to confess our sins before the Creator.

A good way to capture the children's imagination during your explanation of the Communion elements is to invite your pastor to conduct a Communion service in the classroom. He or she should use a loaf of bread to be broken and a pitcher or goblet of grape juice to be poured into individual cups.

Call the children's attention to the basic actions of the Lord's Supper, which are based on New Testament stories of what Jesus did during the Last Supper: He took the bread, gave thanks, broke it, and gave it to the disciples. After the supper he took the cup, gave thanks, and gave it to his disciples.

Seeing the bread broken can remind children of Jesus' suffering and death. The action of giving thanks to God can help children understand that even in suffering, we recognize God as being with us and providing for us. The act of giving can teach that Jesus gave himself willingly on our behalf. The pouring of the wine, which represents shedding of Jesus' blood, teaches that Jesus was committed even unto death to show God's tremendous love for all the world. Sitting around the table will give the children a sense of fellowship and mutual love for one another as they participate in the ritual of Communion. A note should be sent to parents telling them their child will be participating in communion.

5. Hear From a Communion Steward

Invite a Communion steward or the chairperson of the committee that prepares for Communion to come in and tell the children what the stewards do to prepare the Lord's Supper. Ask if it would be possible for the children to help prepare the elements or to simply watch the elements being prepared. Allow the children to ask questions.

6. Get Parents Involved

Invite parents to spend time sharing with their child what Communion means to them. Ask parents to remind their child when Communion is coming up in church. Encourage them to take Communion together as a family, signifying the unity of the family within God's kingdom. Tell the parents what their child is learning about Communion in your class, so that they can reinforce your teaching at home.

7. Make Communion Bread

Ask the pastor if it would be OK for your class to bake the Communion bread for one service. Use any recipe for flat bread or baking powder biscuits. Schedule time in the church kitchen or in your home for this activity. It probably should happen sometime on the Saturday before the bread will be used. Give all the children an opportunity to participate in some aspect of the making and baking.

8. Make Banners

Banners can bring life to the sanctuary. Have a banner-making party and invite the children to use bright colors and a variety of fabrics to make a Communion banner.

Have on hand all the materials and supplies: fabric, paper, scissors, glue, glitter, and so forth. Have the children cut from fabric some key words of Communion such as *love, joy, Communion, fellowship, peace,* and *salvation*. You may also use symbols such as the cross, the table, a chalice, a loaf of bread, a sheaf of wheat, grapes, and a grapevine. Look for design ideas in *Banners for Worship,* by Carol Jean Harms (available from Cokesbury). Ask your pastor whether you may display the banner in your church sanctuary.

Preparing children to participate in Communion is an important teaching task. I hope that these tips will benefit you as you introduce God's children to Holy Communion.

The Reverend Zachary C. Beasley is a pastor in Mississippi.

Dancing Before the Lord

by Beth Teegarden

Peek inside a children's play area and what do you see? Children jumping, running, skipping, turning, rolling, bending, kneeling and just about any body movement that can be done. Children love to move and to be active. They love to express themselves with their hands, arms, and legs. It only seems natural they would like to dance. Dance is defined as "a series of rhythmical motions and steps." In an unorganized way the children are already dancing. They just need an "organizer." Being the organizer is not difficult, and by using the following suggestions, you can organize these energetic children into dancers.

Why Dance?

Dance is not new to our religious beliefs. David was "dancing before the LORD" all the time (2 Samuel 6:14; 1 Chronicles 15:29; Psalm 30:11). Dancing was a way for the people to rejoice and praise God. Today we can follow the ways of the Israelites and "Praise Him with tamborine and dance" (Psalm 150:4).

Dancing and moving also are ways for children to express their feelings. Many times children may not be able to adequately say how they feel about God, but ask a child to show you how he or she feels and you will quickly get the picture. We need to give our children this opportunity in church.

Dancing and moving is also a wonderful teaching tools. When we move, we feel; when we feel, we remember; and when we remember, we learn. Dancing helps us do this.

What Can You Dance To?

If you're going to dance, you must have music, right? Yes and no.

By all means, music is beautiful to dance with. Children's music is generally very descriptive and easy to choreograph. You could try looking for songs in the curriculum, the hymnal, children's songbooks, Bible school songs, praise choruses, folk tunes, and children's choir anthems. Most music found in these sources will be easy for the children to learn and some may even have movement suggestions with the music.

But music is not the only source for dance. The spoken word can be enhanced with the use of movement. A litany, a prayer, a Psalm, a Scripture reading, or a Bible story could all become more visual with the use of dance. Many of the same sources for music will also have prayers and litanies in them and, of course, the hymnal and Bible will be of use. You may also be adventurous and try writing your own, or let the children work together and write something they would want to dance to.

Creating the Dance

You may think this is what you can't do, but with patience and imagination you will be able to create a dance. The first thing you will want to do is take whatever you are going to dance to and look for given words. These are words that tell you what to do, for example: kneel, clap hands, stand, turn around, pray, jump for joy, and so on. If possible, include the actions these words describe in your dance.

The next thing you will want to do is to visualize the other words of the song or text. Ask yourself "What do I see when we say *praise* or *world* or *baby* or *people* or *stable?*" This will give you visual ideas of the pictures you are trying to make.

Finally, you will want to decide what you want the dance to communicate. What is the message? When you decide this, make sure all the movement and pictures you have created are communicating the message. Put all of this together and you have a dance.

Can All Ages Dance?

Absolutely! The only thing you need to be careful about is age-appropriate movements. You want the children to be able to enjoy what they are doing and not become frustrated with the dance. A good motto to keep in mind is "the simpler the better." This will make

the dance easier to create, easier to teach, easier to learn, and more usable in the classroom.

Preschool and younger elementary children have a hard time accomplishing movements that involve using two or more large motor skills at the same time. They would have difficulty moving their arms up and down while marching in place. On the other hand they could do both of these movements if done separately. This age will also have difficulty doing partner or group movements. Holding hands and walking in a circle is a good group movement for this age, but anything harder will be frustrating.

Older elementary children can accomplish most anything you would want them to do. They will welcome a challenge and most likely will want to help create the dance. Some children may be shy about moving at first, but with encouragement and a loving atmosphere within the group, these children will begin to feel more comfortable.

When and Where?

A great time to begin a dance is when a season of the liturgical year changes. In the later part of November you could create a dance that could be used during the Advent season. This way the children can learn the dance well and get to do the dance more than once or twice. As the liturgical season changes, you could then change to a different dance. To begin you might want to incorporate dance into your classroom setting as part of your lesson. You could spend a small amount of class time each week to teach parts of the dance, and once the dance is learned, you could then use it for several weeks in the worship section of your lesson. After this is accomplished, you may want to do the dance for other classes in the church, at children's worship, or even Sunday worship services.

Another great opportunity to use dance is vacation Bible school. Since the children meet each day, you can easily teach them movements to the songs, stories, or theme of vacation

Bible school. This could be a rare opportunity when all ages of children could learn the same dance and do it together.

Other places you could incorporate dance would be day school and day care, church picnics, church camp, retreats, Confirmation, and special programs such as Christmas and Easter.

Above all, it is important to remember that dance is just another way we can worship God. Teach your dancers that they are not performing a dance for entertainment, but are showing praise to God with movement of their bodies. With this kind of attitude, each and every time we dance we are truly "dancing before the LORD."

Beth Teegarden is Associate Director of Music and the Arts at a church in Brentwood, Tennessee.

When You Don't Have What You Need:
Apt to Adapt
by Joyce Brown

You need fifteen cardboard tubes by next Sunday so that children in your Sunday school class can make sheep. Three plans come to mind:

Plan A: You live in paradise, and your church's supply room has a huge stock of cardboard tubes. You collect the tubes a week ahead and place them in the well-equipped supply closet in your well-equipped classroom.

Plan B: You make fifteen phone calls, asking friends to save toilet paper rolls and to bring them to your classroom next Sunday. Next, you worry. What if a friend forgets or three children bring their visiting cousins?

Plan C: You take a deep breath and adapt.

For every Sunday school teacher who has a perfect room and endless supplies, there are scores of teachers who must adapt. They go to their kitchen or bathroom cupboards and turn their imaginations loose, looking for something that will work for a specific project.

The following suggestions are intended to get your creative juices flowing. When you need something you do not have, consider these ideas or —better still —come up with some of your own.

Classroom Equipment

Chairs: Let the children sit on carpet squares or paper grocery sacks. They can personalize the latter with markers or crayons.

Tables: Hand out bulky magazines or 8½-by-11 pieces of cardboard for the children to use as lapboards. For messy projects, let students work on an old shower curtain spread on the floor.

Shelves for Supplies: Create a Busy Box and Busy Bag. See the shaded box for instructions.

A Bulletin Board: Tie heavy yarn between two chairs and use clothespins to clip paper to the yarn. Or drape a sheet over two chairs and pin pictures to the sheet. Or stack and tape together cardboard boxes. You can tape or pin pictures to all four sides. Or hang yarn from the ceiling and pin pictures to the yarn.

Building Blocks: Stuff shoeboxes or paper bags with newspapers and cover the boxes or bags with self-adhesive vinyl. (Get your youth group to help.)

Family Living Center: Use five large cardboard boxes that later can be nested for storing. Cut a door in one box to make a refrigerator. Draw stove burners on a second box. Add a tablecloth to a third box. Place a square baking pan or a plastic dishpan on the fourth box to make a sink. Put a baby blanket and a small pillow in the fifth box for a doll bed. Show the children how to become rocking chairs by sitting cross-legged on the floor and rocking back and forth.

A Dynamic Duo: Busy Box and Busy Bag

Busy Box and Busy Bag are designed to keep children busily engaged in learning activities. Used indoors or outdoors, Box and Bag provide supplies for helping children learn through art, music, drama, and writing. Box and Bag may not contain materials specifically requested in a lesson plan; but these twins contain something that can be adapted. Use the following ideas to create your own Busy Box and Busy Bag.

Busy Box

Create compartments in an 8-inch by 13-inch zippered insulated bag (the kind that holds twelve soft drink cans) by filling the bottom of the bag with cans and plastic jars and gather a few pint and quart zip-type freezer bags.

Fill the box with the following items: pencils, three pairs of scissors (sharing is encouraged), a glue stick, a six-inch ruler, clear tape, crayons, colored chalk, felt-tip markers, food coloring, drinking straws, craft sticks, chenille wires, cotton swabs, clothespins, pieces of sponge, a paper punch, crepe paper streamers (rolled and secured with rubber bands), guitar picks, craft wire (bend it and twist it for a safe needle; or mold it into wire sculpture), jingle bells (who knows when you will need to make music), metal paper fasteners, safety pins, adhesive bandages, an eyeglass repair kit (magnifying glass plus small screwdriver), paper clips, thumbtacks, straight pins, a single-edged razor blade (safely enfolded in cardboard), birthday candles, matches, a small stapler and staples, one die of a pair of dice (moving six spaces is plenty in a Sunday school game), index cards, an ink pad, 3½-inch coffee filters (for dipping into food coloring dye, for folding into flowers, and for making smiley-face puppets), adhesive labels, self-stick removable notes, and reusable adhesive tack (for attaching things to walls and, in a pinch, for making tiny clay sculptures).

To transport Busy Box, zip the cover closed and use the carrying handle.

Busy Bag

Slip 8½-inch by 11-inch pieces of cardboard into gallon-sized zip-type bags (instant lapboards) and add one of the following to each: a blue sheet of paper (can be used to make a bulletin board, a tent, or a pool of water), construction paper, computer paper (leave the sheets connected for a mural; tear them apart for drawing paper), notebook paper, file folders, pocket folders, 22-inch squares of fabric and pantyhose waistbands (for Bible-times head-coverings).

Place the filled zip-type bags in a large canvas tote bag. Add a small battery-operated keyboard and a small cassette tape player to the tote bag and you have a dandy Busy Bag.

Pair Busy Bag with Busy Box for a dynamic duo that's ready for any teaching challenge.

Supplies

Watercolors: Add five drops of food coloring to every two tablespoons of water.

Paintbrushes: Bend twelve-inch chenille wires in half. Clip clothespins to small sponges or to cotton balls. Hand out cotton swabs. Blow through drinking straws to move paint on paper.

Stapler: Use tape, glue, safety pins, or paper fasteners.

Glitter: Add several drops of food coloring to salt or sand, then spread it on paper towels to absorb the moisture. Or add powdered tempera paint to salt or sand. Place either mixture in plastic containers with lids. Use a paper punch to cut colored paper into tiny circles. Cut colored paper into small pieces.

Craft Sticks: Use drinking straws or chenille wires.

Clay: While stirring constantly, cook 1 cup salt, ½ cup boiling water, and ½ cup corn starch over low heat until the mixture is stiff. Cool. Knead, adding drops of red and green food coloring until the mixture reaches a gray-brown color.

Cardboard Tubes: Roll and tape 4-by-6-inch index cards or heavy paper into tubes.

Sock Puppets: No socks? Make puppets from paper bags, paper plates, paper cups, cardboard tubes, or nylon knee-highs stretched over coat hangers.

Props: Draw them on cardboard and "nail" them together with paper fasteners or chenille wires. Drape sheets over chairs, tables or a music stand. Draw props on paper and tape them to a wall.

A Piano: Use a guitar, a battery-powered keyboard, or sing along with a cassette tape.

Puppet Theater: Drape a table with a sheet. Turn a table on its side. Use an accordion-fold cardboard cutting board.

Bible Costumes: Cut head holes in the center of 24-inch by 60-inch pieces of fabric. For belts use rug yarn or waistbands cut from pantyhose. Slit up brown paper grocery bags, turn them wrong side out, cut holes for head and arms, and decorate with crayons or markers.

Joyce Brown is an associate in Christian education and a certified teacher of teachers. She teaches third- through fourth-graders in Sunday school. As a curriculum consultant for Cokesbury, Joyce helps churches discover exciting ways to use curriculum resources.

Especially for First-Time Teachers

by Elaine Alling Lilliston

In the midst of a district Sunday school teachers' meeting, new teacher Carolyn announced, "The gifts survey recently completed by our church family showed that I have no gift for teaching!" We laughed at her admission. I asked why she had agreed to teach. "I don't know. I just love the Lord and I enjoy children." I don't know anything about the paper survey she had taken. I do know that Carolyn's love for God and her deep understanding of children made her a perfect prospect for being a teacher.

> ## You can open yourself to the excitement that comes from joyful teaching.

A month later I checked on Carolyn. She was exuberant about her class of young children. They were fun. They were a high point of her week. She could not stop beaming and bragging about "her" children.

As we talked, she noted that the teachers' meeting had helped her to "relax and to be open to the faith experiences of the children."

You, like Carolyn, can have the teaching skills to relax and celebrate the joy of our faith.

Another new teacher, Jenny, suggested this key to her enjoyment of teaching. "Call the children by name and plan a lot of meaningful activities. If Sunday school is fun, then everyone will learn more and will want to come back."

You can open yourself to the excitement that comes from joyful teaching and creatively sharing our faith in age-level-appropriate ways. Together, let us look at possibilities to assist you as you prepare for a very special journey in faith through the eyes of children.

Take Time to Identify Your Prospective Class Members

Search Known Lists

You may have been given a list of class members. Sometimes this is complete. Sometimes, even in smaller churches, it is not. Children may have been dropped from your list for a variety of reasons. There are some ways to make sure you are reaching all your potential class members:
- update previous class rolls;
- look for church school dropouts;
- reach out to church visitors;
- follow up on special-event participants (VBS, summer days away);
- reach out to the children who may be connected to your church through grandparents, neighbors, or friends;
- discover the names of your class members and create a new listing with addresses, phone numbers, and parents' names.

Reach Out and Introduce Yourself

Send postcards and colorful notes, make phone calls, and personally visit in homes to introduce yourself to the children.

Children enjoy receiving mail and phone calls. Even if you've known the child for many years, this is a new relationship of teaching and learning together. And if you don't know the child, this is a great way to begin.

Jesus met people where they were. When he helped persons feel comfortable, they were drawn closer to God. Your introductions may become the beginning spirit of hospitality for your class.

Personalize Your Room

Create a welcoming atmosphere in your room. Use class members' names in a bulletin board. Put names on doors, walls, ceiling mobiles, or banners. Easy-to-do ideas include:
- paper name balloons with curling ribbon strings;
- member pictures glued on apples on a tree;
- graffiti-style names on a classroom banner;
- paper name bricks on a wall outside your room;
- symbols from your curriculum strung with fishing line and dangling from the ceiling.

For nonreaders, a color-coded or thematic welcoming door or entry display might help children find appropriate classroom areas. Each age level might agree on an identifying color or simple symbol. For example, children might be encouraged to "look for the red door," "come to the sheep grazing on a green hill," or "find the door with purple grapes."

Pray for Your Class

As individuals and as a class unit, begin to pray before your first meeting. If you have a large class, group the children and pray for three or four each week.

Take Time to Explore Your Resources

Use user-friendly resources that invite you to grow in your personal faith as you guide others. Psychologists have discovered that we retain 95 percent of lessons taught. You are about to embark on a major adventure in learning together with the children you teach. To make better use of your resources, try the following:

• Discover the overall focus of the unit for the entire quarter. Look at the goals for each week in the quarter. Make notes as you read through the material of activities you might use, stories you remember, and supplies you might need.

• Reflect on your needs and gifts and the needs and gifts of your class members as you read through suggested lesson ideas. Remember to personalize each lesson for the special group.

• Choose activities and discussion starters that will encourage both individual and group growth.

Biblical background for teachers and concise activity directions with readily accessible materials will allow you time to concentrate on building relationships.

Christianity is not a cut-and-paste activity for the refrigerator door. It is a relationship! Allow activities to become personal reflections of the participants and part of the learning process, not simply "cookie cutter crafts."

Take Time for Age-Level Needs

Reflect for a Moment

• Identify the age you will teach and remember when you were that age.
• Where did you live?
• What did you enjoy doing by yourself and with friends?
• What adjectives would have described you?
• Who were the significant persons in your life? What do you remember about each?

The members of your class may be a lot like you were as a child. They may have similar likes and dislikes. As concerned adults, we at times "miniaturize" Christianity, challenging children to be like adults. We impose our adult perspective on children rather than allowing them to experience God's love with the awe and wonder of childhood experiences. With Jesus' model of teaching, you will be teaching persons first; content will follow!

Take Time to Discover Your Classroom Space

Visit the Area

Look at your classroom space as a "first-time visitor" might. What do you notice? Is it clean? Is it neat? Does it look like a space where a child would come in joyfully? Discover what things need to be taken care of before the children arrive, considering the following:

_____Is this a safe place for children? Examine toys, equipment, and furnishings.

_____Is this an appropriate place for children? Check furnishings, equipment, and room arrangement.

_____Do I have what I need to be able to teach? Look for basic supplies such as pencils, markers, paper, and scissors.

_____Can the parents and children find the space? Ask for or make directional signs from entry doors to your area.

Visualize Yourself in the Room or Area

Allow yourself to imagine the children present in this space. how will they move in the room? Is there so much furniture that they fall over it? Is the room arranged so that they can't find what they need? Is the bulletin board low enough for them to see the display? In what ways, if any, do you feel you might want to change the basic area arrangement?

If you share space, consult with others utilizing the same space to determine the best arrangement for all persons who use the room. While most resources will probably be eagerly shared by all groups, other areas may need to be specified.
• Color-coded fabric shelf "curtains" might help separate one group's supplies from another's
• Reversible bannerlike "announcement flags" can be used and flipped for multi-use spaces.
• Clothespin name clips help personalize clothing hooks and can be changed for each group.

Prepare You Area

_____Refresh bulletin boards;

_____Clean out and clear out out-of-date resources;

_____Gather basic supplies in an accessible spot.

Take Time to Plan the Class Session

"Bee" Intentional

Focus on the learner with introductory activities, room arrangement, and personal words of greeting for each arriving child.

Providing a variety of opportunities will help to meet individual needs and will maximize class time and effectiveness.

Depending on the child's arrival time, attention span, and involvement level with various tasks, he or she will vary in the number of tasks accomplished. All children do not need to do all activities in order to have a meaningful lesson. For example, the names of the disciples might be discovered through a "word search" leaflet activity or a "Bible verse discovery card," or by finding a dozen hidden plastic eggs in the room with a name on each. Children can choose which activity best suits their learning style.

Thematic learning centers allow a child to choose activities to meet individual needs while encouraging the child to become involved in and responsible for the learning process. Leaflet puzzles and games, activity booklet sheets, and ideas from the teacher's guide may readily become "learning center activities."

A "learning center" is a designated area with instructions and supplies to accomplish a special purpose. It may be part of a table, a bulletin board, a box on the floor, a windowsill, a clothesline with plastic zippered bags of activities, a picture on the wall with arrowed reflection questions, a contemplative corner, a snack area, a book-nook area, an easel, a roleplay area, a loft, a listening-responding center with or without headphones, or a "sheet" tent. The possibilities are seemingly endless! Instructions may be written, illustrated, or tape-recorded.

Talking with children allows you, the teacher, to discover what children are thinking about the lesson. This will enable you to reinforce concepts covered in a lesson and to ensure that the activities you have used are meaningful for the children.

Celebrate worship/group time. Use the insights you have gained from your introductory activities, the learning centers, and your conversation with the children. This is affirming to children, and you can clarify and expand lesson concepts. It is exciting to allow children the opportunity to share new knowledge!

"Bee" Prepared

Preparation is a must! After his baptism, Jesus took time to prepare. Through reflection Jesus gained strength for his ministry.

Give yourself the gift of preparation *before* Sunday morning. Know what you want to accomplish. Have your supplies ready. Relax and enjoy the class as you learn and grow together.

"Bee" Present

Recently I asked a group of teachers with children, "If the soccer game begins at four-thirty, what time does your child need to be at the field?" In unison I heard, "At four o'clock!" I prodded, "Why four o'clock? The game is not going to begin until four-thirty!" I was quickly reminded of the need for preparation, the need to warm up, the need to feel part of the team effort, the need to be supportive of one another, and the need to hear the coach's game plan.

I then said, "If Sunday school begins at nine-forty-five, what time do you need to be present?"

Like the sports coaches and team members, we have preparation to do before the session begins. Our timing is a visible, unspoken witness of the priority of this session for our budding Christians. We have heard, "Actions speak louder than words!" In order to be ready, we must be present in both mind and body before the first child arrives.

Take Time to Evaluate

Informal evaluation is an ongoing process as you observe the way children interact with presented ideas. This informal evaluation causes us to move to "plan B" if one idea is not meeting the needs of the group.

Another form of evaluation is also needed. After the children have left, reflect on the overall session. Ask yourself, *What went well? What would I do again? What flopped?* Remember the children as individuals, and assess the ways in which each had specific needs met by the lesson and the opportunity to be part of the class experience. Adjust your plans for the next session based on your newly acquired information and insights.

Take Time for Yourself

Know That You Are Not Alone

For nearly two thousand years teachers through the ages have done what you are doing. Venturing out in faith, persons have shared themselves so that our Christian heritage might be passed from one generation to another. You are joining a long parade of teachers! And God is with you!

BULLETIN BOARD

Basic Classroom Supplies:
A box, bucket, or laundry basket can hold:
classroom Bibles
paper (plain and colored)
pencils, markers, crayons
scissors
glue, paste
masking tape
chalk, eraser
stapler, staples
newspaper (table protection)

Scrap craft materials:
yarn
fabric
ribbon
beads
old jewelry
sequins
glitter
fishing line
clothespins

Additional handy supplies:
paper punch
paper clips
brads
ink pad
paint (water color, tempera, and finger)
paper plates
lunch bags
margarine containers
egg cartons
paper tubes
greeting cards
salt boxes
baby food jars

Additional Resources

• *The Official Sunday School Teacher's Handbook,* by Joanne Owens (Meriwether Publishing, 1987).

• *7 Ways of Teaching the Bible to Children, by* Barbara Bruce (Abingdon Press, 1996).

• *Teaching the Bible to Elementary Children,* by Dick Murray (Discipleship Resources, 1997).

• *Teaching Young Children*, by Mary Jane Pierce Norton (Discipleship Resources, 1997).

• *Transforming Bible Study with Children: A Guide for Learning Together,* by Patricia W. Van Ness (Abingdon Press, 1991).

Elaine A. Lilliston is a diaconal minister and a certified lab leader, with twenty years experience in Sunday school teaching. She and her husband, Andy, teach together in Rocky Mount, North Carolina.

From Crayons to Tissues and Beyond
Equipping Your Room for the Expected and the Unexpected
by Lynne Stillman Froning

A Young Children's Room

It was early one Sunday morning. As I walked through the halls of our Sunday school, I saw Johnny arrive at his room. Mrs. Johnson, his teacher, suggested that he say good-bye to his family and join her.

Johnny had been waiting all week to play with the firefighter's hat and the fire engine that had suddenly appeared in the building center last week.

Mrs. Johnson remembered that play is the work of the young child. She had equipped her preschool room with a wide variety of toys and materials to encourage cooperative play and exploration of the children's world. She knew that the short attention span of young children requires many activity options and frequent movement for the children.

While Johnny played with the fire engine, wearing his hat of course, other children were arriving. Some headed directly to the family living center to care for the babies or to prepare lunch. Still others began to explore the books casually arranged on the carpet near the worship center.

One child was invited into the world of art by an easel that had been supplied with paints in bright colors. Old shirts were available for covering Sunday clothes, and a large piece of plastic covered the floor beneath the easel to protect against accidents.

An Elementary Room

As I moved down the hallway, I stopped at the fifth- and sixth-grade room. Here too children were already busy. Several were working on a relief map of the Holy Land using a variety of materials. They had begun their project several weeks earlier, researching, designing, and constructing as the weeks went by. Other children were involved in research using the Bible, dictionaries, a concordance, and maps. At another table children were working with a teacher to make biblical costumes for a play to be presented to other classes.

The equipment and supplies in these two classrooms are totally different. Attention spans vary. Skill levels and mental abilities are different. A single lesson plan will not work for both age groups, so the rooms must also reflect the differences among the children and affirm the children in their developmental growth.

All Classrooms Need the Basics

While differences exist in equipment needs for children, there are also some common needs to consider. Children need space in which they can move about comfortably. They also need space and clean floors or carpet on which to sit, as well as tables and chairs appropriate to their size.

Basic supplies for all classes include:
▲ Bibles (variety of translations for older children);
▲ crayons (large ones for small hands; small ones for larger hands);
▲ pencils, felt-tip markers (washable for young children);
▲ scissors, both left- and right-handed (blunt-ended for preschool children);
▲ drawing paper and construction paper in a variety of colors;
▲ masking tape, glue or paste;
▲ paper punch, stapler, and staples;
▲ facial tissue, napkins and cups for snacks, wastebasket;
▲ clean-up supplies, including a bucket for handwashing, paper towels, and gentle liquid soap;
▲ a first-aid kit (easily accessible to all teachers) containing antiseptic cream, bandages, and so on.

Every Sunday school room should have a special place for a worship center. This affirms the central purpose of Christian study and fellowship. The following are basic items that might be found in a worship center.
▲ a Bible open to the verse for the week;
▲ nature items, such as a growing plant nurtured by the children;
▲ a magnifying glass to examine those nature items;
▲ a picture to focus children's attention;
▲ perhaps a candle;
▲ an offering plate;
▲ Advent wreath during Advent.

What Young Children's Rooms Need

There are also specific needs for specific age groups. Rooms for young children should have available:
▲ a basket for storybooks (change the books often);
▲ cardboard blocks, vehicles, wooden animals, and people;
▲ toys for small- and large-muscle activities, including dolls that represent a variety of ethnic groups if possible, dress-up clothes, mirror, unbreakable dishes, small broom, small rocking chair,

child-sized kitchen appliances, telephone;

▲ play dough;

▲ flannelboard and supplies for use with it (flannelboard tape is available to convert any picture into a flannelboard item).

Low, open shelves help the children find the equipment and return it to its proper place when the signal comes to clean up and gather for story time. A carpeted area near the worship center is ideal for sharing conversation, stories, and music.

What Elementary Children's Rooms Need

Teachers with younger elementary children will appreciate, in addition to the basic supplies, a map of the Holy Land or a globe and storybooks and floor puzzles supporting the curriculum. Older elementary children should have available Bibles of various translations, maps, a concordance, and Bible dictionaries.

To Further Enrich Learning

Supplies and equipment that further enrich children's learning include:

▲ hymnals and a keyboard, piano, or autoharp;

▲ record player or tape recorder;

▲ a teaching picture file from previous years to supplement the current class teaching packet;

▲ carpet samples for sitting on the floor.

Central Supply

A central supply area, which could be housed in the corner of a classroom, if a separate room is not available, might include:

▲ extra construction paper, newsprint in various sizes, posterboard;

▲ tissue paper, crepe paper, wax paper, graph paper for creating games and time lines;

▲ three-by-five cards;

▲ clear adhesive paper for preserving special work;

▲ modeling clay or play dough, tempera paint and brushes;

▲ pipe cleaners (telephone wire works great for modeling and is often available through the phone company);

▲ yarn;

▲ collage materials (seeds, bark, ribbon, fabric scraps, and so on);

▲ potting soil, seeds, paper cups;

▲ slide-making materials;

▲ butter containers;

▲ socks for puppet shows, and paper sacks;

▲ small, medium, and large balls;

▲ rhythm instruments (ones you buy or ones you make);

▲ catalogs and magazines or family pictures, wallpaper books;

▲ old newspapers;

▲ cotton balls, cotton swabs, and egg cartons.

Some items may be used occasionally but might not be kept in the room permanently. These might include seasonal items such as pine cones; worship cloths for each season of the church; Nativity scenes, some made of cloth and readily handled by small children; Advent wreath materials; old Christmas cards; balloons for Pentecost; costumes for role-playing; and carpenter supplies. Store these items in the central supply cabinet.

Additional Ideas

Storage space a problem? Ask for specific items through your church bulletin at the time they are needed. The key is to plan ahead. Church members, especially the older adults, love to provide materials for Sunday school projects.

A VCR/TV monitor is helpful to supplement curriculum with one of a variety of video resources available for sale or through your annual conference media center. *Always* check before class to make sure the equipment is working.

Don't have a piano but would like to teach a song? Ask someone to tape the accompaniment for you; reserve a tape recorder or bring one from home. For a special treat, ask a guitar player, possibly a youth, to come help you for a few Sundays.

Storage still a problem in your church? Get cardboard storage boxes or plastic tubs or crates that stack and store. All your supplies will be together and will stay neatly organized.

Plan and Organize

All churches need to provide the basic resources for their Sunday school classes. Teachers need to make their rooms or teaching spaces comfortable, orderly, and attractive so children will have good learning experiences. Rooms that invite children to participate say, "We care for you, and we want you to enjoy learning."

The two classrooms described at the beginning of this article showed advance planning by the teachers, a sense of direction, readiness for children's participation, and an understanding of children at a particular stage of development.

Use the space you have and the supplies available to you. Then add the items you feel will enhance your teaching. Mix in your own creativity, your love for sharing the gospel, your care for the children you teach, and your own enthusiasm for the task. Then be amazed at how rewarding the results will be!

Lynne Stillman Froning is a diaconal minister of Christian education in Lincoln, Nebraska.

What Do They Remember?

by Julia Kuhn Wallace

*D*o you ever wonder what your students remember after class? Could they tell the Bible story? Would they recall the names of the characters? Could they repeat the Bible verse? Maybe; maybe not. But their memories are important! What children remember is critical to how, or even if, they grow in faith. Memory has the power to renew and sustain an individual long after the class is over.

As a child, I learned Psalm 100. In an exciting learning atmosphere, I made musical instruments, sang, and danced. Coming to class during that time was like attending a party. I heard the words and message in a variety of ways. For example, the class divided into groups and acted out different sections. Since then, each time I encounter this Psalm, my understanding of it deepens. I had a great foundation on which to build. To this day I can still recite the verses, even though I first learned them over 30 years ago. Children today are just like us. They need to remember and recall what they have learned for it to have meaning and purpose in their lives. What can be recalled has the power to renew.

I heard an old man in a hospital emergency room mumbling the words to the 23rd Psalm. At first the words were hesitant and unsure; then they became more confident. When he finished, the man shared that his wife had had a heart attack and he was trying desperately to pray for her. In the midst of his anguish, the only words that came to his mind were this psalm.

When did he learn the words? His third grade Sunday school teacher had each child make a banner with alphabet noodles. "Do you know how long it took me to finish the banner and learn the psalm?" the man asked. Sadly, the man's family moved that year and he never went to church again. Yet years later, he remembered words that comforted.

Do we teach as if every lesson is a student's last opportunity to hear God's Word?

Ways to Impact Memory

There's truth in the proverb: "I hear, I forget. I see, I remember. I do, I understand." What can we do to help students understand and remember the Bible? Here are some ideas to focus your attention:

1. Take the power of memory seriously.

Webster defines memory as the "power or process of reproducing or recalling what has been learned and retained." To memorize is to learn by heart!

Religious memory brings faith development. What are we doing to

Teaching Tips for Terrified Teachers

build religious memory in children? If a computer does not have enough memory, it cannot run software applications or process data. How much "memory" are we giving our students? And children can remember: I've heard three-year-old children chant intricate commercial or musical jingles, and watched a five-year-old child program a VCR.

Repetition is key to impacting the memory. I'm not endorsing rote memorization alone. Be creative! How many times and ways do you teach a story or verse? How does content spill into the next week or even into another lesson? Is there a way to review what has been taught for several weeks? I make learning centers from activities used in previous lessons. This helps recall and deepen the awareness of a Bible story or verse.

Do you teach a Bible verse to the group with techniques like echo pantomime? Ordering index cards with a word from a Bible verse written on each and then removing one card at a time as the class recites the verse together is creatively repetitive. Sing scriptural songs repeatedly.

Another key is surprise. Bring wonder and the out-of-the-ordinary into the classroom. Have a costumed Bible character visit your class to tell her or his life story. Encourage him or her to converse with the children. Visit a place in your community that explains a setting, tradition, or custom in a Bible story to make the idea alive and real.

For each lesson and unit, be clear about what you want the children to recall. Don't be afraid to ask at the end of a class or at the end of a quarter: What have we learned? Show posters from the class pack, and examples of completed projects to jog memories.

2. Focus on how children learn.

Know your students well enough to understand how they learn best. Name each child in your class and list two or three learning activities that he or she enjoys. As you choose learning activities keep this list in mind. Be sensitive—match the method with the students. Some children learn best with music. Others remember when movement is involved. For some students, discussion and conversation are vital; while others appreciate creating or seeing visuals. When we design a lesson, it is imperative that we begin with the child in mind and that we use a variety of methods to teach instead of just the ones we like or are comfortable using. We should use curriculum that is appropriate for the ages we teach.

Children memorize best when they are encouraged to understand what they are learning, find the patterns in it, and relate it to something they already know. This goes beyond busy-work.

3. Create a church-wide climate for learning.

The entire church teaches in ways beyond words. The location, size of the class space, and the way it is maintained speaks volumes. The condition of the furniture and equipment also communicates. The choice of curriculum and learning activities shares beliefs. Recognizing and training teachers focuses the attention of the congregation, including the learners, on the importance of teaching and learning.

Do bulletin boards in the main locations share what is being learned in your church? How does what happens in worship intersect with lesson topics? Where do children have an opportunity to share what they've learned, talk about the Bible, or ask questions? Are there mission projects, field trips, and intergenerational activities that reinforce learning? Multiple settings in our faith communities enhance our understanding of God and what it means to be a Christian disciple.

At *Disciple Bible Study* training, I marveled at a woman who shared the Gospel during the closing worship. Instead of reading from her Bible, she held the book open and looked us in the eye as she recited the scripture. She had memorized the entire passage! Afterwards, I remarked on this. Quietly she told me that was how she grew up. The expectation in her church had been to become so familiar with the Bible that you knew it by heart, and lived it.

What are the expectations in your congregation about what your students are learning? Is memorization of the Scripture encouraged? Is basic biblical knowledge taught and applauded?

John 8:31 tells us: "If you continue in my word, you are truly my disciples". This passage reminds us of the power of memory. We want our students to continue in the Word, to be comfortable and familiar with the Bible, the songs and hymns, and the traditions of our faith. It's our job to help them discover and incorporate God's Word. Can we afford to do anything less?

Julia Kuhn Wallace is the Director of Small Membership Church and Shared Ministries at the General Board of Discipleship in Nashville, Tennessee.

Telling Bible Stories

by Dr. Michael E. Williams

*S*o you think you're not a storyteller.

When was the last time someone asked you about your recent trip? What did you tell them? A story, most likely. Or what did you say when you saw that friend you had not seen for years? Didn't you swap stories of the years since you last met?

Most of us tell some stories each day, even if it is just to let a spouse or friend know how our day has gone. Storytelling comes so naturally to us that most of us don't realize that we are practicing the same art that brought us the stories of the Bible.

Susan Harrison

Why Tell Stories?

As teachers of children, you tell Bible stories as naturally as talking to your closest friend. The goal of telling Bible stories is to show, through the ancient narratives of faith, God's presence in the students' lives today. Keep in mind that storytelling in the classroom is not performance or entertainment; biblical storytelling is acquainting listeners with biblical family and deepening the loving relationship you have already begun with your students. Most important, you are deepening each student's relationship with God.

When you tell Bible stories to your students, you:

• let them know that they belong to the family of faith;
• provide companions for their spiritual journey;
• provide them with the basic content of faith through examples of God's creative presence with our ancestors;
• and let them see God's creative presence in their own lives.

As the storyteller, you are serving as tour guide through the ancient world of the Bible. Although many of you may feel more comfortable in the role of teacher than in the role of storyteller—you each bring all the necessary tools—all you need is a body, a voice, and an imagination! Without your guidance and knowledge, your students will miss incredible sights, sounds, smells, and experiences. Be sure each story you tell invites their senses. And don't worry! Much of the information you will need can be found in the lesson material, but sometimes it will be helpful to look at a Bible dictionary, commentary, or other biblical reference book. (Check your church library.) These additional resources will help identify characters, objects, and customs of particular interest.

Using Your Imagination

Your imagination as a storyteller can spark the imaginations of your students. The information you gather from the lesson, a Bible dictionary, or a laymen's guide can help create the world of the story. Don't be afraid to embellish the story with details that "might have been." Give students enough information to imagine for themselves. Imagination simply involves offering enough detail for your listener to actively participate in creating the story world. The artistry is in giving enough detail without overdoing it, and without getting bogged down in too many details. You want to allow your students enough imaginative room to do their part in creating the story.

What About Gestures?

How comfortable are you with your body? Your use of movement in storytelling will depend on your comfort with your body and its range of movement. A simple gesture can show an emotion or the size of an object or the height of a character. Rhythmic motions allow young children to participate more fully and help hold their attention. You can lead the movements and ask them to mirror your actions. It is always appropriate to sing a song or portion of a story; many Bible story songs are available. With older children, involve them in acting out the story after you have told it.

Emphasize With Your Voice

Your voice is the most effective tool you have to communicate the energy and feelings for an effectively told story. If a character you are describing is happy, sad, afraid or ashamed, your voice must communicate that. If the tone of a story is somber or suspenseful or fanciful, show it by the tone of your voice. If you are having a difficult time holding the attention of your listeners, use a trick that storytellers have employed for centuries: instead of raising your voice, speak more softly. This will draw your listeners into the story, sometimes encouraging them to literally lean in to hear more clearly.

Storytelling With Young Children

What will they remember? If you teach preschool age children, you may wonder what these little ones will remember of the stories you tell. In truth, they may recall little of the content immediately. That does not mean that our storytelling and teaching will have no positive effect on their faith and lives.

Often I will ask groups of adults to recall the first story they ever heard. Many times those stories come from early childhood. Although sometimes people will remember the content of the stories they were told, more often they will remember who told it to them, where they heard it, and how they felt when they heard it. Usually they recall a warm, close relationship with the teller and the sense of belonging they experienced. So your person and your presence outweigh the content of your stories.

Through your stories, young children may experience for the first time the sense of belonging to a group outside their immediate family. In later years they may hear these Bible stories again, and the stories will seem familiar. They probably will not remember where they first heard them: they will have known them all their lives. As they encounter others who know these stories, they will experience the kinship of being a part of God's family. Ultimately, if young children go away with a sense of belonging to the family of God, then you have given them a great gift.

Storytelling With Early Elementary Children

During the early elementary years (grades 1-3), the role of storytelling expands as the students get to know the members of their biblical family. The characters in these Bible stories become their familiar companions and will then accompany them through life, reminding them of their faith and of the values of those who follow the Scriptures and Jesus' teachings. When we tell stories to this age group we are both populating and strengthening their inner world.

Bible people made real through storytelling accompany children, teens, and adults through life. When children must move out of familiar surroundings, say to a strange house and neighborhood, Abraham and Sarah will go with them. When they face their worst fears, young David will stand beside them with his sling and five smooth stones. When they are the new kid in class, feeling very much like a foreigner, Ruth the Moabite will speak words of hope and courage. When they go off into the "far country" of disobedience and alienation, Jesus' prodigal son will whisper words of forgiveness and home and they will look for the welcoming father figure.

Bible stories, and our telling and retelling of them, help us make wise and loving choices when we are confronted with important decisions. They form our character as people of God, set apart to be a blessing to all the world.

Storytelling With Older Elementary Children

Older elementary children like stories too! In fact, the characters and stories often seem more interesting to older elementary children when the teacher reads or tells the stories aloud. Our students simply hear the stories in different ways at different ages, building their household of faith upon the foundations that have been laid previously. Therefore we do not ignore one level of story in order to go to another. Each level of experiencing the story builds upon previous learning.

Older elementary children (usually grades 4-6) can deal with more of the content of faith than younger children. This may include the historical or cultural background that can be found either in the lesson or any good Bible dictionary or a resource like *The Storyteller's Companion to the Bible* (Abingdon). To complement the story, encourage the students to put the story into action by constructing scale model buildings from the period, making costumes, and acting out the story.

We know that stories shape decision making. We Christians are a people with a specific set of stories that we claim are sacred to us. Those stories are contained in the Bible. The choices we make are a reflection of the stories we live. So our ethics take shape as we learn the stories of our faith tradition. Stories that are not from the Bible, but that are drawn from the history of the people of faith, can also be helpful as we are formed in the peculiar people God has called us to become.

Perhaps the most important thing to remember in telling Bible stories to persons of any age is that, as Christians, the story we have to tell is a love story. We are like children on the playground passing along a love note to a beloved child that reads "Did you know God loves you?" This is our calling: To tell stories about the God who loves all of us to people we have come to love. This is also one of the greatest privileges anyone can have.

Dr. Michael E. Williams is a storyteller and pastor in Nashville, Tennessee and is editor of The Storyteller's Companion to the Bible *(Abingdon Press).*

How to Teach Songs to Children

by Birdie C. Scott

Few things are more pleasant to hear than the voices of young children singing joyfully and enthusiastically. Music contributes to a happy church school experience that is encouraging and rewarding to the child.

You do not need to be a skillful musician in order to guide the musical development of your class. In Sunday school, musical skill is not a primary consideration for valuable learning to occur; you can, however, work toward these outcomes: children singing more easily and in better tune; children dramatizing their songs and rhythms more freely and with increasing creative expression; children playing rhythm instruments more rhythmically and with growing discrimination of their sounds; and children showing greater pleasure in listening to music. Let the children sing in a normal situation, without "special singing seats."

Of course, not all members of your group will respond to music in the same way. If your group is typical, some children may take part in music activities readily and easily, while others seem to have little desire or ability to do so (sometimes perhaps because of physical conditions). Your goal should be to help each child find personal pleasure in singing, playing, and participating with the group.

Seek ways of adjusting classroom musical experiences to include *every* child. The student who does not gain control of the singing should be given a part in dramatizing; playing the drum, bells, or sticks; or in doing any other activity that you have created for the purpose.

Be careful not to decide that a child is unrhythmical, however. Continue to provide opportunities for enjoyable activities, and someday he or she will develop with the music.

Use of Recordings (Tapes or CDs)

The audiocassette or compact disk that is part of your Sunday school curriculum not only provides interesting and rewarding listening, but is also a natural and helpful auditory aid for musical learning, quickly giving children a clear idea of each song and what it has to say. Play a song several times at one sitting until the class can hum along with the song in its entirety. When the children are familiar with the tune, then begin teaching the words.

Use the classroom cassette frequently for activities other than singing. With a focus on listening, children can pay closer attention to the music and may discover by self-evaluation ways to improve their singing. Hearing an artistic performance, the children will try to sing the song expressively and in its true spirit.

Help children become aware that the song material on the classroom cassette reflects many different cultures. Discuss the instruments used and why these particular ones were selected for the song.

Learning a song with the help of a cassette does not mean that the class should sing only with the cassette. Once a song is learned, it can be sung like any other song, either unaccompanied or with the piano, keyboard, guitar, or other instruments. Ideally, your class experience should include frequent singing with a variety of rhythm instruments such as tub and hand drums, maracas, a tambourine, triangles, a wood block, jingle bells, finger cymbals, and sticks.

When a new song has been learned, tape record the children singing it. They love to listen to themselves. Develop each student's sensitivity to how his or her voice can blend with others and contribute to the group singing.

The Smallest Singer

Use these suggestions when you teach a song to very young children:
- Play the Echo. Sing the words of the song phrase by phrase as the children listen. Have them echo you after each phrase.
- Talk about the words of the song to ensure understanding. If a child is not certain of the words, he or she will have difficulty following the melodic line.
- Use visual aids such as pictures, charts, puppets, and masks (for characters) to help the child remember the sequence of words.
- Add pantomime or finger plays to help children remember the words.
- Repeat the song many times; play the cassette *often.* Children learn through repetition and are delighted to sing familiar songs time and time again.

The Elementary-Age Singer

An attractive tune does wonders in encouraging elementary-age children to sing. After listening to the cassette many times for the purpose of learning the tune, the elementary-age student is ready to "see the song" by using a songbook or a song sheet. Although the children will have the music and the lyrics in their hands, do not expect children to learn the music note by note. Children sing tunewise rather than notewise, so the tune should be picked up as a whole. Control of pitch will develop in time.

Children of this age group tend to sing on a rather low pitch level (throat voices), especially the boys. Higher-pitched singing (head voices) should come as a natural development and not through forcing.

In any good song, words and music are closely united. Help children feel and understand the words they are singing. A feeling for the lyrics can help elementary-age children not only with the expression (loud, soft, fast, slow) but also with the up and down of the melody and with the rhythm.

When children leave the elementary grades, each will take along a musical instrument (his or her voice), a greater understanding about how to use that voice, and the many songs you and other teachers have taught. Each child will be aware that the joys of singing can be with him or her anywhere. Every child should have had the opportunity to develop a personal set of values regarding the kinds of music he or she finds satisfying and the place music will fill in his or her life.

For Your Confidence

Music is a language of sound. It involves listening and paying attention to how the music sounds. Learning to sing any tune requires this kind of attention. The more songs children learn, the more easily they learn them. For example, as children hear the fourth song, they learn it more easily and more accurately than they did the third song. As they gain this additional security, they learn new songs more readily and enjoy all of their participation.

The same is true of *teachers*. Your first task in helping children learn songs is to relax. God has given you a special blessing: to be in ministry to children. You want to do so as a sympathetic helper and not as a critical perfectionist. You help create the environment of learning through which children explore the music of humankind. As you and they discover this rich heritage, you both will grow in the ability to understand, appreciate, and interpret musical ideas.

A Piano in the Classroom?

And now for the hard question: When should a piano be used with singing? A piano should *not* be used to teach songs. If you are able to play it, use a piano in connection with a song in the following ways:

1. After you have sung the song without the piano in order to give the children a clear idea of the words and melody, sing it again with the piano.
2. Play the song while the children listen, either to recall the song as something they have heard or merely to suggest a mood.
3. For the smallest singers, play the song while the children rest—not expecting any particular response or reaction from them.
4. After the song has been well-learned by the children, play the piano while you and the children sing the song.
5. Even if you play well, the children should frequently sing without the piano and should never become dependent upon it.

In music, as in many other areas of learning, the sequence for the learner is (1) to do, (2) to discover what he or she is doing, and (3) to gain confidence that he or she can do it well. The third step depends on your reinforcement and on your frequent praise for improvement, even though the results may not always be as good as you would like.

Enjoy the music!
Enjoy the children!

Birdie C. Scott, a public school teacher for thirty-seven years, is now retired. She is the director of the Children's Enrichment choir and chairperson of evangelism for her church in Phoenix, Arizona.

Working With Children With Special Needs

by Brett Webb-Mitchell

This story is a Holy Surprise. The "Surpriser" was Sal, whose place in the body of Christ was to hug the stuffing out of all the other members. She would wrap her legs and arms around you and look up into your face with a big grin, hair always disheveled, and tell you how glad she was to see you. Sal was "developmentally delayed," "hyperactive," and had a speech impairment, but this didn't hold her back from being engaged with life and God.

She had been living in a unit for young children in a residential treatment center where I had worked as Director of Religious Life. Sal would come to the "Religious Story Time" that I held in her unit once a week, quietly sitting as close to me as possible, if not on me, while the group sang Christian folk songs, recited the Lord's Prayer, and read children's stories.

In one session, I had begun singing "Jesus Loves Me," when Sal's jaw dropped; she jumped up from my lap, and while leaping around the room, exclaimed, "I like that song! I know that song! Watch!" While I sang the words, Sal provided the "Holy Surprise": she began to do the precise hand gestures that go with the entire song! All the staff and the other children were stunned by her beautiful performance. What was truly remarkable was that no one, including the staff and the speech therapists, was aware that Sal knew American Sign Language. As I finished the song, she finished the hand gestures. She told everyone in the circle that that was her favorite song, and she asked if we could sing it again. And so we sang it again, six more times.

Where had she learned that song and its gestures? Sal's mother told me that Sal would always attend worship on Sunday morning at her neighborhood church. She would watch the children in the front during the children's sermon, not allowed to go forward because of her sometimes uncontrollable gestures. Apparently the song and its gestures "rubbed off" onto Sal's imagination.

> Inside many children with disabilities is a person who has been blessed by God with gifts and talents that are of great value in the body of Christ.

Be on the Lookout for Holy Surprises!

While many people think that they know what is going on in the life of a person who is visibly disabled, inside many children with disabilities is a person who has been blessed by God with gifts and

talents that are of great value in the body of Christ. The trick for the church is realizing that many of the children who seem to have "less" really have "more." A compassionate community, engaged in caring gestures, will enable all to participate in the body of Christ.

The reason that children with disabilities are to be part of the classroom in the church is that they are part of the kingdom of God. In Luke 14:15-24, Jesus explains to the listeners that the kingdom of God is like a great banquet feast, where God is the host, and Jesus the servant among other invited guests. As the story unfolds, none of the invited guests makes space for the kind invitation to the feast. Frustrated at such an indignity, the host sends the servant out to the streets, inviting "the crippled, the blind, and the lame." Though perhaps hesitant at first in accepting the invitation, they are the ones who come to the banquet, realizing that this invitation is at God's initiative, grace in action, for there is nothing that any of those persons could do to repay the kindness of the host. And that is why children with disabilities must be part of the church, whose very nature is prefigured by the kingdom of God.

Expecting Changes in the Classroom

Here are some helpful steps to prepare for, welcome, and accept the presence of children with disabilities into a congregation's classrooms:

● *Educate the learning community that someone new is coming to the community.* Read aloud some children's books from the church or public library about people with disabling conditions, or perhaps show a filmstrip or videotape from the denominational resource office about disabilities. In Walt Disney's film *Dumbo*, the focus is on an elephant who is different from the others and whose "differentness" becomes a wonderful gift to the entire circus.

The puppet troop, "Kids on the Block", also provides a good teaching tool, since the "kids" in this presentation all have specific limitations and abilities.

Invite the children in the class to talk about some of the tasks they can do in the church and those tasks they are *not* able to do in the church. The focus here is on teaching children that all humans have limitations and abilities.

● *Find out what the child with the disability can do. Ask the parents or guardians or the child.* It is only natural to ask someone who appears to be different what he or she can and cannot do. Surprisingly, children are more apt than adults to ask a person

with a disability why he or she is in a wheelchair or has a Seeing Eye dog. And most children with disabilities and their parents would rather you ask what the child can and cannot do than assume you already know, for your assumptions may be wrong. The other children in the class and the educator should assume the role of "students" and let the children with the limitations, or their parents, do the teaching, telling the class who they are and what they can and cannot do. Some wonderful learning will take place among God's people in that class, and the class will become more open to the wonderful diversity of the body of Christ.

There are ways to approach a child with a disability that only the family, therapists, or special educators may know about. By talking with these people, you can learn the specific activity and approach that will work for a specific child. You and the class are helping by reinforcing a certain helpful program, *even* in the context of a church.

● *Choose a "Best Buddy."* For children with more restrictive disabilities, you may want to find another child in the class or an older child to help the child with the disability in the classroom. The

choice of a "Best Buddy" should be a mutual one, if at all possible, and should not be forced upon either child unless the children, the educator, and the parents agree upon the arrangement. If possible, try to have the child with a disability and the "Best Buddy" "choose" one another.

● *Create and maintain a least-restrictive environment in the classroom.* The last things that children with disabilities need in the classroom are physical and learning barriers. There are simple things that you can do to make all the children feel included.

- If a child is in a wheelchair, place other furniture in such a way that the child can go freely to learning centers or can participate in circle activities.
- If a child has a visual impairment, warn the child of any changes in the room arrangements.
- If the child has a hearing disorder, be sure the child can see the faces of the people speaking.
- If the child has a learning disability or mental retardation, tell the stories to the entire group rather than making some children read the story and selectively choosing the child with the disability to be read to.

Focus on Certain Christian Gestures

Many children feel excluded and on the margin of certain activities because they are not able to participate in the task assigned. Many classes continue to focus upon learning God's story by using primarily written and verbal methods of communication.

Instead of focusing on writing and memory-learning exercises, begin to bring to each class session a certain Christian gesture. A gesture is an important action of body or limb, used as an expression of feeling or thinking. It is a bodily movement that communicates a message from one person to another.

Jesus loves you.

I love you. or I love you.

> **Christian gestures are what we use in the Christian community to express and receive the story of the Gospel.**

Christian gestures are what we use in the Christian community to express and receive the story of the Gospel. For example, to hug a person in the Christian community expresses "I love you because God first loved us," without saying a word. Sometimes, in a moment of grieving, a hug is all that needs to be said, for words are hard to come by at that time.

The learning community could work on creating, developing, or learning other gestures of the church. In class, teachers and students can learn certain gestures that all can use. These gestures can be part of a welcoming ritual, like learning how to pass the peace of Christ between members in a class, as in congregational worship. New gestures also can be created to convey meanings that are deeper than the spoken or written word. Some examples are:

- shaking hands when seeking reconciliation;
- getting a chair if someone needs one in an activity;
- learning acts of caring for others, such as drawing pictures instead of words for "thank-you" notes;
- putting an arm over someone else's shoulder when the person needs some caring;
- moving down on the pew if someone is looking for a seat.

Another important place to practice gestures is in singing songs in class. When hand and body gestures in songs are used, *all* children may be able to participate in ways they otherwise might not be able to do.

The class can also work on learning the significance behind the gestures of the sacraments. For example, baptism is a richly complex dance of many gestures, with the high point being placing water upon the head of the child. Eucharist is a larger, intricate pattern of smaller gestures in the act of worshiping and celebrating the presence of God among us, in the breaking of the bread and drinking from the fruit of the vine.

What is important about expressing and receiving the Gospel using Christian gestures is that more children, including those with certain limitations, will be able to participate in ways that the spoken and written words may only hinder. Some adaptations will need to be made, but the possibility exists that more children may be able to participate in such faith-filled actions.

The Abilities Disabilities Make Possible

The church is not the school. In public schools children are rewarded for their academic, artistic, and physical abilities. In the church children with disabilities bring to the classroom an opportunity to address the "moral slowness" of

many children whom society has labeled "normal" or even "gifted and talented." Learning to walk more slowly at someone else's pace is a wonderful lesson of empathy. Communicating by means other than verbal and written language, such as American Sign Language, is a wonderful way to learn about the multitude of ways we communicate. Asking someone if he or she needs help before jumping in and taking over a project is a lesson in patience. Receiving a gift of love, from a hug to an artistic creation, from someone whom others may consider "less fortunate" challenges our expectations of what people can and cannot do.

Most importantly, the children in the church will begin to understand how beautifully diverse and intricate God's Banquet Feast is, as they learn to care for and be cared for by one another, regardless of abilities or limitations. If some children learn that each person at God's Banquet Feast has his or her own unique place setting, made incarnate by the wonderful diversity found among children found in the classroom, what a wonderful surprise awaits the greater church. For while we may all have different place settings around the Table, what we share is our common dependence upon the love and grace of God that alone sustains our lives. Perhaps this is the Holy Surprise waiting to be found as we welcome all children into our classes in the church!

Brett Webb-Mitchell teaches courses in Christian nurture at Duke Divinity School. He is president of the Religious Division of the American Association on Mental Retardation. His book, God Plays Piano, Too, *continues to explore themes used in this article.*

"THE WELCOME TABLE"

Teaching a Child With ADHD

by Dr. Millie S. Goodson

He runs from activity to activity. He is the first one finished with projects every time. He just can't seem to sit still. He fidgets and squirms, he refuses to pick up the toys. He blurts out answers and can't wait his turn. He has great difficulty getting along with the other children because he misses their social cues. He runs from you and often makes you wonder why you decided to teach Sunday school in the first place. He could possibly be a child with ADHD: Attention Deficit Hyperactive Disorder.

More Boys than Girls

Actually, this child could be a boy or girl, although ADHD affects more boys than girls. When a child has ADHD, he is suffering from a glitch in the chemistry of his brain. If you and I were sitting across from each other talking and there was a red soda can between us on the table, we could talk for a long time and never notice or touch the can. An ADHD child could not. He doesn't have the filters in his brain which tell him what information is important, what to focus on and what to ignore. An ADHD child will stop in the middle of a busy street to pick up a piece of shiny metal, or run and scream when he hears a loud noise.

Five ADHD Characteristics

There are five basic characteristics which ADHD children have to varying degrees. Hyperactivity is the first. The ADHD child gets out of his seat, wiggles and taps, wanders around the room, runs or climbs or perhaps talks excessively. A child can be ADD without the hyper-activity. This child will exhibit the other characteristics but has no difficulty remaining in her seat. Yes, there are more girls than boys who are ADD.

The second characteristic is (extreme) impulsivity. The impulsive child literally can't wait his turn. He blurts out answers. He jumps to conclusions. He is impatient. He basically acts without thinking. An impulsive preschooler may run and grab. He may glue one piece and be done with what you had planned as a fifteen-minute project. The elementary child who is impulsive may push others aside to get materials, may blurt out answers and may not seem to care about others' feelings. He cares, it is just difficult to filter out the important things to do in a situation.

Inattention is a third characteristic of children with ADHD. An ADHD child may seem to be a slow learner because he can't follow directions. This can be because there are too many directions given at once. Such as, "Go to the table and get some construction paper and cut out your leaf to glue on the mural." The ADHD child may catch "glue on the mural" and think he is supposed to go to the mural. Also, this child is easily distracted so giving him directions is difficult. He doesn't seem to listen and gives up easily. But be aware: Sometimes parents will say, "He can't be ADHD because he can watch a video for two hours or play with Lego blocks for a whole hour." Even though children with ADHD have trouble focusing their attention, they can

> **Transitions are very difficult for a child with ADHD.**

sometimes get "locked" into an activity. Then it is difficult to move them out of that activity. Transitions are very difficult for a child with ADHD.

Difficulty controlling anger or aggression is another characteristic of ADHD. The ADHD child is usually frustrated. Because of inattention and hyperactive behavior adults are constantly "on his case," telling the child what he did wrong, punishing him, calling attention to all the behavior difficulties. Often, a child can't take all the criticism. His defense systems go up or he lashes out at anyone who is going to put him down . . . again. He is constantly in 'lose-lose' situations. Lack of self esteem and peer approval become big, unresolved issues as children move into the older elementary years.

Finally, learning difficulties characterize the ADHD child. A learning disability means the child has difficulty reading, writing, and processing information. Though this child is usually of average to above-average intelligence, he has trouble with learning activities. He is often disorganized, has poor handwriting, and gives up easily.

What can you do to help this child maintain some kind of purpose and order in your classroom?

Preparation

Plan—Spend extra time planning to avoid problems before they happen. Offer choices of activities instead of just one activity for everyone. Then when the child finishes early give him a clear choice of activity a or b.

Evaluate—Think about what did not work last time and don't do this again. Try a new approach.

Reexamine your classroom—Try to look at your room through the eyes of a child who is easily distracted. Are there too many things hanging from the ceiling, walls, windows, and door?

Pray—Ask God to help you care for this child and his parents. Try to think of the good you see in this child. Focus on the things the child is able to do and ask for God's guidance in helping the child use his talents.

Activities

Create choices—The activities you plan can guide an ADHD child and help him to focus. Besides creating choices, try to find out what the child likes to do and incorporate that activity into your lesson.

Extra ideas—Have your pocket full of other things to do when the things you have planned don't work.

More than reading and writing—Plan more than just reading and writing activities. ADHD children have the most difficulty with these and need other avenues of learning.

Listening Center—Create a listening center where children can put on earphones and listen to the stories you have recorded.

Plan for active learning—Incorporate games and outside activities in your lessons. ADHD children often learn best by experiencing the story. Petting sheep, building a pretend campfire outside or walking to Jericho all provide the child with a chance to move and learn through experience.

Keep changing—Vary the types of activities you plan. Have some that are individual and some with partners and some with small groups. Often it is easier for an ADHD child to focus when there are fewer children.

Teaching Style

The way you approach an ADHD child can help him control his behavior.

Praise—"Catch" the child being good, if only for a moment. Say, "Charlie, I like the way you are sitting at the table."

Overlook some things—Try to ignore some disruptive behavior, unless someone will get hurt because of it.

Set parameters—Set an atmosphere in which the children know both the rules and the consequences for failure to follow them.

> # The way you approach an ADHD child can help him control his behavior.

Set a schedule—Set up a regular schedule so the children will know that, for example, choices are first, then group time, then a group project, and then final worship.

Look him in the eye—Give directions face-to-face to the ADHD child after you have given them to the group. Make them simple.

Be patient—Don't blame the child or the child's parents for a chemical imbalance in the child's brain.

Often, the best teaching style for the ADHD child is the best teaching style for all children. It includes lots of activities, a feeling of love and community, and is structured and well planned.

Working With Parents

Parents of an ADHD child often feel helpless—they have tried everything and don't know what else to do. Sometimes they feel guilty, thinking their actions (or inaction) cause the poor behavior. They are often embarrassed by the child's behavior, frustrated by the lack of support, and feel the silent criticism of themselves and ostracism of their child. You can help initially by not blaming them for improper or inadequate discipline. Asking questions about their pregnancies or deliveries in an effort to discover why the child has problems also just makes the parent feel at fault. Here's what you can do:* Show love and concern for the parents.

* Ask the parents what works for them.

* Share good work the child has done with the parents. They hunger to hear something good their child has done.

• Keep in touch with the parents about activities in your class so they can help the child succeed with projects and assignments. Use a variety of ways to communicate with parents: notes, telephone calls, e-mail, and posters on the classroom door.

• Approach the subject of the child's behavior gently. Parents of ADHD children are battered and torn already. Tossed from specialist to specialist, from principal to team consultations, asked to come in for conferences and told of the horrible behavior their child exhibits—many parents become depressed, angry, or may deny there is a problem altogether. Sometimes even divorce is a result. Focus on the exact behavior that is creating a problem in your class. Is it ADHD or aggressiveness? You may say, "I am having trouble with Judy throwing blocks and have worked out a reward system for her when she plays nicely with the blocks. I just wanted to let you know what I have worked out."

• Inform yourself. There are many books and pamphlets about ADHD and learning disabilities. Tell the parents you would like to learn more and let them supply you with articles. Or you can discover materials to share with parents.

God calls us to ministry with all children. Some are more challenging than others, but all are important in God's sight.

Dr. Millie S. Goodson is a professor of early childhood education at Tennessee State University.

How to Talk With a Parent

by Cheryl W. Reames

As you walk down the hall of a church, how do you hear teachers talking with parents?

Teachers of younger children greet parents as the children arrive, ask about the child, and find out any special concerns or needs. When the parents pick up the child, the teacher and parent may talk again—about how the time went, anything significant that happened in the class or to the child, or how the child seemed to adjust and interact with others.

Down the hall teachers of younger elementary children may give a parent a quick greeting as the child is dropped off. You might hear, "Christina looks so cute today" or "We missed Brett last Sunday." When parents pick up the children, teachers may give other quick comments, such as "We were glad to have Jaime here today" or "Daniel has a note about the children's program."

What kinds of talk would you hear between teachers and the parents of the older elementary children? It might be similar to what you hear at the younger elementary classroom. Or perhaps no talk is taking place, since older elementary children usually do not want to be accompanied to their classroom door by a parent, and parents usually meet children elsewhere after class.

Why Talk to Parents?

Why should Sunday school teachers talk with parents? Parents can provide a wealth of information as you seek to help their children grow in faith, knowledge, attitudes, and skills. They can tell you what background, if any, their child has on the topic of class study. They can let you know what faith questions children are asking that you may want to talk about in class. They can help you understand special needs and interests of their child. All of these can help you as you seek to guide the child in learning about and growing in the Christian faith.

> **Parents can provide a wealth of information as you seek to help their children grow in faith, knowledge, attitudes, and skills.**

You are a resource for parents. You can help parents understand what the child is studying in class, so that parents and children may focus on these topics at home, if they wish.

Build a Team

Whether you teach young children, younger elementary, or older elementary children, strive to build a team by talking with the parents of your students. When teachers and parents are working toward common goals, the child's learnings and growth will increase.

Make contact early. If you don't know a parent, introduce yourself. A quick introduction as a parent drops a child off for class might be a beginning, but try to find time for a more significant early talk.

Learn the parents' names. A parent's last name might not be the same as the child's. Use the parent's name when you talk with him or her. When you know their names and use them, you show that your students' families are important. It shows you care when you talk to both parents, rather than to the same one all the time.

Refer to the correct child when you talk with a parent. Don't tell Jennifer's mother how wonderful Jessica was today!

Be positive. Nothing makes a parent happier than to have another adult make a positive statement about his or her child. "Nikeea sang so well with us today." "Bradley reminded us to pray for homeless children." One-sentence positive comments can lay a good foundation for good communication with parents.

Greet parents briefly and cheerfully if you see them before or after class. If you teach young children, you may need more time with the parents to discover particular needs of the child for that day or to give parents a report of how things went for their child that day. If you teach older elementary children, you may not see the parents. Whether you usually see parents or not, plan some unhurried time to talk to the parents of each of your students.

When Talking With Parents

Talk to parents and ask some questions before problems can develop. "What are some things I should know about Meghan to help her have good experiences in our class?" An open-ended inquiry gives a parent a chance to tell you if Meghan needs help relating to others, if she has difficulty reading aloud and might be embarrassed if asked to do so, or if she has a medical condition that might affect her participation.

Always say something good about the child. Parents want to think you like their child and enjoy teaching him or her. Even with a disruptive child, you might make an honest statement admiring his or her tremendous energy, cleverness, smile, or some other positive trait.

Ask about the child. You can relate what you are teaching in class to the child's life if you know about a child's interests, the child's fears and concerns, the child's home life and religious practices, and what is happening in the child's life. Did the child's grandparent or pet recently die? What was the child's reaction? What questions has the child been asking that relate to God and faith?

When Trouble Happens

How do you talk to a parent when there are problems? If possible, talk to a parent after you have had a chance to think about the problem and consider what you should say.

Focus on behavior and skip labels. Say, "Today Katrina scratched Gretchen." Avoid saying, "Katrina was really bad today." Labels are judgmental and may seem to focus on a negative quality of the child. A description of behavior focuses on what happened in an objective, less judgmental way. It may help to keep parents from feeling they are being judged or attacked.

Seek understanding. Ask parents to help you understand more about why a child may engage in certain behavior. You might ask, "Could you help me understand more about Katrina?" or "Dan seems to have a hard time sitting still and paying attention during class. What do you think I could do to help him get more out of our lessons?"

Seek solutions. Focus on "how can we handle or resolve this situation." Talk in terms of the

> # Parents want to think you like their child and enjoy teaching him or her.

child's needs—for example, what a child needs to learn or to do. Instead of saying, "Robert constantly bothers the other children," try saying, "Robert needs to learn to keep his hands to himself during class. Can we think of some ways we might help him do that?"

Seeking to help the child develop appropriate behavior lets parents know you are trying to find positive ways to help the child develop to his or her greatest potential.

During and After Talking

Listen to the parent. Make notes to help you remember what a parent has said. It may seem enough to remember that the dog of one of the class members died this week. Thang won't appreciate it when you forget that it was her dog and think it was Alex's.

Record contacts with parents. Use a notebook with a page or two for each student. Jot down the date you talked and significant information. As you gain information, you will learn more and more that can help you be a better teacher and friend to each child.

After you talk, follow up. If you say, "I'll let you know what happens," parents will expect to talk to you again. Do whatever you said you will do—or let parents know why you can't follow through.

Plan to talk with parents soon. You, your students, and the parents will be glad you did!

Cheryl W. Reames is a Christian educator and parent. She teaches first- and second-graders in Herndon, Virginia.

Keeping in Touch With Your Children's Parents

by Carolyn C. Brown and M. Franklin Dotts

This article is the result of a conversation between Carolyn Brown and Franklin Dotts. Some of the ideas come from Carolyn, others from Franklin.

Those of us who work with children in the church have to maintain many important relationships, but one of the most important is our relationship with the families of our children—with their parents, with the other children in the family, and with other adults who may live with the family also.

Nurture the Relationship

In fact, as a teacher of children you should nurture a close relationship with the total family situation in which each of your children lives. Find many ways to maintain active communication with your children's families.

• Use notes or phone calls that give specific suggestions. For instance, your note could say, "Our class is studying the Lord's Prayer. Since we pray it in our worship service, make sure that when you sit with your child in church, she or he is praying it too." Suggest to parents times for the whole family to pray the Lord's prayer together at home. Give specific suggestions such as at meal time, when the child is getting ready for bed, or in the car on the way to school. Make your messages practical. Show you care.

• Involve parents in some way in what's going on in your class. Make sure parents are aware of the sections in their child's curriculum that are aimed at adults at home. Find out how they are using those suggestions. Give concise suggestions on what parents can do at home to reinforce what you are doing in your class.

• Invite parents to help with a specific activity or project and to be part of it. Often they will be glad to help with specific jobs for a limited amount of time. For instance, if your class is making lunch for the people building a Habitat for Humanity house, bring some parents along. Let the parents help you organize the kids to make sandwiches. Let them observe as the children plan the blessing they are going to use. Then the parents can talk with the kids about what's happening in this mission project of the church. And they will be able to share with their children and go home and tuck them into bed that night and say, "Hey, we did God's work together today!"

• Find a time to meet with parents to talk over what your goals are and how you hope to accomplish them with their children. Explain what you do in class and why you do it. Some parents have never finger-painted, or worked with clay, or used a Bible concordance. They are usually glad to know why certain activities are used in certain ways. Such a meeting will give them a whole new perspective on what happens in class and why.

Add your own ideas to this list of suggestions, but do all you can to strengthen your relationship with parents. Once parents get involved, they will understand more clearly what you are trying to accomplish and why it is so important. You can draw parents into their child's educational process by giving them specific information.

And sometimes parents will find out that teaching is fun. In fact, involving parents is often a good way to find teachers!

There are a lot of adults who really care about their children and who really want to do well with their children's religious education, but many of them haven't a clue about how to start. They don't know how to communicate what they believe to their children, so they depend on the church to do it. And that's where you come in.

Children and Worship

Worship is another area where many parents may need your help. Be ready with some practical suggestions.

Lots of families who have young children choose not to attend the weekly worship service because they have no idea how to deal with a worship hour with a seven-year-old. Give them some very specific directions.

• It is true that hymns are hard for some children, but most seven-year-olds know their numbers well enough to look up the numbers of the hymns and tear off a corner of the bulletin to mark the page. And then even if they can't read every word, they can turn to the hymn and stand up and hold the hymn-book with you and watch for words they do know.

The word *God* is wonderful, for example. It has only three letters, and most kids can say, "There's one word I know! and there's another one. I know *Jesus*."

Or you may come upon certain other words in the hymns. When Easter comes around we have lots of *Alleluias.* In the hymn "Christ the Lord Is Risen Today," for instance, children can sing the *Alleluias* and count to see how many there are.

• Older children can also mark the Scripture passages to be read in the service. If your sanctuary has pew Bibles, have older children help younger children find the passage and mark it with a slip of paper. Then when the Scripture passage is read, they can read it together silently as it is read aloud. If your sanctuary does not have pew BIbles, suggest to parents that they bring a Bible from home so that their children can do this.

• And then there's color. Most church sanctuaries have lots of colors. Does your church use the colors of the church year on paraments and vestments? Give your parents information about those colors (it's often in the curriculum, so the children know about it!) and suggest that they help children look for the colors and watch for times when they change.

Does your sanctuary have colors in the windows? in banners hanging in the sanctuary? in kneelers or upholstery at the chancel? in robes and stoles worn by worship leaders and choirs?

Suggest to parents that children might search one week for as many colors as they can find and write them down. Then another week they can search for all the green, or all the purple, or all the gold. And then when families go home, parents and children can talk about where the colors were. Let the children explain where they saw each color. Make it a learning experience for both the children and their families.

The same things can be done with people and symbols. How many images of Jesus can the children find? How many different kinds of crosses? How many different Christian symbols? Suggest to parents that each of these searches can become the focus of conversation and learning together at home.

The goal in each of these suggestions is to get the children more actively involved in the worship experience. Gradually they will become more used to the worship setting, more comfortable with what's going on there, and more involved in the flow of worship. It takes a while, and parents must be patient. But you as teacher can give parents some directions on how to help children grow into the worship service in your congregation.

The Informal Times

You will have many unplanned opportunities to relate to the families of your children. Make the most of them!

• You're in the supermarket. You're intent on searching up and down the aisles for that one last item you cannot find. And suddenly from down at the end of the row you hear "Hi, Mrs. _____!" And there is Andy and his father. The look on Andy's face gives it away! He's glad to see you. It's been two weeks since Andy was in class because his mother has had a new baby. And Andy's been staying with his grandparents. What an opportunity to visit with Andy and his dad and inquire about the new baby, ask about Andy's mother, and talk about how much you missed Andy in Sunday school. Seize the moment! Show how much you care!

• You and your wife are at an adult couples class bowling party. You see the recently divorced mother of Melissa Cassidy, one of the children in your Sunday school class. You and Mrs. Cassidy visit awhile and talk about Melissa and the hard time she's having right now. You say how glad you are to have Melissa in your class, how alert she is, and how well she seems to relate to the other children. Mrs. Cassidy's face brightens. That's good news. She says she's glad Melissa has a male teacher right now, and you agree to keep in touch regularly. Seize the moment! Show how much you care! These are but two examples of unplanned times when you can nurture the relationships with your children's families. There are many others: at the playground, in PTA meetings, at the public library, and at little league games.

Make It a Cooperative Venture

You and your children's families are a team, working together to form Christian disciples.

Most parents are working as hard as they can to do the very best job of parenting they can manage in their circumstances. And some of them have really tough circumstances.

As you work together in the process of forming the children as disciples, you can all grow as Christian disciples—parents, siblings, other adults at home, and perhaps most of all, you. What a wonderful team you make! Work at it together!

Carolyn C. Brown is director of Christian education at First Presbyterian Church, Charlottesville, Virginia. She has written a number of books dealing with the Christian education of children, including

Forbid Them Not: Involving Children in Sunday Worship.

Franklin Dotts is a retired editor of children's curriculum for The United Methodist Publishing House.

The ABCs of Classroom Discipline

by Alice Kirkman Kunka

A friend reminisces about rumors of his childhood school's electric paddler, which was supposedly hidden in the principal's office. We have often joked about the occasional need for that electric paddler in our Sunday school.

While Sunday school teachers realize that corporal punishment would hardly convey the positive atmosphere we desire for our children, we are sometimes at a loss about just how to discipline effectively to ensure an optimum environment for learning. Here are some fundamental strategies—some ABCs of classroom discipline—that will help the children learn appropriate and acceptable behavior patterns.

 pply logical and natural consequences. A logical consequence is one that is related to the behavior and of which children are aware in advance. For example, if a child refuses to share markers, the child knows that the markers will be taken away. A natural consequence is one in which something is allowed to occur that would naturally curtail the behavior. For example, when you leave the cap off a marker, it dries out and you are no longer able to use it.

e in the classroom early, before the first child arrives. If you've ever walked into a classroom of twenty-three whooping children who are already out of control, this tip probably makes a lot of sense. Have some type of "sponge" activity (an activity to soak up extra time) before you officially begin the class.

reate a cool-down corner. As a last resort it may be necessary to remove a child from a group situation temporarily. For a younger child, this may be a cool-down corner in the room. For an older child it may be asking the superintendent to come and take the child out of the room for a time. It is important not to make this a fun-filled time of privilege for the child. Provide a Bible storybook for an older child or a stuffed animal for a younger child. Ask children to let you know when they're ready to try to be with the group again.

 istract and divert attention when needed. This works best with younger children, whose attention is more easily swayed. Older children should be encouraged to find alternatives when a situation gets out of hand.

nlist the help of the superintendent or a parent. Sometimes a situation may require more knowledge about the child than is available to you. The superintendent or parent may provide insights into working with a particular child and may offer support for improving a child's self-discipline outside the classroom.

 ollow through on logical consequences of inappropriate behavior. Children need to know that you will consistently employ logical consequences. "Getting away with it" only reinforces the inappropriate behavior.

 ain a child's attention using his or her name and making eye contact. Nothing will attract a child's attention more than the sound of his or her own name. Use a tone of voice that is calm but firm, and look the child directly in the eyes.

 elp children understand that their behavior affects the rest of the class. If a child is disrupting class activities, he or she is spoiling the fun for the rest of the children. Point out the unfairness of this situation.

ncorporate every child in whole-group activities. If one child is allowed to be outside the circle, he or she will prove to be a disruption for the rest of the class. If a child refuses to participate, have the child go to the cool-down corner.

oin children in their small group activities. Don't expect to give children a learning task and have them run on auto pilot, especially if the activity is new for them. By joining the children initially and by clarifying their questions, you may avoid disruptive behavior from children who just don't understand what is expected.

 now each child. Find out why a child behaves in a discourteous or disruptive way. Perhaps the child is having problems at home. The child may have been diagnosed as hyperactive, and his or her parents may have decided not to place the child on medication while at church. Knowing these situations will make it easier for you to encourage and affirm each child.

 ove each child. A loving, kind attitude that builds children up will go a long way toward earning their love and respect. In a climate of acceptance in which all children are really listened to and never criticized, children will be encouraged to share their feelings, thoughts, hopes, and dreams.

Teaching Tips For Terrified Teachers

Make music a means of managing the class. Having trouble gaining a noisy group's attention? Sing your directions to a simple tune such as "My Bonnie Lies Over the Ocean" or "London Bridge Is Falling Down." Music can calm the noisy classroom. Play soft music during rest time for younger children and create put-away time songs to sing as everyone picks up toys before the next activity. Older children enjoy listening to music as they participate in crafts and games.

Notice the activities the children in your class enjoy. For four-year-olds, for example, playing outside may be a favorite activity; five-year-olds may enjoy more imaginative play. Be sure that the activities are developmentally appropriate for the children in your class so that children are not frustrated.

Offer a choice. Ease a sticky situation by giving a child two or more appropriate choices. Ask: "Would you rather wait in line for the next art easel or join the group that's playing the game?"

Pray for each child in your class. It would be a mistake to think that we can handle all discipline problems by relying on ourselves or on the information in good books or articles on the subject. Ask God for insights in dealing with the children in your class. Thank God for the opportunity to help children develop appropriate behavior.

Quiz children periodically on the classroom rules. For example, when a child runs in the hallway, ask: "What are our rules about running? What can happen when someone runs in the hall?"

Recognize a child's feelings. Sometimes it helps to let a child know that you understand his or her feelings. "I know you want to be first, but everyone can't be first. We have to take turns."

Schedule monthly classroom meetings to help children learn to discipline themselves. Before each meeting, you and the children should make a list of problem situations that have occurred in the last month. Gather the class into a circle and help children tell how these situations make them feel, using "I" statements. Children can role-play the problems and then brainstorm solutions.

Talk to a disruptive child one-on-one. Making general statements to the class about an individual child's disruptive behavior probably will not cause that child to change. Walk over to the child and bend down so that you can use a calm voice to talk one-on-one.

Use every opportunity to build up the children. Find positive words to encourage individual children and the group as a whole. By creating a climate in which children know that they are loved, valued, and respected, you will be modeling the behavior you want the children to imitate.

Vary the pace. Boredom breeds disruptive behavior. After a quiet activity, have children go into a more rousing activity for a few minutes. Realize that after a period of high activity, it will take children several minutes to return to a quiet mode.

Wait to get their attention. Look around the room and make sure that all eyes are on you before you speak. Use a positive approach such as "I see Emily's eyes."

X-ray" the children. Not literally of course, but find out what is happening inside them. Have they had a bad day before they came to class? Are they not feeling well? All could contribute to behavior problems.

Yield your notions about a perfectly controlled, quiet classroom all of the time. This is only a dream. Recognize that there will be times when the noise level will be above what you'd like it to be but that learning can and does take place at those times too.

Zero in on the reason for the problem. Is Christina picking on Jason because she is frustrated by the reading level required in the activity? Such insights can help you determine whether the child is misbehaving to attract attention, to get revenge, or to deal with the frustration of tasks that are too easy or too difficult for him or her.

Keep in mind that no one strategy will work with each child or in every situation. But by beginning with the ABCs, you can then build your repertoire to include additional approaches that work and that will meet the needs of your particular situation. Classroom discipline based on positive internal discipline will enable you to create a nurturing environment that children will look forward to returning to each week.

Alice Kirkman Kunka is a director of Christian education and mission in North Carolina. She holds a Ph.D. in Educational Communications and Technology.

Don't Forget the "Every-Other-Sunday" Child

by Mary Alice Donovan Gran

We all have them. Yes! Even you! Most Sunday school classes today have at least one child (and probably more) who because of a family configuration is missing from Sunday school with some degree of regularity.

Who Are These Children?

These are children whose families are affected by separation or divorce, children who may visit a parent or grandparent frequently (perhaps every other weekend), or children whose resident parent works a rotating shift Sunday mornings or Saturday nights. It is easy for us to overlook the fact that these children need to be included and involved when they are unable to attend Sunday school with their friends.

Look carefully at your Sunday school attendance chart. Look for patterns of nonattendance. Do you know why children don't attend? Don't just assume you know the answer. A telephone call to the parent or parents expressing your concern may provide important insights.

How Can You Maintain Contact?

It is hard to let a child know he or she is an important part of your class when that child is not present regularly. But it is not impossible!

It takes deliberate effort when planning your class sessions, and it takes additional time at some other time than Sunday morning. It is not easy. But it is worth every effort you make.

Think back to your own childhood. Do you remember an adult outside your own family with great fondness? Why? What made that person special? Perhaps you can be that special adult for your missing children.

Do You Need to Do Something Differently on Sunday Mornings?

Maybe. Maybe not. Ask yourself the following questions.
• Do I reassure *all* the children in the class that we are glad they come whenever they can?
• Is attendance of *all* the children rewarded by a friendly greeting as they walk in the door?
• Do I ever say anything that might make the "every-other-Sunday" child feel different from other children?
• Are any special rewards given to *every* student on random Sundays? (Remember that monthly or quarterly attendance contests are negative experiences for children whose family situations make weekly attendance impossible.)
• Do we try to finish activities in one Sunday instead of carrying them over to "finish next week"? (Or, as an alternative, do we plan so that activities cover an extended period of time so that *each* student gets *equal* opportunity to work on the activity?)

Your answers to these questions will tell you if you need to make any changes.

How Can You Start?

The most important action you can take is to pray for each child by name each day of the week. The connection you have with each child through prayer will pay high dividends.

Prayer alone is not enough, however. Children need concrete reassurance that they are remembered and important. The reassurance comes when they continually feel accepted and included.

As the teacher, you are the primary key to that reassurance. What you plan and what you do does make an important difference.

Each week as you plan, include some of the following ideas. Start with one new idea and then add additional ideas as your new routines become more and more comfortable.

Planning for "Every-other-Sunday" Children

1. Send a note home regularly to all parents telling "what's ahead at Sunday school." Informed parents can be extremely helpful to their children and to you. Knowing what the class will be studying and doing on a particular Sunday that the child is absent can help the parents help the child stay current. You might want to include a note with each

Sunday description, "If your child is absent, . . . *[fill in here an idea of something the parent can do with the child that relates to what is happening in class]*."

2. In mailing information to parents include both parents, even when one parent lives in another town. Talk to the resident parent first to make sure this will be appropriate.

3. When planning class outings or special events, make sure parents know details well ahead of time. Then it may be possible that "being gone" plans can be negotiated and attendance might be possible.

4. If pictures of children are taken to be used on a bulletin board, banner, or some other display, plan to take pictures over two or three Sundays so that every child can be included.

5. Make a take-home bag. Cloth bags with handles can easily be made. Or, small boxes with lids can be covered and decorated appropriately. When any child knows on Sunday that the following Sunday he or she will be absent, send a bag home with the child. In the bag could be Sunday school leaflets and activity book sheets for the next Sunday; a small Bible storybook; an activity to make; a daily list of something to do (Monday—write a prayer to say at dinner; Tuesday—visit an elderly neighbor; and so on); a small toy; a small box of crayons; and a note from you. Put a different set of activities in each bag. Update and change the items in the bag regularly.

6. Recruit an adult Sunday school class whose members will "adopt" your class members. Their task would include regular contacts to encourage and nurture the child. Every child in your class should have a "special friend" from the adult class. (*Hint:* Some adults may not always be reliable in these projects for a variety of reasons. Write clear directions or expectations for the adults. Remind them throughout the year. Be prepared with substitutes.)

Remembering "Every-other-Sunday" Children

7. Prepare messages or pictures for absent children during class. Notes from other children or child-made gifts are very meaningful. Delivery can be made by you personally, by asking another child's parents to go with their own child to make the delivery, or by mail to the absent child.

8. Send postcards with a friendly, positive message during the week. Mail is extra special to children who usually receive very little addressed directly to them. Postcards can be made from greeting card covers or heavy card stock in color or white and illustrated with a few quick lines of a marker or with cheery stickers carefully placed.

9. Call an absent child during the week. Invite the child to tell you about his or her week. Then tell the child about what happened in class (and in worship) on Sunday.

10. Give each child a special something (a kind of "warm fuzzy") to keep to remind the child of her or his friends at Sunday school: a pom-pom of yarn, a cross to carry in a pocket, a small New Testament, a photo of the whole class waving "Hello!", and so on.

Involving "Every-other-Sunday" Children

11. When you know ahead of time that a child will be absent, send with him or her a leaflet or an activity book sheet for the Sunday the child will be absent, along with a blank cassette tape. Include an instruction sheet that asks the child to record on the tape something specific from the curriculum for that day, such as answers to a question or a reading from the Bible. The rest of the children can then listen to the tape on the following Sunday as review.

12. Older children can create a class scrapbook in which children are encouraged to add memorabilia from their times away, such as a photograph, a poem about a special activity, and illustration of their experiences, postcards, and so on.

13. At the same time the child is absent, ask the classmates to make a cassette (or video) tape recording for the absent child. It can be personalized and include some telling of the class's learning for the day. End with the whole class sharing an appropriate greeting—perhaps a closing from one of Paul's letters, a traditional class closing, or just "See you next Sunday!" Be sure to see that the tape is delivered to the child promptly.

14. If there are younger children in the family, ask your child to "teach" Sunday school to the younger sister or brother, using the items found in the take-home bag. If you teach young children and there is an older sibling, have the young child ask the older brother or sister to help him or her have a "personal" Sunday school class.

As you try these ideas, it is most important to be intentional about being inclusive and caring. You should also involve the resident parents as much as possible, so you have their support.

As the teacher, you become a strong symbol of God and of the church to your children. They may not remember any particular activity, but they will remember the feeling of love, caring, and acceptance you have provided as they grow in the faith as members of the church family.

Mary Alice Donovan Gran has taught Sunday school and worked with Sunday school Teachers for twenty-five years. She was a single parent for thirteen years. She came from Ames, Iowa to Nashville, Tennessee to work with children through the General Board of Discipleship of the United Methodist Church.

Seasons: How to Be Sensitive to Single Parents

by Jenni Duncan

Your job as a teacher goes beyond keeping children interested and out of trouble. You also minister to children's families. If single-parent families are represented in your classroom, you need to be particularly aware of some of their concerns related to holidays—especially Mother's Day and Father's Day.

Be Aware of Feelings

Holidays can evoke powerful feelings of loss and grief for single parents. On Father's Day and Mother's Day, when churches give children flowers to give a parent or when they have the honored parent stand with the child, what if . . .

- my child has just moved in with the other parent?
- my child is with the other parent and doesn't call?
- for the holiday dinner honoring me, I drive, pay the bill, and settle the fights among the children about where we'll go because I never have a break from being Mom or Dad?

Mother's Day and Father's Day can intensify a single parent's feelings of being totally responsible, alone, and overwhelmed. How can you help?

Broaden the Church's Celebrations

Suggest that leaders use language that helps children and families identify support from their family of faith. A teacher might say, "Remember when the young adult class stood with Robert when his son was baptized, because they are a family to one another? Who in the church could be like a mother or father to you?"

Emphasize the idea that your entire congregation is a family of faith. Ask some persons to talk in worship about their foremothers and forefathers in the faith.

Reevaluate traditions. Maybe you should skip the recognition of those with the most children attending on Mother's Day or move your mother-child brunch to a weeknight meal. Consider a dutch treat get-together for any single parents with or without children that particular week.

Use Inclusive Examples

When you give examples or show art samples, be careful to include examples of more than one kind of family. Follow up on your church's emphasis on the family of faith: Show old photos or scrapbooks of the church family.

Focus on the Festival of the Christian Home

Help your students answer "What makes a home? What makes a family? (love, eating together, living together [or sometimes not], helping one another).

Craft ideas might include:

- filling a house-shaped drawing or cutout with activities and items important to our home, drawn or cut out from magazines;
- filling a heart-shaped drawing or cutout with drawings of our important people.

Use Appropriate Class Activities

Go ahead and have children make the traditional card or gift for Mom or Dad. You are in ministry when you help the children make their parent a gift. Plan to have the children make the gift over several Sundays so that every-other-week children can participate.

If you've heard stories from one parent about how the other parent has been a jerk, ignore the memories. If the child wants to make a gift of love for one parent, the other parent will appreciate someone else taking care of it. Don't be surprised, either, if the child wants to make a card for a grandparent or other special friend. Help children acknowledge family in whatever form it comes.

While you're at it, offer some hope. When children make the ever-popular handprint, help them also write or record their answers to
- I thank you, (*parent*), for . . .
- My family is . . .
- I hope that . . .

In class play Hot Ball, where a ball or any item is passed around a circle. When you say, "Stop," whoever is holding the ball answers a question. Repeat the following several times (since different people will be answering):
- What I like about my family is . . .
- What I like about my mother (or father) is . . .
- Something my family likes to do is . . .
- Something great about my mom (or dad, or family) is . . .
- I want to tell my dad (or mom) . . .

Bring It Home

Strengthen the home by helping children and parents communicate:
- Start a notebook in which child and parent write to each other. For younger children, supply stickers or labels with prewritten messages: "You have a great smile" or "I'm proud of you" or "Thanks for all your help." Leave

some pages blank for them to continue.
- Invite one parent per child for a prayer time. (That way children of divorced parents don't feel conspicuous.) Ask each duo to write or name some hopes for their family, tell each other some prayers they remember, and name two or three people to pray for. Then ask that every duo pray quietly but out loud all at once. When everyone seems to have finished, allow a few moments of silence, then close. You may have started something.

Be Sensitive Each Season

Mother's Day and Father's Day are obviously touchy times for single parents. Other holidays can also be painful. At Easter a single parent may think . . .
- Is it my year to be Easter bunny, or will I see my children at all?
- In the midst of my joy and hope in Christ is the reminder of the split in my family.
- With the turmoil we've been through, can I believe that resurrection—transformation and new life—is possible for us?
- I can have faith in God's grace, because others express their hope and faith. I don't have my own faith back yet.

You can affirm the hope of Easter. Help a single parent understand that people can change through Christ and that God can bring about wonders when people think that things are hopeless.

Be sure to save some Easter party treats for your every-other-week child. Or invite the child to come to Easter festivities with the other parent. If one parent got "custody of the church," the other parent may feel hesitant to venture into the territory of the former spouse. You might help put aside these concerns with your invitation.

Offer ways for single parents to help at holiday activities—bringing cookies or volunteering together. But remember that when singles volunteer, they need a nursery for any babies or toddlers. Some singles may want someone to sit with.

It can take a great effort for single-again parents to walk back into a church. When parents observe that the church is sensitive to their needs, then seasonal activities with their children can become an entry or growth point. Where parents go, children often follow.

Jenni Duncan is a Minister to Families with Children in Little Rock, Arkansas. She enjoys spending her time with her blended family (four children).

Special Friendships With Older Adults

by Janet P. Westlake

"Why don't I have a grand-mother like Joey does?" Sarah asked. "You do have a grandmother; she just lives in another state," her mother answered.

Sarah said, "I want a grandmother to see in church just like Joey has!"

Growing up without an extended family may leave children feeling lonely and isolated at times. The church is ideally suited to provide significant relationships both for children in families living without grandparents and for older adults existing without opportunities for shared affection. There are many situations and manners in which these interactions can occur.

As a Class

• Host a party with an adult class. One group provides the food and decorations; the other provides the program. Programs could include talent shows, themes based on the generations involved, or dramatic performances.
• Ask an adult class to adopt your class. The adults can send birthday and Christmas cards to the children.

They may be able to provide funding and physical labor to enhance the classroom space. They can also serve as substitute teachers. This would assure a consistent group of people that the students would be familiar with and would allow for deeper involvement in the class sessions.
• Invite an older adult to tell biblical or personal stories to the class. Some older adults who may not be physically capable of working with young children may be excellent storytellers when provided with the opportunity.
• Plan a Special Friend Day, and ask every child to invite an older adult. The day can include a special program and opportunities for the participants to interact with one another. Calling it Special Friend Day instead of Grandparents Day removes the concerns of children who may not have grandparents locally available.
• Adopt a church member whose ability to leave home is limited. Have the class participate in research about the person's life.

Hang up the member's picture and pray for him or her. Send him or her birthday and holiday cards and audiocassettes or videocassettes of dramas or songs prepared by the class. (Provide the audiocassette player, VCR, or other equipment.) Individuals may record some of their interests on an audiocassette. Include a class picture that the member may keep. Ask the person about a convenient time to visit him or her. Take cookies and crafts made by the class.
• Make seasonal cards, gifts, or party favors to send with hospital callers or with meals being delivered to individuals. The recipients will enjoy the gifts, and the children will be involved in service to others.

As an Individual

• Encourage families to invite an older adult to share a holiday or festive meal with them. Church staff often know of people who will be alone for the holidays.
• Take photographs of children and older adults and ask them to pray for one another for an assigned period of time. Gather information about specific concerns and personal interests.

Teaching Tips For Terrified Teachers

- Pair an older adult mentor with a child who is having problems adjusting to school, church, or family situations. The older adult can provide a listening ear and counsel from personal experiences.
- Distribute addresses, cards, and stamps so that children can send cards to adults whose ability to travel is limited. Include information about the adults' interests.
- Find older adults to sit in worship with the children of choir members and worship leaders. The adults can guide the children in using the hymnal and worship bulletin. Worship companions will also improve the behavior of all parties involved.
- Ask an older adult to assist in the nursery by rocking the children. The nursery staff is often busy providing care and may be unable to offer extended time for stories, songs, and personal attention. The nursery staff should be prepared to bring a child to the adult in the rocking chair if the adult has problems lifting or getting up and down.
- Provide an individual whose ability to leave home is limited with cards and stamps to send birthday and Christmas cards to children.

As a Church

- Hold a "Christmas Around the World" celebration. Pair each children's and youth class with an adult class and assign the pair a country. The partnership can present a carol from that country and assemble a display of special Christmas customs, foods, crafts, and games from the assigned country.
- Offer classes for children in woodworking, knitting, crocheting, or whittling; ask older adults to lead the classes. Many adults have talents and skills that are not being passed on to new generations. Children enjoy learning new skills from people who have time to share with them.
- Use children and older adults together to light the Advent candles. This reinforces the intergenerational or multigenerational nature of the community of faith.
- Have older adults greet children arriving for Sunday school. These adults can greet the children and still be able to attend their own Sunday school classes. They can also welcome visitors and guide them to the appropriate classes.
- Use older adults as counselors for summer camp or after school ministries. Many retired individuals have more time to spend in the program and have the patience to deal with the children.
- Assign an older person or couple to serve as a baptismal sponsor. He or she can spend time with the child, sharing his or her faith and offering deeper support to the family within the community of faith.

As a Community

- Link children having problems in school with older adults who serve as tutors. Tutors can work with the children on their homework, review basic skills, or teach new skills that the children need to learn.
- Take children into retirement facilities to read to and to play games with the residents. The residents may know games the children are not familiar with and may enjoy teaching new games. Hearing good stories is a treat for a person of any age.
- Build a shared facility for day care. One wing can provide childcare for preschool children and the other can provide care for adults who need daytime supervision. Design a common space so that they can interact together.
- Ask children to participate in cleaning the yards and homes of older adults. This allows the children to interact with the older adults and those that accompany them in the work project.
- Staff a telephone line with older adults who can help with homework, read stories, or offer advice. Some telephone companies can provide the capability for the people to do this from their homes on a rotating basis.

Children and older adults can learn and grow through shared time and activities. Children today need the wisdom of older generations. Adults need to be reminded of the energy and optimism of children. Teachers in the church are instrumental in making these connections happen.

Janet P. Westlake is a Christian Educator in Beaumont, Texas and serves as a training instructor and consultant.

When Children Have Experienced a Death

by Dr. Judith Johnson-Siebold

When I was a child, my mother died. The church we were part of rallied around my family and did their best to comfort us. It felt good to have their support, but some of their verbal expressions of sympathy were less than helpful. From that experience I learned some of the statements that church members, especially Sunday school teachers, would be well advised not to say.

Don't Say . . .

"God needed your mother more than you did."

This statement does not reflect a positive concept of God, who must be either weak or mean to need a young child's mother more than he or she does. Further, the statement is not helpful for the child of the deceased to hear. At best it leaves the child resentful of God. At worst it could turn the child away from the church permanently.

"You mustn't ask why. God's ways are not understandable to us, and we mustn't question God."

This statement, again, is not helpful for dialogue. If we're not supposed to question, why were we given inquisitive minds? People in mourning need to be able to ask why as myriad questions pour forth from the recesses of their spirits. To stifle such questions closes down dialogue and causes the mourner to feel guilty for the very questions he or she needs to ask.

"God called your mother home."

This statement may reflect a pretty notion, but it still leaves the impression that God is insensitive to the needs of the child left behind.

"The good ones die young."

This popular phrase leads the child to wonder, *Then are the ones who didn't die bad? If I'm good, will I die?*

"I know how you feel."

No, you don't. You may have had similar experiences, but they were not identical; and you are not identical to this person and his or her experience. Everybody is different, and our uniqueness results in differing emotional reactions to death.

"You must feel terrible."

Maybe not. Maybe the child doesn't feel anything just yet (a common response to death), leaving the child to wonder, *Are you suggesting that I should feel terrible? If I don't, am I bad?*

Do say . . .

With all these examples of statements that are inappropriate in the face of death, you may be wondering if it's safe to say anything at all. It is; but the simpler, the better.

"I was sorry to hear about your mother."

"How are you feeling?"

"Would you like to talk?"

When a Pet Dies

Not all deaths that come into children's lives are those of *people* they loved. More often, the death is of a pet; and such deaths give rise to questions about an afterlife for animals. Adults are torn between wanting to tell the truth as they understand it and wanting to minister to a grieving child. I have found it helpful to say that no one really knows for sure, one way or another, about what happens to animals after death but that God holds all things together and that God will take care of our beloved animals in God's own loving way.

We are fortunate, indeed, to be able to point to the hope of our faith. At the same time, we can appreciate and make use of the findings of social science that remind us that ages and stages play a part in the mourning process.

Age Levels and the Mourning Process

An article by Paula Westmore in the Spring 1996 issue of *Childhood Education* reminds us that three-year-olds to five-year-olds may view death as temporary or may liken death to sleep and may fear falling asleep (a good reason not to use the prayer "Now I lay me down to sleep . . ." with this age level). Children this age also may hold themselves responsible for a death.

Six-year-olds to eight-year-olds realize that death is final and want to know what happens after death. Nine-year-olds to eleven-year-olds are afraid that their parents may die and leave them without resources. Children this age may use joking to cover their fears and grief.

Stages of Grief

Westmore also reminds us that grief occurs in stages and that, generally speaking, the entire grieving process can take two years. Grieving has four stages:

1. **Shock and Disbelief**—Children may feel numb and apathetic; they may appear withdrawn or abnormally calm.
2. **Denial**—Children may appear not to understand, may refuse to acknowledge any loss, or may use fantasy to escape.
3. **Growing Awareness**—Children may feel anger, guilt, anxiety, and depression.
4. **Acceptance**—Children adapt to their changed reality.

Our Response

The ideal way of helping children experience the death of a loved one is to have had communication on the subject before it was needed. Discussion about death can occur naturally in children's classes as part of a study of Holy Week and as part of a spring emphasis on new birth and the life cycle.

Sometimes events in the church or in the lives of the children provide teachable moments. Increasingly, I see the children I know being confronted with the knowledge of violent deaths. My own school-age children have already lost friends to accidents and violence.

Books such as *The Day Grandma Died* (Paideia, 1987; ISBN 0-88815-565-4) or *The Tenth Good Thing About Barney* (Simon and Schuster Children's Books, 1987; ISBN 0-689-71203-0) are helpful for approaching the topic of death with children.

Activities we can encourage to help children cope with death include self-expression such as drawing, painting, music, and journaling. Planting flowers or trees in memory of the deceased can also be helpful. Being sensitive to the ways music can affect the bereaved is also appropriate. When someone plays a CD of "our song" or a particular hymn brings forth tears, the sensitive teacher will understand and sympathize.

The point behind reading books about death or having activities that are related to losing a loved one is to provide an atmosphere in which children feel comfortable approaching this scary subject. They need us to listen, to provide reassurance that all our loved-ones are in God's hands, and to answer their questions honestly and with gentleness.

The promise and hope of eternal life enables us to help children cope with death. Although they—and we—may mourn, we do not do so as those without hope (1 Thessalonians 4:13).

The Reverend Judith Johnson-Siebold is an ordained elder serving in Wyoming. She holds a Ph.D. in Education with emphasis on curriculum and instruction from Syracuse University.

Helping Make the Transition to Youth Ministry

by Todd Outcalt

Moving from sixth to seventh grade can be like leaping the chasm with Indiana Jones when he's seeking the Holy Grail. It's inescapable, huge, and calls for courage. Or so those children-almost-teens think! By spring of the sixth grade year, most girls and boys look toward the junior high grades with all the excitement, fears, and challenges that accompany this significant transition. For many, this will involve a change of schools, a change of status, and a loss of familiarity. This promotion also means changes in their church classes and groups.

Moving to the youth Sunday school class and to the youth fellowship group is part of leaping that chasm. Some children are filled with uncertainty; others are looking forward to being a part of the church youth group; and some may be ambivalent about their role in the life of the church. No doubt you've seen changes during the last year. Girls, who often show signs of maturity before the boys in their class, are dressing with more care. Boys may still look like boys: many have not had a "growth spurt," have few signs of approaching puberty, and are often shorter than the girls. Beyond these generalities, are the children at the extremes: those who have matured earlier than their peers and those who are still waiting. Because these children, and our culture, place such a premium on outward looks, the transition to junior high school, Sunday school, and youth group is frightening because those are places where preteens think everyone will be looking at them.

As the sixth grade Sunday school teacher, you can help make the transition to seventh grade Sunday school and youth fellowship group a positive experience for your entire class. Regardless of whether your church promotes children at the end of the school year (June) or near the beginning of the new school year (August), here are some ideas for your teaching ministry.

Introduce the Youth Leader

Invite the youth group leader or primary adult counselor to come to your class. Schedule her or his visit well before the first activity to which they, as rising seventh-graders, will be invited. Ask him or her to give a brief, inspirational talk about the youth group and extend an invitation to your students. Plan to have a question and answer time as well. Your church may have one group for all youth from grades seven to twelve, or may be divided into a junior high group and a senior high group.

You may want to invite a current junior high student, active in the group, to visit and bring flyers, schedules, or a small welcoming gift. Talking face-to-face and hearing directly about plans and activities will help your students grow in their excitement and anticipation of being a part of the group.

Parent/Teen Sunday

Working in conjunction with your junior high youth leader, plan to invite all sixth graders and their parents to a junior high "Parent/Teen Sunday." Make this a party with plenty of color and festivity, perhaps a punch bowl and cake (or juice and hot rolls). Use this time as a send-off or recognition event for all the fine work the sixth-graders have accomplished in your class. Then allow next year's Sunday school teacher or the youth leader to welcome the students into the youth ministry of your church.

Inviting adults to an event such as this further cements the important relationship between youth leaders and parents. It gives parents an opportunity to know more about the junior high group and what will be expected of their son or daughter. Select a meeting time that is convenient for parents and preteens; perhaps a Sunday morning breakfast meeting, or a luncheon. The Sunday school hour may or may not be the best time for this meeting.

Teaching Tips For Terrified Teachers

Summer Sunday: Mix It Up!

Arrange to combine your class with the seventh grade or junior high class in their setting for one Sunday in mid-summer. Work with the current seventh grade teacher to plan an interactive session where the youth have opportunities to share and discuss. Cooperatively share the lesson preparation and presentation. If space allows, meet in the seventh grade classroom.

Meet for Mission

Form new bonds of friendship between the rising seventh graders and the older youth by including them in a summer mission project. Talk to your youth leader, pastor, or mission chairperson about the local possibilities. A good junior high mission project can be as simple as organizing a local outing to paint homes for shut-ins, cleaning up the premises at a local charity or church agency, or working in a soup kitchen. (There are also national organizations like Appalachia Service Project and Mountain T.O.P. that take junior high youth groups to other regions for work camps and service projects.)

Fun Day

Young teens love amusement parks, water parks, or other summer activities. Working in conjunction with your youth leader, organize a fun outing to help the kids get acquainted with their new friends in the youth group.

In order to promote mixing within the group, it always works well to pair one set of older junior high students with a set of younger ones. This way, teens get to know each other in a fun and relaxed setting. And on the way to the amusement park, don't forget those great bus games to promote laughter and bonding.

Kickoff Sunday

Talk to your youth leader about promoting a Kickoff Sunday with your students. This event will be the first meeting to include the rising sixth-graders and should have plenty of fun, games, and food. Many churches use the kickoff event as a way of organizing the junior high youth group before the new school year. But it could also be used as a primary way of welcoming new students into the life of the group.

Be certain to talk to your youth leader about this event, and ask for promotional materials as they become available.

Pool Party

Ask a church member with a pool to "host" a pool party. Invite both the sixth-graders and the junior high kids for a pitch-in pool party. The kids each "pitch in" by bringing some food (snacks and soft drinks are fine). Open and close the time together with name games and mixers.

Campfire Worship

Locate an acceptable place to hold an evening campfire rendezvous. Bring together the youth group and the rising sixth graders for a wiener roast. Tell ghost stories. Share jokes. Close your time together with an evening vespers service. Plan ahead to include several of the teens in the worship experience (readers, singers, liturgists). Invite your pastor to serve Communion if you like.

And as an option, you could plan to sleep overnight in tents—if you are the outdoor type!

Weekly Words

Each week leading up to promotion Sunday for your sixth graders, invite the youth leader or counselors to stop by at the beginning of class to give a one minute invitation to the youth group. Encourage her or him to hand out flyers or brochures with specific information.

Your intentional plans to guide these sixth graders across the chasm to seventh grade and junior high will pay off. Many new seventh graders will become actively involved in the junior high youth group, in the seventh grade Sunday school, and in the worship life of the congregation. Most importantly, these new teens will grow in their faith and daily Christian living.

Todd Outcalt is a pastor in Indiana.

Hallowing Halloween: Putting the Hallow Back in All Hallows' Eve

by Ron Mills

The calendar page turns from September to October. Pumpkins and witches pop up on lawns. Ghosts and skeletons dangle from trees throughout the community. Giant spider webs appear in nooks and crannies. Bright orange and black messages drape the landscape. "Boo!" shouts Halloween.

The popular celebration enjoys immense media and cultural support. Huge marketing strategies proclaim the holiday. Halloween is second only to Christmas in the revenue it generates! Halloween candy, Halloween cards, Halloween costumes, Halloween parties, and Halloween decorations abound in near Mardi Gras spirit. Halloween costumes and parties for adults frequently outnumber those for children. It's all around us!

Murmurs begin in your classroom. "Can we have a Halloween party?" The question confronts the sacredness of the church with this "sinister" celebration. You want to encourage free-spirited fun; but images of death, fear, and the ghoulish parade through your mind. Ghosts and goblins in church? As a Sunday school teacher, are you ready to say no to Halloween? No wonder church school teachers like yourself long for a way to redirect Halloween's focus.

the eve of the New Year, spirits of the dead might roam the land. These ghostly wanderers could torment the living, wreaking havoc on crops, houses, or buildings. The Celts set out food to appease the spirits; they roasted nuts over a fire for good luck in the new year. Likewise, the first person to retrieve an apple from a large tub of water with his or her teeth would be the next one to marry. Most of the Halloween customs we know—costumes, jack-o-lanterns, tricks or treats—came to the U.S. from these Celtic descendants, often via English and Irish immigrants to America.

As superstition increased in the Middle Ages, witchcraft flourished. October 31 was understood to be a more potent day for spells, incantations, and predictions than ordinary days. Hence, the more ominous symbols of Halloween—black cats, witches, bats, and skulls—swirled into the seasonal mix. No wonder Christians began to withdraw from this holiday.

Reclaiming Halloween

Did you know that originally Halloween was a celebration of the church year? It was.

As a children's Sunday school teacher, you can define this holiday with God's light; you are positioned to reclaim Halloween's darkness. You can grant the children's wish for a party, encourage their fun and celebration, and teach them a valuable lesson of faith. All this begins with the simple desire to hallow Halloween.

History and Traditions

Many traditions have influenced the present day Halloween. And yes, some practices do have roots in early pagan festivals. In pre-Christian England and Ireland, the Celts celebrated a festival of summer's end, which also marked the eve of the Celtic New Year, November 1. In Celtic religion, transitions such as the passage of one year into the next were considered times when the veil between life and death thinned. On

Declaring Life and Light

As Christianity spread to Europe during the first centuries, Christian themes invaded the pagan culture. All the while, God's church was honoring its martyrs through holy days of worship and prayer. As early as the fourth century, evidence for a service celebrating all saints, not just martyrs, exists. By the seventh century the feast of All Saints was secured as a regularly celebrated day of the Christian year.

As the fall landscape lay withered and barren, and as the days darkened, death's images loomed. As a way to proclaim God's grace and celebrate life over death, the Church set November 1 as All Saints' Day. In confronting pagan interpretations of reality, the Church proclaimed a joyous celebration of life now and of life to come. Death, then, is not a veil separating the living from goblins and dark spirits, but is the passageway through which we travel to become whole in the presence of God! The faithful who die are not consigned to desolate eternal wandering. They live abundantly with God, released from incompleteness, suffering, and want.

All Saints' Day carries powerful affirmations of our faith. Believers then and now participate in something holy beyond the framework of their own lives. We learn we are a congregation not only in space but also in time.

Origins of "Hallow's Eve"

Where does Halloween fit into all of this? Traditionally feast days, such as All Saints, called for a day of preparation of heart and mind, in order to properly observe and celebrate the feast. Prayerful preparation preceded the holy day. An earlier title for All Saints' Day was All Hallows' Day (to hallow is to consider something holy, sacred; to honor). The day before, then, is All Hallows' Eve, which became Hallows E'en and finally Halloween.

Emphasizing the "Hallow"

Contemporary society celebrates a Halloween void of any real meaning; fun but empty. The church, however, possesses a Halloween full of meaning. It can be a hallowed evening again. Here are suggestions for hallowing Halloween.

• **Gather festively on October 31.** Celebrate the joy that comes from believing in God. Encourage costumes accordingly: heroes and heroines; noble people; saints. Emphasize the phrasing, "All Hallows' Eve" as opposed to "Halloween" on flyers, posters, or invitations. Have a greeter and a doorkeeper. The greeter may give each participant a "key" to the celebration. The doorkeeper will allow only those with this key to enter. For example, the greeter would distribute slips of paper with a phrase from the Apostle's Creed on it "I believe . . . in the communion of saints and the life everlasting." Children, youth, and adults must recite this to the doorkeeper to gain entrance to the party! Life is affirmed at the door!

• **Maintain or renew traditions.** Bob for apples, make candy or caramel apples, pop popcorn, serve fruits and nuts—all reminders of the harvest time. Have an apple peeling contest. The longest unbroken peel promises a good long life. (Give 'Life' Cereal as the prize!)

• **Give "soul cakes."** Make shortbread cakes in a gingerbread man shape. In early England, soul cakes were distributed to All Hallow's Eve beggars who came knocking. You can give your soul cakes raisin eyes, noses, and so on. You may want to use soul cakes to remember the names of family members who have died and are now with God.

• **Make doughnuts.** One legend tells of a cook who wanted to make a soul cake that made the beggars think of eternity with every bite. She made a cake, punched a hole in the middle of it to create a circle—the symbol of eternity—and the doughnut became part of All Hallow's Eve. Have a doughnut frying booth and let the children see if they can "taste eternity in every bite."

• **Play games.** Alter a version of an old favorite, "Pin the Tail on the Donkey." Create a child-size "saint" with white robes; attach it to the wall. Add a gold crown and play "Pin the crown on the Saint!"

All Hallow's Eve is your opportunity to focus on the powerful theme of life in the presence of God, both now and forever. Then Halloween again becomes a hallowed time of joyful community on earth now, and a reminder of the promise of life in heaven. It's time to put the "Hallow" back in All Hallow's Eve!

Ron Mills is a pastor who lives and writes in Martinsville, Virginia

Celebrating All Saints' Day

by Christina C. Zito

At this time of year when we turn to thoughts of football games, harvest festivals, pumpkins, and candy apples, and decorate our homes, businesses, and offices with the trappings of Halloween (next to Christmas the holiday for which most people nationwide decorate), the church turns its thoughts to things more "saintly."

What should the church do, or not do, about Halloween? Where should your focus as a Sunday school teacher be as All Hallows Eve approaches? Maybe you've forgotten just what it is the eve of.

How It Began

Let's take a brief look at the history of All Saints' Day. The Celts of ancient Britain and France, led by their priests the Druids, believed that a lord of death sent evil spirits into animals who then roamed around all winter playing evil tricks on people. To escape these evil spirits, it was believed that each autumn persons must build bonfires and offer sacrifices to frighten the spirits. In addition, it was believed that people had to wear a disguise so that evil spirits would think they were one of them.

Early Christian Celebrations

Early Christians tried to change the holiday from a festival of fear to one of joy. All Hallows Day became the Christian alternative as a day in which the "holies" (those people who had died faithful to Christ) were remembered and honored.

Originally the Roman Church set aside the Holy Day of Obligation to honor all saints who were martyred. In the fourth century the Eastern Church expanded the list of saints to include nonmartyrs. In A.D. 835 the first of November was officially established as "All Saints' Day" honoring all those who had been canonized.

> # What should the church do or not do about Halloween?

In the tenth century November 2 was set aside as "All Souls' Day," a day in which "ordinary" people were prayed for in hopes that God would allow them to share in the victory of Jesus.

Who Are Our Saints?

What remains today, in the Protestant tradition, is an odd mixture of participation in harvest festivals, memorial services, costume parties, honoring of the dead, bobbing for apples, and celebrating the lives of living saints.

If we are to honor and celebrate saints, we must first define just who a saint is. The Old Testament sees a saint as one who is closely bound to God in love (Psalm 31:23). A saint (holy one) is one who is set apart and dedicated to the service of God (Daniel 7:27). A saint is one who has remained faithful (Psalm 16:3).

The New Testament refers to saints as being "called to belong to Jesus Christ" (Romans 1:6-7). Paul names every living Christian believer a saint. It seems clear that any person, living or dead, who is set apart because of his or her relationship to God is a saint.

Saints are not perfect humans, but have been made saints through the process of sanctification, of growing into what God has already made us in Jesus Christ.

How Will You Celebrate?

How then are you, as Sunday school teachers, going to celebrate All Saints' Day? Here are some suggestions that may work for you.

● Kids love the adventure of costumes. Fantasy is an important part of childhood. Why not encourage your class (and you too!) to dress in Bible costumes? Choose historical figures with positive images! Others could guess who you are by receiving biblical clues. You can learn about the lives of saints as you act them out.

● When talking about the dead, constantly remind your class that those who die faithful to Christ are not dead at all but alive in Jesus Christ. Talk about the good times as you discuss family members and loved ones who have died.

● It is often difficult for young children who have not yet experienced the loss of a loved one to understand memorializing of saints. Have children talk about the living saints in their lives. You could

HOLIDAYS

Art by John Ham

have your students write letters of thanks or make special gifts for those people.

● Talk about other times when you hear about saints celebrated in the church: St. Valentine, St. Nicholas, St. Patrick, St. Peter, and St. Paul are just a few. You might want to explore the traditions behind the calendaring of special saint days.

● Perhaps your church is named after a saint. Investigate your church history and the history of "your" saint.

● Write a history of your congregation (you might want to illustrate it or include photographs) and include the saints (clergy and laity) who have had an impact on lives in your church and community.

● Visit a local cemetery. Do grave rubbings (you may have to get permission first) and display them in your church.

● Know what will happen in worship on All Saints' Day. Encourage children and youth to participate in the service, preparing them for the special celebration of saints which may include such things as:

1. a special floral or candle arrangement symbolizing the lives of those persons in the congregation who have died during the past year;
2. a period of silence to honor the dead (perhaps with the tolling of bells);
3. Eucharist using the ritual in the *Book of Worship* for All Saints' Day;
4. words of witness memorializing individuals;
5. an opportunity to name and pray for individuals who have been saints in your life;
6. or Easter (resurrection) music that celebrates life eternal.

● Finally, be sure you encourage children to live as saints (holy ones set apart from others) every day of the year. Perform small miracles—practice random acts of kindness for other people. Challenge your students to use the creativity of the Creator to celebrate light and life in this world and Christ's victory over evil.

Christina C. Zito is a diaconal minister in northern New Jersey. She is serving as a director of Christian education.

Using Chrismons in Christian Education

by Robin Knowles Wallace

*C*hrismons, signs for Jesus Christ and his saving deeds, have been around since the earliest days of Christianity. In the 1950s a Lutheran church in Danville, Virginia, decorated an evergreen tree with ornaments made solely of these symbols. The idea caught on, and soon churches across the United States and Canada were placing Chrismon trees in their sanctuaries during Advent through Epiphany. Whether or not your church has a Chrismon tree, you can use these symbols in your teaching.

The word *Chrismon* comes from combining the words *Christ* and *monogram*. The first Chrismons used the first two Greek letters for Jesus' name: *Chi-Rho*.

One early Chrismon, still familiar today, is the fish, a symbol used as early as the second century A.D. This symbol is related to baptism and, in Greek, to the acrostic "Jesus Christ, Son of God, Savior."

Chrismons have been found in the catacombs and on door frames, on jewelry and on utensils of the early church.

There are many Chrismons today, both ancient and modern. They are based on biblical symbols for Jesus, from both Old and New Testaments. Some are drawn from his name, some from his life, and some from the meaning of his life for our salvation. Chrismons range from simple crosses and stars to complicated combinations of symbols. They are made primarily of white (symbolizing the purity of Jesus Christ) and gold (symbolizing his majesty). Other colors may be added, but sparingly, as accents.

Using Chrismons in the Classroom and in Worship

In addition to the fun of making them, Chrismons may be used both in the classroom and in worship. If you have a Chrismon tree in the sanctuary, have someone explain some of the symbols during worship or during Sunday school devotions. (Adults will be interested, as well as the children.) In the classroom, Chrismons can be used to symbolize a point you are teaching or as a focus for classroom devotions. For example, one Chrismon shows the

cross on top of the world. Even young children can understand that this Chrismon symbolizes that the world belongs to God and that Christ's power (shown on the cross) works in the world for good.

Another example would be to use the Chi-Rho Chrismon where the *Chi* looks like a manger and the *Rho* like a shepherd's crook.

Point out these symbols to the children and then pray: "Dear Jesus, We are excited about your coming as a baby in a manger. Thank you for watching out for us like our shepherd. Like a shepherd, lead us safely every day. Amen." The children could make and take home this Chrismon as an evening prayer reminder.

Different-shaped star Chrismons tell the story of faith. The five-pointed star of the Nativity is also called the Bethlehem star. The six-pointed star of David reminds us of the great king of Israel, God's chosen people. Stars with seven or more points tell of God's wonderful creation. A rose centered on the Nativity star symbolizes Mary and her decision to do God's will, which made the star of Bethlehem possible.

Along with sharing the meaning of these stars, read together the biblical passages that speak of them: Matthew 2: 1-2, 9b-11; Psalm 8: 1, 3-5; Genesis 1:14-18; Luke 1:26-28, 30-31, 38.

Making Chrismons With Children

Chrismon making can range from simple to difficult and might be done either in the classroom or at a special Advent workshop or tree trimming. For younger children, precut simple shapes from white paper, felt, or nonrecyclable white plastic foam meat trays. Then let the children add gold accents with crayon or glue-on sequins or glitter. Use gold in the Chi-Rho Chrismon on the cross that makes the manger, on the cross over the world, or on the rose on the white Nativity star.

To make tree ornaments either prepunch holes in the Chrismons and thread with yarn or ribbon, or prepare clear plastic lids with holes and string. The children could glue the symbols onto the plastic lids. Since many Chrismons include an outside circle, using lids will make the children's Chrismons look more like the ones they might see on a Chrismon tree.

In addition, elementary children could make gift bookmarks with Chrismons on them. The children could draw or glue Chrismons on two-inch-wide construction paper strips that are fringed on both ends. More elaborate bookmarks could be made by using a twelve-inch length of ribbon. The children could fold and glue or sew each of the ribbon ends into a point to strengthen it, then sew a pipe cleaner fish and cross near one end.

Older children could make cards with a Chrismon on the front for church members who are ill or who cannot attend services. The children could write an explanation of the symbol and a Christmas message on the inside of the card.

Older children could also make tree ornaments or mobile symbols by drawing, cutting out, coloring, or gluing sequins or glitter on paper. Or children could shape Chrismons out of pipe cleaners. The Chrismons could be made into a mobile, using dowels or straws and yarn.

Using Chrismons With Youth

Youth might find it interesting to experiment with combinations of symbols, once they have discussed them, either by drawing the symbols or forming them from wire and beads. (Find patterns and instructions from those who have a Chrismon tree, at your local library, or in books on Chrismons.) As a mission project, youth might want to make Chrismons to give to persons whose ability to travel is limited.

Since many youth enjoy wearing crosses, discuss with the youth the different kinds of crosses in Christian symbolism, all of which are used as Chrismons.

An *ojo de dios* (OH-hoh deh DEE-ohs), Spanish for "God's eye," which is often made at summer camps, is appropriate as a Chrismon. Ojos can be made by youth or elementary children, using yarn and toothpicks, straws, craft sticks, or dowels.

The Power of Chrismons

Because Chrismons have been used for hundreds of years, they have a history of helping Christians to understand our faith in a different way than words do. This makes them particularly useful for prereading children. But it is also important for readers to let God speak in different ways. In the case of Chrismons, God speaks through a symbol that stands for Jesus Christ.

Suggest to the children that when they are in worship, sitting quietly during the sermon, they look at the Chrismon tree or other symbols in the church (in stained-glass windows; on the baptismal font; on paraments on the pulpit, altar, or lectern) and let their minds focus on what each symbol tells them about God and Jesus Christ. Ask the children to think about how the symbol tells about God's great love for humans. Chrismons can also become focal points for prayer. Meditate while looking at the Chrismon and listen for what it tells you about Jesus Christ and about your own life.

Use Chrismons and let these rich symbols of faith speak of the love and salvation offered to all by God through Jesus Christ.

Robin Knowles Wallace did her P.h.D work at Garrett-Evangelical Theological Seminary in the areas of theology and worship. She has had experience with children's choirs and music in Christian Education.

Christmas Activities From Around the World

by Jacqulyn Thorpe

Christmas is universal—or at least international. Children can experience this Christian holiday and feel connected to children from other countries by doing activities and crafts that children from other countries love to do.

As the teacher, you can enhance any of these suggestions if you can visit an international store or shop that offers merchandise from any of the countries mentioned, and can see Christmas materials, decorations, and ingredients firsthand. Visit your church or community library and search the card catalogue for Christmas-around-the-world resources with pictures.

Presents

There is a funny thing about presents at Christmas. Around the world, the beliefs about where they come from differ from one country to the next.

In Latin America, presents come from the wise men. In Germany, presents come from the Christ Child. In France, presents come from *Pere Noël* (pehr noh-EHL), Father Christmas; and in Sweden, presents come from little elves.

In the Middle East, children believe that presents come from "The Little Camel," rewarded with immortality by baby Jesus. According to legend, it gallops about the desert, delivering presents on Christmas Eve.

Talk with older children about these customs and about their memories of receiving gifts at Christmas. Then move into a more serious discussion of why presents are exchanged (to symbolize God's gift of Jesus and to celebrate goodwill).

Wreaths and Candles

One of the loveliest uses of a wreath and candles for beginning the season is the **Advent Wreath** from Germany.

In Sweden, young girls wear a **Saint Lucia Crown,** a wreath with candles, on their heads on December thirteenth. Dressed as Saint Lucia, wearing a white dress with a brilliant red sash and the crown of pine boughs haloed with the light of seven candles, one girl in every family awakens the other family members by bringing them coffee and Lucia buns on a tray, thereby proclaiming the arrival of the Christmas season.

Under supervision, children of all ages could make and wear the wreath crown. Do not light the candles. Let the children pretend to be in Sweden on Saint Lucia Day (December thirteenth) and to be awakened by Saint Lucia with her treats. Let one girl dressed as Saint Lucia pretend to awaken the others from sleep as she offers them sweet buns from a tray. Prepare a favorite hot drink to be pretend coffee; but to avoid spills, serve it at a table rather than putting it on the tray.

Stars

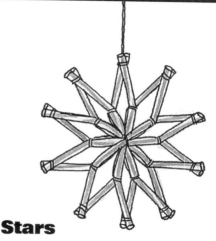

The star has long been used to celebrate Christmas everywhere. In Europe bands of star singers carry poles topped with a star. Let the children (all ages) become star singers by affixing large construction paper stars to the tops of wooden dowels, by parading, and by singing carols.

Or make **Drinking Straw Stars** from Sweden.

Supplies: drinking straws, red thread

1. Tie ten drinking straws together at the center. Tie ten more in the same manner. Tie the two bundles together so that you have twenty straws.
2. One inch from the center, tie the straws together in groups of four, using red thread and tying a tight knot. You will have five ties on each side of the center, ten ties in all.
3. Then tie two of the four straws from each group to two of an adjoining group at the outer ends of the straws. Doing so will form a ten-point star.
4. Think of ways to display the stars.

HOLIDAYS

Wall Hangings

In Denmark, Norway, and Sweden, Christmas wall hangings are created by drawing a scene on tapestry-like fabric. Elementary-age children can make a hanging for your classroom or a hallway. Below is a pattern to enlarge by copying the lines in each square onto a corresponding larger square in a grid lined off on fabric.

Supplies: a large piece of burlap, tempera paints, and brushes; or felt, scissors, and fabric glue

1. Draw a Christmas scene on the burlap. One possibility is the three wise men, shown below, holding their gifts for Jesus.
2. Paint the scene with tempera paints. Or if painting is not convenient, use felt cutouts and fabric glue to create the wall-hanging.

Poinsettias

Did you know that the poinsettia plant came to our country from Mexico in 1825? It is called *Flor de la noche buena,* (flor deh lah NOH-cheh BWEH-nah). Let the children say the Spanish name with you. Bring a poinsettia plant and let the children look at it as they draw and color a poinsettia plant. Don't forget to bring red and green crayons and markers.

Christmas Candles

Candles are used in churches, homes, and neighborhoods to celebrate Christmas, because Christians believe that Jesus is the Light of the world. In addition to being used on wreaths, candles are used in **Luminarias** in Mexico and other Spanish-speaking countries. Children of all ages can make luminarias for your church.

Supplies: small brown paper bags or colored bags, sand or gravel (about three cups per bag), and short votive candles

1. Fold down the sides of the paper bags to make them square-shaped.
2. Fill the bags half full with sand or gravel.
3. Put a candle down inside the center of the sand or gravel in each bag.
4. Line a sidewalk, stairs, steps, a porch, or the front of a stage with the luminarias.
5. Light the candles. What a beautiful Christmas welcome.

In China, Christians use candles in lanterns to observe Christmas. Older elementary-age children can make an adaptation of the **Chinese Christmas Lantern,** a six-sided lantern with a pointed top covered with several shades of transparent paper. Inside are figures of the wise men and a star over a house.

Supplies: glue, tinted plastic wrap, clear tape, old Christmas cards, a heavy saucer-sized cardboard circle, six thin 6-inch dowels, six thin 12-inch dowels, red yarn

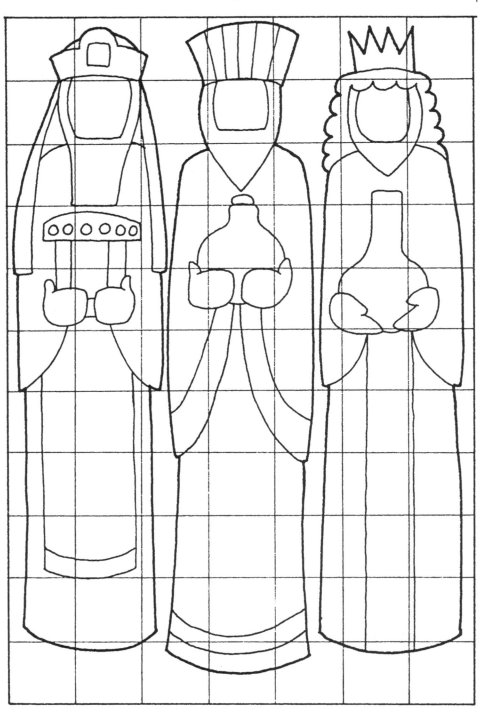

1. Using an awl or one blade of a scissors, punch holes at six equidistant points around the edge of the cardboard circle. Twist the awl or scissors blade to enlarge the holes until the twelve -inch dowels fit snugly into them. For sturdiness, put a drop of glue on each dowel.
2. From used Christmas cards cut out figures of the wise men and a star over a house or manger. When cutting, make a tab at the base of each cutout.
3. Fold the tabs at the bottom of the cutouts to make them stand up. Glue the tabs to the cardboard circle so that the figures stand.
4. Gently wrap tinted plastic wrap around the outside of the dowels.
5. For the roof, arrange six six-inch dowels like the spokes in a wheel and tape them onto a twelve-inch circle of plastic wrap.
6. Gently lay the roof across the top of the lantern so that each dowel in the roof is touching a dowel on the base. Allow for the roof to be pointed, but let the roof dowels stick out beyond the sides of the lantern. Glue each roof dowel and side dowel together where they touch.
7. Make tassels from red yarn and attach them to the ends of the roof dowels.

A real lantern would have a candle inside and would be hung from a hook. This adaptation is more fragile and will need to sit on a table.

Christmas Recipes

Even very young children can enjoy helping you bake Christmas cookies.

Gingerbread Cookies are a kind of Christmas cookie common to both Denmark and Iraq.

Supplies: gingerbread mix, coffee, a rolling pin and board, flour.
1. Add just enough coffee to gingerbread mix to moisten it. The dough should be stiff.
2. Form the dough into a ball and roll it out on a generously floured board.
3. Cut shapes with a gingerbread cookie cutter.
4. Bake on a cookie sheet at 350 degrees for ten to twelve minutes.

Kings' Cake
In France, where the Twelfth-Night Feast is celebrated each year to remember the wise men's journey to see the newborn Jesus, the dessert is a flat cake called *La Galette des Rois,* or Cake of the Kings. A bean or figurine is baked in the cake. The person who finds it in his or her piece is named king or queen of the feast. This person "rules over" the dancing, games, and other festivities of the evening.

Supplies: cake mix of any flavor, eggs, oil, water, measuring utensils, mixing bowl, cake pan, and one dried bean
1. Mix the cake according to the directions on the box. If there is not enough time during class, mix the batter just before class.

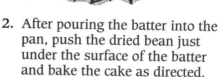

2. After pouring the batter into the pan, push the dried bean just under the surface of the batter and bake the cake as directed.
3. Before cutting the cake, explain the custom of the Kings' Cake.

In Africa **Christmas Plum Pudding** is eaten. The following recipe is unbaked, with a gelatin base. Let a small number of children help you put it together. Children can do much of the preparation. Be sure that only you do the stove top cooking.

Supplies: 1½ teaspoons unflavored gelatin, ½ cup currants, 1 pint milk, 1½ squares chocolate, ½ teaspoon vanilla, 1 cup seeded raisins, 1 cup cold water, 3 egg whites, ½ cup sugar, ¾ cup dates, ½ cup nuts, and salt; a double boiler, an eggbeater, and a nut chopper or sharp knife
1. Soak the gelatin in the cold water about five minutes.
2. Put the milk, currants, raisins, and dates in a double boiler and warm them over low heat.
3. Melt the chocolate and add a small portion of the sugar and a little milk to make a smooth paste.
4. When the milk is hot, add the chocolate paste, stirring to blend. Add the soaked gelatin, sugar, and salt.
5. Remove the mixture from the heat; when mixture begins to thicken, add vanilla and chopped nuts.
6. Fold in egg whites, beaten stiff. Turn the mixture into a mold lined with whole nut meats and raisins. Chill. Serve with whipped cream, sweetened and flavored with vanilla.

Nativity Scenes

In France a Nativity scene called a **Crèche** (kresh), which includes not only the Holy family but also persons from the modern-day village (mayor, priest, policemen, butcher, baker, miller, and farmer), is arranged by the children and placed in their living rooms. Suggest that the children bring small rocks, branches, and moss to make a setting for a manger in your classroom. Use little figurines to represent the Holy Family, the other characters in the Nativity story, and the people of the village. Or let the children make simple figures, using gift wrap rolls that have been cut to three-inch lengths for bodies and plastic foam balls for heads. Be creative, using scraps of fabric, yarn, and paper to decorate the figures.

In Poland, children put a nativity scene in a box, and it is called a **Szopka** (SHOP-kah). The children proudly carry their Szopka around, and they also carry it during processions. Decide with the children how to make the tiny stable scene in a box and let them make a Szopka and carry it during a parade or procession.

In Thailand there are full-sized manger scenes. Let the children dress up as Mary, Joseph, baby Jesus, and shepherds; and take a picture of them reenacting a full-sized manger scene.

In Mexico, the manger scene is called a **Nacimiento** (nah-see MYEHN-toh). It can be very simple, with just Mary, Joseph, and Jesus. Or it can include wise men, shepherds, farmers, and townspeople. Usually the scene is placed on an altar in a home. Larger figures are sometimes placed outside in the community.

Piñatas

Christmas in Mexico always includes the children playing their traditional game with a piñata (peen-YAHT-uh). Middle and older elementary children can make a piñata.

Supplies: newspapers, a balloon, flour, water, string, tissue paper, glue, a bowl, scissors, candy, a blindfold, and a stick

1. Blow up a balloon and tie it.
2. Mix a paste of one part flour to two parts water.
3. Tear newspaper strips about one inch wide by three inches long.
4. Dip the newspaper strips into the paste and layer the pieces around the balloon. Apply about three layers, leaving an opening around the stem of the balloon (this will be the top of the piñata).
5. Let the piñata dry for several days. Pop the balloon.
6. Decorate the hollow shell by gluing strips of colored tissue paper fringe around it. Curl longer strips to hang from the bottom.
7. Make two small holes in the sides at the top and run a string through the holes for hanging.
8. Put candy into the piñata. Hang it high and let the children break it by taking turns hitting it with a stick while blindfolded.

A Warm Weather Christmas

Some Christian groups in Africa have had a continuous history from the first century onward. The Christmas season centers around the church. The weather is hot in some places and warm everywhere else in Africa at Christmas. Thousands of people cover the hillsides, praying and chanting sometimes throughout the night before Christmas morning.

African Christians, who are mostly Egyptians and Ethiopians, sing carols by candlelight, read and reenact the Nativity, and go to church.

The "Hallelujah Chorus" is a well-known music masterpiece. Listen with the children to a recording of this song and let the children respond freely through movement. Tell them that they are celebrating Christmas as African Christians do.

Because the weather is so warm, activities such as fireworks displays, open-air dining, swimming, and outdoor parades with string and wind instruments are popular. Let the children draw any of the scenes described and make a montage called "Africa—A Warm Weather Christmas."

"Joyeux Noel" from France. "Feliz Navidad" from Mexico. "Fröhliche Weihnachten" from Germany. "Sheng Tan Kuai Loch" from China. Merry Christmas.

Jacqulyn Thorpe, a diaconal minister of Christian education in the Washington-Baltimore Conference, serves as adjunct lecturer of Religious Education at Howard University School of Divinity.

Let Your Light Shine!

by Nancy M. Victorin-Vangerud

Stars and light, wise travelers and a baby—Epiphany is the season of mystery, discovery, and transformation. As a teacher, you are preparing to invite your students on an exciting journey. The star in the sky is the sign. It beckons you and your class to come and discover a king, but what surprises wait ahead!

The name of this season, Epiphany, comes from the Greek word *epiphaneia,* which means "appearance" or "manifestation." The Greeks used this word in reference to a wondrous appearance of their gods, especially in a time of great human need. In the Christian churches, we celebrate Epiphany as the season of God's manifestation in Jesus, our Savior.

Epiphany's central symbol is light. With the arrival of the wise men from the East, symbolizing the nations of the world, we realize Jesus is more than a Savior for a particular people in a certain time and place. Jesus is the Light of the World and a Savior for people in all times and places. What begins as a mysterious birth in a poor stable soon has far-reaching implications, even for the powerful and the mighty of many lands.

Epiphany Ends the Twelve Days of Christmas

Epiphany traditionally begins with the Feast of Epiphany on January 6, and we celebrate the Sunday before January 6 to bring Christmas to completion. As a season, Epiphany includes the Feast of Epiphany, the baptism of Jesus, and the Transfiguration. Central colors for the Epiphany season are white (symbolizing light) and green (symbolizing growth).

Epiphany invites children to join in the journey of the "wise ones" to Bethlehem. While our traditional Christmas pageantry

> Epiphany invites children to join in the journey of the "wise ones."

speaks of three kings, any number of children can join in the search. The Scriptures refer to the travelers—without specific number and in the plural—as Magi, or learned men, possibly from Persia, who interpreted the star's appearance as a profound cosmic event. Thus, in experiencing the Epiphany story, all of the children in your class— boys and girls—can become "wise ones" setting off on a journey to discover the child.

Take an Epiphany Journey

In preparation for the "journey to Bethlehem," map out a path through your church. Like a treasure hunt, hide a crèche figure or picture of the baby Jesus at the culmination of the path. For a star leading the way, have each child make his or her own star from construction paper, foil, or colored cardboard. The children may decorate their stars with glitter or pieces of colored tissue paper. Punch a hole through one of the star points and thread yarn through the hole to make a hanger. Carry the stars on the journey.

To add excitement, have the children dress up in costume. Make head coverings from scarves, towels, or pieces of cloth. Use strips of cloth to tie the scarves to their heads. In keeping with the tradition of the kings, the children may make and decorate crowns from construction paper.

With younger children, stop at certain points along the way to tell the story from Matthew 2:1-12. As you talk, invite these younger children to pretend that they are stopping for rest or for water.

With older elementary children, plan clues for different "wayside stops" along the path. At each stop, hide a scroll with another part of the story and the next clue. The children can take turns reading the story and figuring out the clues. Take pictures at each stop. The children can use the pictures to make an Epiphany bulletin board to inform others in the congregation.

When the children find baby Jesus, sing some Christmas carols together. Take a different route back to your classroom, since the Magi were warned in a dream not to let King Herod know where Jesus was living.

If you have access to video equipment, several children can pretend to be correspondents on the journey. Record the rambling path through the church and interview "wise ones" on the way. At each stop, tape the reading of the story and the discussion of the next clue. Show the videotape at an Epiphany party with another children's class, an adult group, or with parents.

HOLIDAYS

Epiphany and Mission

In contrast to the intense commercialism during the weeks prior to Christmas, Epiphany offers a different theme—giving our gifts to Jesus. The theme provides an excellent opportunity to engage children in mission. While the Magi brought expensive gifts, no child's gift is too small.

> **Epiphany offers a different theme from Christmas —giving our gifts to Jesus.**

In our church last Epiphany the children participated in two mission projects. On Epiphany Sunday the children brought gifts to the worship service. During the service, the children placed these gifts around the altar. We still had a large crèche set up at the base of the altar, so our children were able to sit and hear the Epiphany story along with the other "wise ones." The gifts were then given to several organizations serving children's needs here.

The second project linked our children with children in Jalapa, Nicaragua. For several years our church has been sending an adult Short Term Volunteers in Mission team to Jalapa to help build a community medical center and to help with children's Christian education. This year the team happened to be leaving during the Epiphany season. Two weeks after Epiphany Sunday the team led our children's chapel service. They told stories about their work and showed slides of children living in Jalapa. Then the children and the team made a large banner for the children of Jalapa. Each child used colored markers to trace his or her hand on the cloth. When the banner was finished, the mission team taught the children to sing "Jesus Loves Me" in Spanish.

The next Sunday the children brought school supplies for the mission team to take to Jalapa. The Sunday before the team left, the children processed into worship carrying the banner along with the team. A litany of blessing was offered for the team, and several children participated as readers. When the team returned, they brought a banner made by the children of Jalapa for our children here.

An Italian Folktale

A wonderful story to expand the theme of giving gifts is the Italian folklore tale of Old Befana. Your church or public library may have a copy of Tomie De Paola's *The Legend of Old Befana.*

Befana is an older woman who lives by herself. She has no time for visitors and spends her days baking and sweeping. One night a glorious star appears. The next day a caravan of kings stops by her home seeking directions to the Christ Child. A camel boy invites her to come along, but Befana declines. Later she decides to go, but she never catches up with the caravan. Instead she visits all the children and leaves them gifts just in case one child is the Christ Child.

Read or tell the story to your class and invite your children to act out the story. The legend of Befana may also be told using puppets. Younger children may make simple puppets on craft sticks. Older children may make puppets from cloth, socks, cardboard, yarn, and buttons.

In Epiphany, the Light spreads out into the world. As you lead children in discovering Jesus, the poor child born in Bethlehem, invite them to help spread the Light. Each child can live the words of the African-American spiritual, "This little light of mine, I'm gonna let it shine!"

Nancy M. Victorin-Vangerud is a minister of eduction in Rochester, Minnesota.

What's On Your Forehead?

by Robi Lipscomb

Have you ever had someone tell you, "There's dirt on your forehead"? Was it on Ash Wednesday? And how have you responded? Or have you seen smudges on other peoples' foreheads and wondered what they got into? Do you connect Ash Wednesday and marking with ashes (called "imposition") with practices of the Catholic Church? Is imposition of ashes unfamiliar to your church and uncomfortable to you?

Within the last twenty years, some protestant denominations have been more intentional about observing Ash Wednesday, not only as the beginning of the Lenten season, but as a holy day of observance, a day marking the beginning of a penitential and preparation period. The whole concept of Ash Wednesday and Lent is new to many denominations, and definitely not as clear as Easter Sunday. Maybe it is because there is no exact Scripture or story in the Bible regarding Ash Wednesday. Maybe it is because most congregations downplay the more somber or sad events of Christian history. We are all so excited about getting to the empty tomb on Easter morning that we don't really notice the road on which we journey to get there. Whatever the reasons, it is important that the journey to the empty tomb purposefully and specifically begin on Ash Wednesday, the day that begins preparing us for a full blessing on Easter morning.

So what is Ash Wednesday? Ash Wednesday was begun in early medieval times as a day of penitence to mark the beginning of Lent—the forty days of preparation for the celebration of the death and resurrection of Jesus Christ. The use of ashes was a reminder of the Old Testament practice of putting ashes on the head as a sign of grief and mourning. During this time of Lent, persons were prepared for their baptism, while those who felt themselves separated from God by sin and from the community of faith were reconciled and restored to participation in the life of the church, and each member of the congregation was reminded of God's mercy and forgiveness as revealed in Jesus Christ. Specific Lenten disciplines were encouraged: prayer, fasting, self-denial, Scripture reading and meditation, self-examination, and repentance. Ash Wednesday marks the beginning of this season.

The ashes, traditionally burned from the palm branches of the previous Palm Sunday, were imposed on the forehead as a reminder of our mortality, that we are created out of the dust of the earth and that it is only by God's grace that we receive everlasting life. In addition to this definition, there are other meanings and traditions woven into Ash Wednesday: the Biblical symbolism for the use of ashes can be found in Genesis 3:19, Jonah 3:6, Esther 4:1-3, and Job 2:8; with references to mourning and penitence by wearing sackcloth in II Samuel 9:1, Genesis 37:34, and Nehemiah 9:1. In each of these verses the dust, dirt, and sackcloth are used to symbolize someone grieving a death or great loss.

Ash Wednesday is the beginning of our forty days of reflection and grieving over the events that led up to our Lord's death by crucifixion. We also use this time to grieve and reflect on our own sins that separate us from our Lord Jesus Christ. The meaning and celebration of Easter Sunday is only fully received with a beginning grounded in Ash Wednesday.

Children and Ash Wednesday

How do you explain Ash Wednesday to children? Keep it simple. Use concrete imagery. Avoid abstract ideas. Appeal to their senses of smell, taste, touch, sight, and sound. What follows are a few simple ideas that you can use that will not only explain Ash Wednesday but will also include children in the event.

UNDERSTANDING THE CONCEPT

From the age of about three years, children understand being sorry. They have experienced their own regrets over doing something they knew they shouldn't. They also have known the regrets of others: "I'm sorry I bumped you and you fell down." Ash Wednesday is a day when we tell God that we are sorry for not being the best boy or girl we could be. God loves us and forgives us. On Ash Wednesday, we ask God's help to talk and act more like Jesus has taught us.

As their teacher, you can guide older children to identify more specifically ways that they have disobeyed God's will, and also, ways that they will intentionally seek to live faithfully, especially during this season of Lent. Some of those ways might include five minutes of prayer when they awaken each day, reading from their Bible daily, or saying or doing a specific act of kindness or love each day.

CHECKING OUT THE BIBLE

Through the Bible verses cited earlier, introduce children to the Old Testament usage of "sackcloth and ashes" as a way of demonstrating grief and sorrow, both to God and to other people. Act out how sick and sad Job was when everything he had was lost. What did his face look like? Act out Mordecai's distress when he heard that all the Jews in the country were to be killed. How did Mordecai look? What did others who saw him think?

TOUCHING THE SACKCLOTH

Bring burlap for the children to touch: notice how rough it is. No one would be comfortable wearing sackcloth: it was a constant reminder of inner grief and sorrow. If possible, get enough burlap sacks for the children to actually try them on.

SMELLING THE ASHES

Using the palms from last Palm Sunday, carefully burn them to ashes. (Watch out for fire systems; warn others in the building that you will be intentionally creating smoke.) Experience the smell of the burning; watch the smoke rise, and remind the children that ancient people understood that the smoke went up to God. Then when the ashes are cooled, mark each child, on the hand or the forehead, with a cross. Explain that this is the mark of a Christian, and whenever they see the ashes, they will know that they are a follower of Jesus. (If palms are not available, ask the children to write either some act for which they are sorry, or an act they promise to do as a gift to God. Burn these as offerings, creating the ashes that you then use for imposition.)

TASTING THE SYMBOLS

One position for prayer is standing with bowed head, arms crossed and hands on shoulders. Circular pretzels remind us of this prayer position, and have become a symbol of the Lenten season. Remind the children that Lent, beginning with Ash Wednesday, is a time of prayer. Share pretzels and prayer together.

Lent was also a time for fasting, or at least for a dramatically restricted diet. One of the foods of Lent were hot cross buns, sometimes containing fruit, but always with the sign of the cross. Enjoy hot cross buns together, noting the Christian sign.

A Brief Ash Wednesday Service for Children

Now that the children are familiar with the symbols and the meanings of Ash Wednesday, you may want to involve them in a worship service. Be sure to talk with your pastor about your preparations. She or he may want to share this with you and the group. You could use this at an after-school program, before or instead of children's choir practice, simultaneously with an adult Ash Wednesday service, in a Sunday school class, or as a family devotional. Choose a worshipful place, whether in a chapel, sanctuary, or the worship center of a classroom.

Ash Wednesday Service

(Play quiet music and light the candles.)
Song: "Lord, I Want to Be a Christian" (Look in a hymnal for this hymn.) vs 1, 2
Silent Prayer
Psalter: Psalm 51 (paraphrased for children)
Reader 1: Wash me clean, O Lord. Touch me gently.
Reader 2: Smooth away my failures;
Reader 1: I know I have let you down.
Reader 2: You are right to be angry with me.
Reader 1: So cleanse me from the inside out.
Reader 2: Heal my broken spirit,
Reader 1: A fresh start begins with a pure heart.
Reader 2: I do not want to be without you, O God. Amen.

The Lord's Prayer. (prayed by all)

PRAYER OF THANKSGIVING OVER THE ASHES

Loving and forgiving God, thank you for these ashes. Let them remind us and others that we are trying to follow Jesus and that we really want to show love like Jesus did. Thank you for your love and your forgiveness. Amen.

IMPOSING THE ASHES

Song: "Lord, I Want to Be a Christian" vs 3, 4

Don't be afraid to introduce Ash Wednesday to children: show them the fullness of the Christian year, and the spiritual journey to Easter. Guide children toward understanding the true love and grace that God gives all of us.

Robi Lipscomb is a director of children's ministry in Orlando, Florida.

A Lenten Tree?
by Carol McDonough

A tree. What better way is there to symbolize new and ongoing life?

Throughout the month of December, churches all over the world are decorated with Advent wreaths and Chrismon trees. Children and adults alike look to these symbols year after year as a way of remembering the significance of the birth of our Lord. Now with the coming of Lent and spring, our thoughts turn even more to new life. And this is the perfect time to include a symbolic tree in teaching your class about the significance of Lent.

You can help your children make the connection between the Christmas tree and the Lenten tree by reminding them that just as Advent is a time of preparation for the coming of Jesus, Lent is a time of spiritual preparation for the events leading up to Jesus' death and resurrection.

Getting Started

The Sunday prior to Ash Wednesday would be a perfect time to introduce the Lenten tree idea. Recruit the children to help you assemble a small artificial Christmas tree and place it near the worship center. Remind them that the tree is not a Christmas tree, but rather a Lenten tree, and that each week during Lent they will be adding new decorations which will help them to remember and understand the events that happened during Holy Week.

Lent

Second Sunday of Lent: The Money Bag

The account of Judas' betrayal can be found in all four gospels. However, only Matthew 26:14-16, Mark 14:10-11, and Luke 22:3-6 tell of the payment Judas received for his act. The money bag symbolizes the thirty pieces of silver.

You can make these by placing several pennies in a small square of nylon net and tying it on to the Lenten tree with yarn.

The Symbols
Sunday before Ash Wednesday: The Evergreen Tree

Tell the children that because this tree does not lose its needles during the winter, it is a symbol of eternal life.

The Color, Purple

Place a purple cloth around the base and add purple bows to brighten your tree as well as to emphasize this color, which is used during the Lenten season. Purple is a symbol of royalty and, during Lent, we are reminded about the time when people recognized Jesus as a king.

Third Sunday of Lent: The Chalice

In the final days before the crucifixion, Jesus chose to eat his final Passover meal with his twelve disciples. During this last supper, Jesus instituted the Lord's Supper by the sharing of bread and wine. Matthew 26:26-29, Mark 14:22-25, and Luke 22:15-20 all tell of the symbolic nature of the bread, representing Christ's body, and wine, symbolizing the blood of the new covenant.

Have the children make a chalice for their Lenten tree by taping together the bottoms of two small paper cups. Cover the cups with aluminum foil, molding the foil to the contours. Punch a hole in the top of the chalice and hang it on your tree with yarn.

Fourth Sunday of Lent: The Pretzel

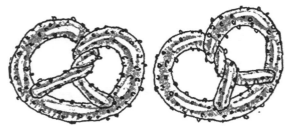

As the time of his death drew nearer, Jesus went to the Garden of Gethsemane to pray. The pretzel was originally shaped to look like hands folded in prayer and therefore has often been used as a symbol of prayer.

Your children can tie a piece of yarn through a pretzel and hang it on their tree to remind them of the importance of prayer.

Fifth Sunday of Lent: The Nail

A simple nail reminds us of the suffering Jesus experienced on the cross.

Tie a piece of yarn around the head of a nail and add this somber symbol to your tree.

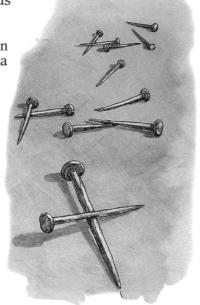

Sixth Sunday of Lent: The Palm Branch

Palm Sunday is the perfect time to remember Jesus' triumphant entry into Jerusalem. In an atmosphere of excitement and anticipation, crowds of people gathered along the road waving palm branches as they anxiously awaited the arrival of their king.

The children can place a live palm branch on the purple cloth at the base of the tree or make a palm branch out of green construction paper.

Easter Sunday: The Butterfly

Following the gloom and despair of Holy Week, we arrive on Easter morning to the glorious realization that

Christ has risen from the dead. A butterfly is often used to symbolize Jesus' resurrection. A caterpillar, entombed in a chrysalis, seems to have died. And yet, suddenly, as if born again, a beautiful butterfly appears. This reminds us that Jesus was killed, but God raised him from death to life.

Now that Lent is over, have the children remove all Lenten symbols from the tree. Replace the purple cloth with a white cloth, symbolizing purity and joy. Make butterflies out of construction paper, tissue paper, or other materials and fill your Easter tree with these colorful signs of new life.

Carol McDonough is an ordained deacon. She currently serves as Director of Volunteer Ministries at a church in Nashville, Tennessee.

Easter Egg Hunts
More Than Just Candy in the Grass
by Betsy Williams

God has provided a beautiful spring day. The blue sky shows a few wisps of feathery white clouds and the sun is shining brightly as the birds are heard singing in the trees. A closer look shows the church yard sprinkled with hundreds of plastic eggs filled with candy as crowds of children gather, waiting impatiently for the signal to begin the Easter egg hunt. Once the signal is given, an exuberance of chaos fills the air as the eggs are collected in a record time of seven minutes flat. Now what? Easter is so much more than just candy in the grass; the children are there with eager minds always ready to take in something new. What a perfect opportunity to take advantage of the moment and provide a closer insight to the Easter season!

With a little creativity and a number of adult volunteers, your Easter egg hunt can be transformed into an afternoon of fun and fellowship as well as Christian education. In addition to the traditional hunting of the candy eggs, you can add substance to your Easter egg hunts by including activity centers BEFORE the actual hunt. Divide the children into smaller groups and invite them to rotate their way through each of the centers. Kids will love them and so will the adults! Here are some different ideas for your activity centers.

Decorate Collection Bags

If the children are not going to bring Easter baskets for the gathering of their eggs, provide lunch bags for that purpose. Set up a center with white lunch bags, crayons, markers and stickers, and encourage children to decorate their own collection bags. Be sure to put each child's name on his or her bag to prevent confusion later.

Storytime

Children love to hear and to tell stories. Find church members with that special storytelling knack. Dressed in biblical costumes, have them tell the Easter story with the help of the children. You may want to use pictures, books, puppets, or other props. Ask the children leading questions and encourage them to tell as much of the story as they remember. The hearing and repeating of stories is one of the best teaching tools and the insight of children is tremendous. You'll be surprised at how accurate some of them can be. You'll also be amazed at how much we, as adults, can learn from a child's perspective.

Make an Easter Banner

As the spring weather warms up after the cold of winter, many of us love to run barefoot—especially children. Take advantage of this natural desire and make a footprint banner. Beforehand, prepare a large piece of white or pastel-colored cloth or section of bed sheet by cutting it to an appropriate size to hang on the wall inside your church. Hem or bind the edges of the cloth. Securely tape a large, simple cross of wax paper in the center of the banner taking care to tape down all the edges of the cross so that nothing can get beneath the paper. Now comes the fun part! One at a time, paint the feet of the children with bright, rainbow colors and have them walk across the banner until it is covered with little footprints. When the paint has dried, remove the wax paper cross. The result is a beautiful banner, created by the children, that might be used to adorn your narthex or sanctuary on Easter morning. Imagine the pride of the children in your church as they make their contribution to the Easter worship experience.

A few helpful hints for this activity:
- do this project outside if possible;
- use paint that will not stain the children's clothing or feet;
- consider testing this procedure on paper first to find the best paint consistency;
- have plenty of adults or youth to help with this center;
- provide buckets of warm, soapy water and towels for foot washing.

Don't miss a learning opportunity! As they are having their feet washed, talk with the children about Jesus and how he washed the feet of his disciples. You may even want to encourage them to help wash the paint off of each other's feet.

Color Easter Eggs

A rule of thumb for children is: If it's a little messy, it's a lot of fun! Again setting up outside, let's color Easter eggs! Provide smocks and paint shirts, plenty of adult or youth supervision, hard boiled eggs, and egg dye. As the children are coloring the eggs, explain that eggs are a Christian symbol of new life just as Easter symbolizes new life in Jesus. The eggs may be used in Easter baskets for shut-ins or possibly given to a meals-on-wheels program to be added to Easter Sunday food trays. If this is the case, be sure to call your local meals-on-wheels headquarters and ask about special handling and preparation instructions.

Mission Table

The possibilities are endless for this center. With a table full of craft supplies, encourage the children to create cards, bookmarks with Bible verses, paper flowers, and drawings that can later be taken to home-

bound individuals or those in the hospital. Another idea for this table might be to make and fill Easter baskets for similar delivery. Always take care to call ahead for dietary restrictions and the best time for visitation. Whether these items are delivered by children, youth, or adults they are sure to brighten up the day of the recipient.

Make Pretzels

In the past, part of the observance of Lent has included a time of fasting when certain foods could not be eaten. Pretzels, made of salt, water, and flour were developed in Germany as a food that could be eaten during these days of fasting. They are shaped to remind us of arms folded in prayer. Talk about this with the children as they make their own pretzels.

Let each child take pre-prepared balls of bread dough (available in the freezer section of the grocery store or made from the recipe below), dip them in flour, roll them out in snake-like fashion, and mold them into the traditional pretzel shape. Salt the tops and bake the pretzels as the children move on to

other activities. At the end of the egg hunt, each child will have a freshly baked pretzel to take home. The pretzels might also be included in the Easter baskets for others with a brief description of the symbolism enclosed.

These are just a few suggestions and ideas to get you started. Jump in with childlike enthusiasm and enjoy your next Easter egg hunt. Happy Easter! Christ is Risen!

Make Pretzels

Dissolve the yeast in warm water in a bowl, stirring until the yeast looks soft. Add one teaspoon regular salt, sugar, and the flour. Mix ingredients until a dough forms. Knead the dough on a floured board. Take a golf ball-size piece of dough and roll it into a strip 15 inches long. Make a loop by twisting the ends together. Bring the ends up and over and press them against the sides of the loop. Place the pretzels on a greased cookie sheet and brush them with the beaten egg. Sprinkle coarse salt over the pretzels. Bake them at 425 degrees for 12-15 minutes.

Pretzels

1½ cups warm water (105-115 degrees)
1 package active dry yeast
1 teaspoon salt
1 tablespoon sugar
4 cups flour
1 egg, beaten
coarse salt

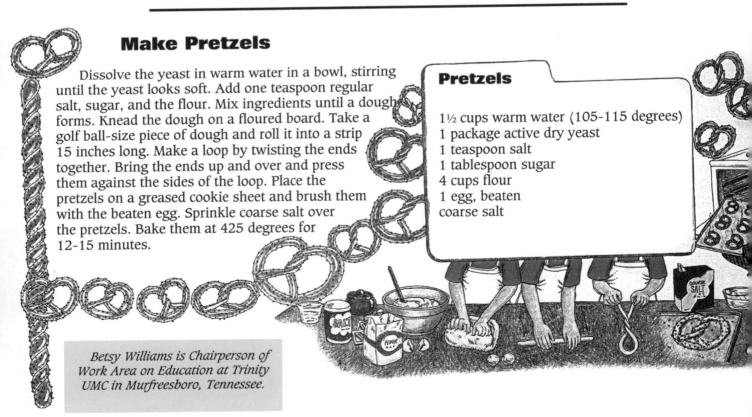

Betsy Williams is Chairperson of Work Area on Education at Trinity UMC in Murfreesboro, Tennessee.

Make a Big Deal About Pentecost!
by Susan Cox-Johnson

Make a big deal about Pentecost! Pentecost, the "birthday of the church," celebrates God's sending of the Holy Spirit, creating understanding and unity among the early followers of the risen Christ. It was originally a Jewish harvest holiday; it became, in the early church, the culmination of the "great fifty days" following Easter. For the church today, Pentecost is almost the only significant Christian holiday that has not been usurped by commercialism, so make the most of it with these terrific ideas for celebrating!

Susan Harrison

With Young Children

Young children will catch your enthusiasm for Pentecost, and will learn that we read about Pentecost in a very special book, the Bible. Preschoolers are eager for parties, especially birthday parties, and will happily celebrate the birthday of the church with cookies or cupcakes and candles. Although they may miss the historical details, together you will establish positive memories about this significant day.

Young children enjoy acting out stories and dressing up. Provide costumes for the children and help them dramatize the story as you retell it. Encourage them to use their hands to demonstrate "tongues of fire" on their heads, and to make the sounds of the mighty wind.

Enliven children's natural awareness of color and shapes by visiting the sanctuary. Help them discover the color red and to find doves and flames that represent the day. Check out stained glass windows and banners for other colors and symbols.

School-age Children and Pentecost

Emphasize Peter's courageous role (especially in light of his earlier denial of knowing Jesus) in the Pentecost story. As fans of action heroes, help your students to understand Peter and the other disciples as brave heroes for their faith.

Middle- and older-elementary children, who are beginning to think symbolically, will enjoy activities that include the symbols of the day: the descending dove, the flames, and other simple Holy Spirit symbols.

Elementary-age children also enjoy helping others. Include activities that emphasize the outreach of the church, such as ways we care for people in need, and how the church ministers across the world.

Ways for Everyone to Celebrate

Adapt these ideas for your age group and class size.
- Have a birthday party! Bring a birthday cake to share (or make a microwavable one during class) and let the children decorate it using red icing and the symbols of Pentecost.
- Instead of having party favors to take home, help the children make simple gifts that they can share with their community. Make Pentecost-related tray favors for the nursing home by drawing doves on cards and decorating them. If there is a daycare or preschool in your church, have children make pinwheels to be shared with the children. Remind the children that when the Holy Spirit came, the Bible says it sounded like a mighty wind (Acts 2:2).
- Make a banner! Explain that the followers of Jesus spoke different languages but were miraculously able to understand one another. Help the children make a poster or banner using the word *peace* in as many languages as possible. Your

HOLIDAYS

local high school foreign language teacher is a great resource for this project. Incorporate the Pentecost colors of red, white and gold.
● Invite persons from different nationalities in your church or community to share how Christians worship and observe Pentecost in their countries.
● Emphasize that the Holy Spirit was poured out "on all flesh" (meaning everyone) (Joel 2:28). Ask your pastor to tell your class about one of the church-supported ministries that show the love and peace that the Holy Spirit brings. Or describe the Heifer Project, Habitat for Humanity, or other ecumenical outreach ministries. All of these activities emphasize the empowerment the church receives from the Holy Spirit.
● Sing church "birthday"songs from your hymnal such as "We are the Church" or "Jesus Loves Me". If you are using a hymnal with other language translations (such as *The United Methodist Hymnal)* use the Cherokee, German, Japanese, and Spanish translations (or whichever translations you have available).

The Coming of the Holy Spirit

Learn about the symbols of the Holy Spirit. Describe the symbols of Pentecost through the newsletter, bulletin, bulletin boards, and through verbal communication. Help members of the congregation understand that red represents the tongues of fire, white represents the dove of the Holy Spirit, and that streamers are often used to represent the wind. Encourage everyone to wear red on Pentecost, and provide red ribbons and pins in case some forget.

Get permission from your pastor for your class to read and interpret Acts 2:1-4 for the worship service

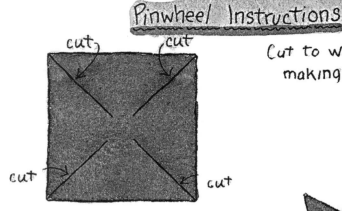

Pinwheel Instructions

cut · cut

cut · cut

Cut to within 1" of center making 4 triangles

Pin left corner of each triangle to center using one pin or paper fastener.

Susan Harrison

on Pentecost Sunday. If you teach older children, ask two children to read the story aloud. Have one child read the narration and another read the places where people speak. Have other children be the "spirit bearers" who, each time the Holy Spirit is mentioned, wave short dowel sticks wrapped with streamers of crepe paper. Children will enjoy developing other actions and sounds for the wind, the voices, and the flames.

Celebrate the presence of the Holy Spirit by singing songs from your denomination's hymnal like "I'm Goin' a Sing When the Spirit Says Sing," "Spirit of the Living God," "Surely the Presences of the Lord," and "Sweet, Sweet Spirit."

A Celebration of Wind

Acts 2:2 tells us that when the Holy Spirit descended, there was a sound "like the rush of a violent wind." We often refer to the Holy Spirit as the "breath of God." Have a celebration of wind by making pinwheels from red, orange, and

yellow paper. Or fly paper airplanes with Pentecost symbols on the wings, blow bubbles, or fly a kite! Let the children take pleasure in the wind that God has created.

Ask children and their families to bring windsocks or wind chimes from home to decorate the sanctuary. The sound of the wind chimes will enhance the worship service for persons of all ages.

No matter how you decide to celebrate Pentecost in your classroom, don't be afraid to make a big deal about it! Use your imagination! The Holy Spirit comes to help us to think new thoughts, and to open us to new possibilities! So make a big deal about Pentecost!

Susan Cox-Johnson is a pastor in Columbia, Missouri.

INDEX OF TITLES

LINCOLN CHRISTIAN COLLEGE AND SEMINARY
INDEX OF AUTHORS

Compiler: Marcia Joslin Stoner
Designer: Adolph C. Lavin

Illustrators: Susan Harrison,
Barbara Upchurch, Cheryl Mendenhall,
Bill Woods, John Ham, Rosemary Berlin,
Jack Kershner, Brenda Pepper, David Gothard,
Keith Neely, Charles Jakubowski

Kel Groseclose (page 51) *is a retired minister who owns a bookstsore in Wenatchee, Washington. He is a regular contributor to publications for church school teachers and leaders.*